David Edgar

CONTINENTAL DIVIDE

Mothers Against

Daughters of the Revolution

NICK HERN BOOKS
London
www.nickhernbooks.co.uk

A Nick Hern Book

Continental Divide first published in Great Britain
as a paperback original in 2004 by Nick Hern Books Limited,
14 Larden Road, London W3 7ST in association with
the Birmingham Repertory Theatre and BITE:04 at the
Barbican, London

Cover image: Kent Barker / Getty Images

Typeset by Country Setting, Kingsdown, Kent, CT14 8ES
Printed and bound in Great Britain by Bookmarque, Croydon, Surrey

A CIP catalogue record for this book is available from
the British Library

ISBN 1 85459 778 7

To Cecilia O'Leary and Tony Platt

Cast and Creative Team

Director	Tony Taccone
Scenic and Projection Designer	William Bloodgood
Costume Designer	Deborah M. Dryden
Lighting & Projection Designer	Alexander V. Nichols
Sound Designer	Jeremy J. Lee
Composer, *Mothers Against*	Todd Barton
Dramaturgs	Lue Morgan Douthit
	Douglas Langworthy
	Luan Schooler
Assistant Director	Randy White
Casting Director	Amy Potozkin
BRT Production Stage Manager	Michael Suenkel
OSF Production Stage Manager	Kimberley Jean Barry

Mothers Against
Cast in order of appearance

Caryl Marquez	Vilma Silva
a pollster	
Don D'Avanzo	Michael Elich
Sheldon's campaign manager	
Connie Vine	Robynn Rodriguez
Sheldon's wife	
Vincent Baptiste	Derrick Lee Weeden
a political analyst	
Deborah Vine	Christine Williams
Connie and Sheldon's daughter	
Mitchell Vine	Tony DeBruno
Sheldon's brother and campaign chair	
Sheldon Vine	Bill Geisslinger
the Republican gubernatorial candidate	
Lorianne Weiner	Susannah Schulman
a commentator	

Daughters of the Revolution
Cast in order of appearance

Michael Bern	Terry Layman
Abby, Beth, Branflake	Michelle Duffy
Ryan, Pat, Snowbird	Christine Williams
Jools, J.C., Rainbow, Bob LeJeune	Jacob Ming-Trent
Elaine, Ash, Connie Vine	Robynn Rodriguez
Ted, Jimmy, Nighthawk, Sheldon Vine	Bill Geisslinger
Arnie, Ira, Eddie, Mitchell	Tony DeBruno
Bill, Troy, Zee, Don D'Avanzo	Michael Elich
Kate, Yolande, Hoola Hoop	Vilma Silva
Dana, Trina, Aquarius	Marielle Heller
Jack, Darren, Sam, No Shit	Craig W. Marker
Blair Lowe	Lorri Holt
Rebecca McKeene	Melissa Smith
Kwesi Ntuli	Derrick Lee Weeden
Lorianne Weiner, Firefly	Susannah Schulman

Berkeley Repertory Theatre

Tony Taccone, Artistic Director and Susan Medak, Managing Director
Founded in 1968, the Tony Award-winning Berkeley Repertory Theatre
has established a national reputation for the quality of its productions
and the innovation of its programming. Under the leadership of Artistic
Director Tony Taccone and Managing Director Susan Medak, Berkeley
Rep's choice of material and bold, vivid style of production reflect a
commitment to diversity, excitement and quality. The company is
especially well known for its presentations of important new dramatic
voices and fresh adaptations of seldom-seen classics. In December
2001, Berkeley Rep opened the Roda Theatre, a 600-seat proscenium
theatre that compliments the existing 400-seat Thrust Stage. In
December 2001, the company opened the Nevo Education Center, home
of the Berkeley Rep School of Theatre. The addition of these two
buildings has transformed what was once a single stage into a vital and
versatile performing arts complex.

Oregon Shakespeare Festival

Libby Appel, Artistic Director and Paul Nicholson, Executive Director
The Tony Award-winning Oregon Shakespeare Festival, located in
Ashland, Oregon, was established in 1935 and is the oldest and largest
professional regional repertory theatre company in the United States.
Since 1995 Artistic Director Libby Appel and Executive Director Paul
Nicholson have continued the OSF tradition of commitment to artistic
excellence and fiscal health, leading OSF to highly lauded seasons in
the last few years. The 2004 season will run from February 20 through
October 31, and OSF will stage 784 performances of 11 plays - four by
Shakespeare and seven by classic and contemporary playwrights - in
rotating repertory in three theatres: the outdoor Elizabethan Stage
(seating 1,190), the Angus Bowmer Theatre (seating 601) and the
intimate New Theatre (seating 260-350, depending on audience seating
configuration). OSF employs approximately 450 theatre professionals
including more than 70 actors and operates on a budget of more than
$20 million, 77 percent of which is realized through earned income. In
2003, OSF was rated among the top five regional theatres in the
country by *Time* magazine.

Acknowledgements
Continental Divide was co-commissioned and co-produced by Berkeley
Repertory Theatre and the Oregon Shakespeare Festival. The original
cast at the Oregon Shakespeare Festival included Mark Murphy, Catherine
Lynn Davis, Mirron E. Willis, Catherine E. Coulson, Nell Geisslinger, James
Ingersoll, Linda Alper, Demetra Pittman and Richard Elmore. The stage
managers were Kimberley Jean Barry and Jill Rendall.

The research for *Continental Divide* was coordinated by Luan Schooler
and Megan Smith. Luan Schooler also assembled the quotations used in
this programme-text. The Spanish translations are by Vilma Silva.

Birmingham Repertory Theatre

Birmingham Repertory Theatre is one of Britain's leading national theatre companies. From its base in Birmingham, The REP produces over twenty new productions each year. Under the Artistic Direction of Jonathan Church, The REP is enjoying great success with a busy and exciting programme.

Throughout 2003 The REP's productions included David Hare's trilogy of plays (*Racing Demon, Murmuring Judges* & *The Absence of War*) Miller's *A View From The Bridge*, Alan Bennett's *The Madness of George III* and *The Wizard of Oz*. This Spring will see new productions of Alan Ayckbourn's *The Norman Conquests*, Alistair Beaton's *Follow My Leader*, and David Lindsay-Abaire's *Fuddy Meers* plus many more. This Christmas, The REP will present *The Witches* and *The Snowman*.

The commissioning and production of new work lies at the core of The REP's programme. In 1998 the company launched The Door, a venue dedicated to the production and presentation of new work. This, together with an investment of almost £1 million over four years in commissioning new drama from some of Britain's brightest and best writing talent, gives The REP a unique position in British theatre. Indeed, through the extensive commissioning of new work The REP is providing vital opportunities for the young and emerging writing talent that will lead the way in the theatre of the future.

Developing new and particularly younger audiences is also at the heart of The REP's work, in its various Education initiatives, such as Transmissions, The Young REP, Page To Stage, as well as with the programming of work in The Door for children.

Birmingham Repertory Theatre productions regularly transfer to London and tour nationally and internationally. Our acclaimed production of Steinbeck's *Of Mice And Men* opened in the West End in October and a new production of *Hamlet*, directed by Calixto Bieito, toured to Edinburgh, Barcelona and Dublin. Previous productions that have been seen in London in recent years include *The Snowman, Two Pianos, Four Hands, Baby Doll, My Best Friend, Terracotta, The Gift, A Wedding Story, Out In The Open, Tender, Behsharam, The Ramayana*.

Artistic Director **Jonathan Church**
Executive Director **Stuart Rogers**
Associate Director (Literary) **Ben Payne**

Performance dates 6-13 March 2003
Box Office 0121 236 4455
Book online at www.birmingham-rep.co.uk

The Barbican and BITE

The Barbican was officially opened on 3 March 1982 by HM The Queen who described it as "one of the wonders of the modern world". It was built as "the City's gift to the nation" by the Corporation of London at an historical capital cost of £161 million – equivalent to between £400-£500 million today. Under one roof are housed a Concert Hall, two Theatres, two Art Galleries, two Public Cinemas and extensive Conference facilities.

In 1995 John Tusa was appointed Managing Director with Graham Sheffield as Artistic Director. Under their leadership the Barbican is now recognised as one of the finest cultural destinations in the world. The truly international nature of our Arts programme and it's vast range, are what make the Barbican unique within arts institutions. It is not only the diversity of events but the interaction between them that is key – artists working across disciplinary boundaries but also across national and cultural boundaries. The "Arts Centre concept" is alive and flourishing at the Barbican.

BITE (Barbican International Theatre Events) is the Barbican international theatre, dance and music theatre programme. Established in 1998, it is the only year round international performing arts programme in London. BITE is defined by the people we work with and the Barbican is proud that many international artists have come to consider us their home. Graham Sheffield and Louise Jeffreys, Head of Theatre, have brought to the Barbican Theatre (capacity 1100) and the Pit Theatre (capacity 180) some of the most influential artists working in the world today, as well as those artists heading the race for the 'greats' of tomorrow. Productions from any country, in any language and with any performance art form are embraced in the BITE programme, which whilst insisting on excellence, introduces it's artistic collaborators to an open platform.

John Tusa, Managing Director
Graham Sheffield, Artistic Director
Louise Jeffreys, Head of Theatre

Performance dates 20 March-4 April 200
Box Office 0845 120 7515
Book online at www.barbican.org.uk

Biographies

DAVID EDGAR
(Playwright) took up writing after a short careeer in journalism. His adaptations include *Mary Barnes* (premiered at the Birmingham Repertory Theatre and revived at San Francisco's Eureka Theatre), *The Jail Diary of Albie Sachs* (RSC, also revived at the Eureka, directed by Tony Taccone), and a Tony award-winning adaptation of Dickens' *Nicholas Nickleby* (RSC in London, Manchester, Newcastle, New York and Los Angeles), a new dramatization of Stevenson's *Dr Jekyll and Mr Hyde* (RSC) and a play based on Gitta Sereny's biography of Albert Speer (National Theatre). His original plays for the theatre include *Death Story* for the Birmingham Repertory Theatre, *Saigon Rose* for the Traverse Theatre in Edinburgh, *Wreckers* for 7:84 England, *That Summer* for Hampstead Theatre and *Entertaining Strangers*, first as a community play for Dorchester and then at the National Theatre. His original plays for the RSC include *Destiny, Maydays* and *Pentecost* (winner of the Evening Standard best play award in 1995 and revived by Tony Taccone at the Oregon Shakespeare Festival and Berkeley Rep in 1997). *Pentecost* was the second of a series of plays about Eastern Europe after the Cold War, following *The Shape of the Table* (NT) and preceding *The Prisoner's Dilemma* (RSC). David Edgar has also written for television and radio, and he wrote the screenplay for Trevor Nunn's film *Lady Jane*. He founded and directed Britain's first post-graduate course in playwriting at the University of Birmingham from 1989 to 1999; he was appointed professor in 1995.

TONY TACCONE
(Director/BRT Artistic Director) is proud to serve as Artistic Director of the Tony Award-winning Berkeley Repertory Theatre, where he has worked since 1988 and served in his current position since 1997. He has directed more than twenty-five plays for Berkeley Rep, including *Surface Transit, Cloud Nine, Homebody/Kabul, Culture Clash in AmeriCCa, The Oresteia, The Alchemist, The First 100 Years, Ravenshead, Skylight, Pentecost, Macbeth, Slavs!, The Caucasian Chalk Circle, Endgame/Act Without Words, Volpone, The Convict's Return, Major Barbara, The Virgin Molly, Serious Money, Waiting for Godot, The Birthday Party* and *Execution of Justice* (with Oskar Eustis). Before coming to Berkeley Rep, Mr. Taccone served as the artistic director of the Eureka Theatre in San Francisco, collaborating for seven years with Oskar Eustis, Lorri Holt, Susan Marsden, Richard Seyd, Abigail van Alyn and Sigrid Wurschmidt. His directorial highlights there included *Road, Boomer!, Fen, Still Life* and *Accidental Death of an*

Anarchist. Mr. Taccone has been pleased to direct at other theatres around the country. His work has been frequently seen at the Oregon Shakespeare Festival where he directed *Othello, Pentecost, Coriolanus, The Cure at Troy* and the world premiere of *Continental Divide*. He has also worked at Actors Theatre of Louisville, Arizona Theatre Company, San Jose Rep and Yale Rep. He had the great honour of co-directing the world premiere of *Angels in America* at the Mark Taper Forum in Los Angeles. Mr. Taccone has served on the faculty of U.C. Berkeley, the board of Theatre Communications Group and has been a regional representative for the Society of Stage Directors and Choreographers.

WILLIAM BLOODGOOD
(Scenic and Projection Designer) is resident scenic designer with the Oregon Shakespeare Festival in Ashland, Oregon, where in 27 seasons he has designed well over 100 productions. Mr. Bloodgood has designed for many regional theatres as well, including American Conservatory Theater, Arena Stage in Washington, D.C., Arizona Theatre Company, Chicago Shakespeare Theater, Children's Theatre Company in Minneapolis, Hong Kong Repertory Theatre, Indiana Repertory Theatre, Intiman Theatre in Seattle, the Old Globe Theatre in San Diego, Portland Center Stage and Syracuse Stage. In 2002, he was honoured with the Oregon Governor's Award for the Arts.

Recent work for Berkeley Repertory Theatre includes *Pentecost* (by David Edgar), *The Beauty Queen of Leenane* and last season's *The House of Blue Leaves*. The two plays of *Continental Divide* mark his tenth production for Berkeley Rep.

DEBORAH M. DRYDEN
(Costume Designer) has designed for numerous theatre companies, including the La Jolla Playhouse, Old Globe Theatre, Seattle Repertory Theatre, Arena Stage (Washington, D.C.), Alliance Theatre (Atlanta), Guthrie Theater (Minneapolis), Huntington Theatre (Boston), Milwaukee Repertory Theatre, Minnesota Opera, San Diego Opera, Hong Kong Repertory Theatre, the Mark Taper Forum in Los Angeles and American Conservatory Theater in San Francisco. She is currently resident costume designer at the Oregon Shakespeare Festival and is the author of the book *Fabric Painting and Dyeing for the Theatre*. Deborah is professor emeritus of design at the University of California, San Diego.

ALEXANDER V. NICHOLS
(Lighting and Projection Designer) Mr. Nichols' design work spans from lighting and projections to scenery and costumes for dance, theatre and opera. For Berkeley Repertory Theatre, credits include *Ravenshead, Culture Clash In AmeriCCa, Menocchio, Surface Transit* (scenic and lighting), *Galileo* (projections), *Civil Sex* (lighting) and *Rhinoceros* (projections). Mr.

Nichols has designed for companies and artists including American Conservatory Theater, Alley Theatre (Houston, TX), Arena Stage (Washington, D.C.), Oregon Shakespeare Festival, California Shakespeare Theatre, ODC/SF, Hubbard Street Dance Chicago, Alvin Ailey American Dance Theater, San Francisco Ballet, Hong Kong Ballet, National Theatre of Taiwan, Paul Dresher Ensemble, Kronos Quartet and Rinde Eckert. He has served as resident lighting designer for the Margaret Jenkins Dance Co., Pennsylvania Ballet, Hartford Ballet, and as lighting director for American Ballet Theatre. Other dance credits include designs for choreographers Christopher d'Amboise, Val Caniparoli, Sonya Delwaide, Dominique Dumais, Bill T. Jones, Jean Grand Maitre, Mark Morris, Kevin O'Day, Kirk Peterson, Stephen Petronio, Dwight Rhoden and Michael Smuin.

JEREMY J. LEE
(Sound Designer) is returning to Berkeley Rep after designing *Pentecost*, for which he was nominated for the Bay Area Theatre Critics Circle award. Regionally, he has designed numerous productions at the Oregon Shakespeare Festival, including *Lorca in a Green Dress* (premiere by Nilo Cruz), *Continental Divide* and *Stop Kiss* (Loretta Greco, dir.), as well as designed for the Chicago Shakespeare Theatre, American Players Theatre, Cleveland Playhouse, Actor's Theatre of Louisville, Rude

Mechanicals (Austin, TX) and Salvage Vanguard Theatre (Austin, TX). N.Y.C. Credits: Resident Sound Designer for Epic Repertory Theatre; *Burn This* at the Signature Theatre (Assistant Sound Designer). Awards: 2002 Austin Critics' Table Award; B. Iden Payne Award Nomination (Austin, TX).

TODD BARTON
(Composer, *Mothers Against*) has been at OSF since 1969 composing original music for the plays and overseeing all musical activities; composed scores for more than 200 plays including the entire Shakespearean canon. Other theatres: *Sunsets & Glories* (A Contemporary Theatre, Seattle); *St. Joan* (Denver Center Theatre Company); *The Tempest* (The Shakespeare Theatre, Washington, D.C.); *The Sea* (Berkeley Repertory Theatre); *The Merchant of Venice* (Milwaukee Repertory Theater); *Copenhagen* (Seattle Repertory Theatre); *Moon for the Misbegotten* (Willamette Repertory Theatre). Other credits: received Special Award in Popular Music from ASCAP for his compositions for the Festival's 1993-03 seasons; his concert works include performances by the Kronos Quartet, the Oregon Symphony Orchestra, the Cavani String Quartet, and the Rogue Valley Symphony; audio tape, Lao Tzu's *Tao Te Ching*, with author Ursula K. LeGuin; Director of Composition Studies at Southern Oregon University; his genome music has been exhibited at many museums across the country; his composition and sound

design for the 2002 production of *Macbeth* was selected for exhibition at the 2003 Prague Quadrennial Scenography Exhibition.

LUE MORGAN DOUTHIT (Dramaturg) is the Director of Literary Development and Dramaturgy at the Oregon Shakespeare Festival and is this year's Dramaturg for *Topdog/Underdog*, *Henry VI, Part One*, *King Lear*, *Humble Boy*. In nine seasons at OSF: *Romeo and Juliet*, *Daughters of the Revolution [Continental Divide]*, *Hedda Gabler*, *Wild Oats*, *The Piano Lesson*, *Noises Off*, *Who's Afraid of Virginia Woolf?*, *Macbeth*, *The Winter's Tale*, *The Trip to Bountiful*, *Life is a Dream*, *Fuddy Meers*, *The Merry Wives of Windsor*, *Three Sisters*, *The Man Who Came to Dinner*, *Wit*, *Stop Kiss*, *The Trojan Women*, *Chicago*, *Tongue of a Bird*, *Les Blancs*, *Measure for Measure*, *Nora*, *The Magic Fire*. Awards: 1999 Literary Manager & Dramaturgs of the Americas (LMDA) Prize in Dramaturgy: The Elliott Hayes Award. Education: Ph.D., University of Washington; M.A., University of Arizona; MFA, Trinity University.

DOUGLAS LANGWORTHY (Dramaturg) was the Dramaturg at Oregon Shakespeare Festival for this year's *The Visit*, *Oedipus Complex*. In seven seasons at OSF: *Present Laughter*, *Mothers Against [Continental Divide]*, *Antony and Cleopatra*, *Wild Oats*, *Lorca in a Green Dress*, *Idiot's Delight*, *Handler*, *Titus Andronicus*, *Saturday*, *Sunday, Monday*, *Enter the Guardsman*, *Oo-Bla-Dee*, *The Merchant of Venice*, *Two Sisters and a Piano*, *The Octavio Solis Project*, *The Night of the Iguana*, *Force of Nature*, *Crumbs from the Table of Joy*, *The Taming of the Shrew*, *The Good Person of Szechuan* (also translator), *El Paso Blue*, *Rosmersholm*, *The Three Musketeers* (also co-adapter), *Vilna's Got a Golem*, *Uncle Vanya*, *Pentecost*, *Blues for an Alabama Sky*, *The Turn of the Screw*. Translations: Friedrich Durrenmatt's *The Visit* for OSF's *The Visit* adapted by Kenneth Albers; Goethe's *Faust*; Hans Henny Jahnn's *Medea* for Target Margin Theatre; Kleist's *The Prince of Homburg* for the Jean Cocteau Repertory, New York; Wedekind's *Spring Awakening* for numerous university productions. Other credits: Director of Literary Development and Dramaturgy at OSF for seven seasons; dramaturg, Target Margin Theatre, New York; former managing editor of *American Theatre* magazine; 1994 National Theatre Translation Fund Award; adapted *In Dark Times*, about Bertolt Brecht's 1947 appearance before the HUAC. Education: MFA in dramaturgy and dramatic criticism, Yale School of Drama; B.A., German, Pomona College, California.

LUAN SCHOOLER (Dramaturg) served on the Berkeley Rep artistic staff from 1998–2003, where she worked as literary manager and dramaturg for *Antony and Cleopatra*, *The Magic Fire*, *The*

*Life of Galileo, Let My Enemy
Live Long!, The Alchemist, The
Green Bird, Fall, The Oresteia,
36 Views, Much Ado About
Nothing, Rhinoceros,
Homebody/Kabul, The House
of Blue Leaves, Menocchio* and
Haroun and the Sea of Stories.
In the Bay Area, she has also
provided dramaturgy for A
Traveling Jewish Theatre,
PlayGround and the California
Shakespeare Theatre, for
whom she most recently
dramaturged *Measure for
Measure.* She has been
honoured to serve as a
dramaturg for *Continental
Divide* since its inception.

RANDY WHITE
(Assistant Director) NYC
credits include Glen Berger's
Underneath the Lintel (15
months Off-Broadway), Carson
Kreitzer's *Self Defense* and
Valerie Shoots Andy,
Strindberg's *Miss Julie,* George
F. Walker's *End of Civilization*
and Howard Barker's *Judith.*
Regional credits include *Into
the Woods, Cat on a Hot Tin
Roof, A Midsummer Night's
Dream, Sweeney Todd, 1776,
Songs for a New World* and
Billy Bishop Goes to War.
Canadian credits include
*Nothing Sacred, Romeo and
Juliet, Dawns are Quiet Here*
and *Richard III.* Mr. White
assisted on Disney's *The Lion
King* and has also
directed/taught for the Yale
Dramat, Penn Players, N.Y.U.
Tisch School of the Arts,
Fordham University and AMDA.

AMY POTOZKIN
(BRT Casting Director) is in
her 15th season with Berkeley
Rep where she serves as

Artistic Associate and Casting
Director and teaches acting at
the Berkeley Rep School of
Theatre. Ms. Potozkin has had
the pleasure of casting for
Aurora Theatre Company,
ACT/Seattle, Arizona Theatre
Company, Bay Area
Playwright's Festival, B Street
Theatre, Dallas Theatre
Company, San Jose Rep, Marin
Theatre Company, A Traveling
Jewish Theatre, Charlie
Varon's play *Ralph Nader is
Missing,* and Social Impact
Productions, Inc. Film credits
include *Conceiving Ada*
starring Tilda Swinton
and Josh Kornbluth's film
Haiku Tunnel and she was a
dialogue coach for *The
Conversation* (Francis Ford
Coppola, Producer). She
received her M.F.A. from
Brandeis University where she
was also an artist-in-residence.

MICHAEL SUENKEL
(BRT Production Stage
Manager) is in his 18th season
with Berkeley Rep and his
10th as production stage
manager. Favourite
productions include *Mad
Forest, Endgame, 36 Views*
and *Hydriotaphia.* He has also
worked with the La Jolla
Playhouse, New York's Public
Theatre, the Huntington
Theatre in Boston and the
Pittsburgh Public Theater. For
the Magic Theatre, he stage
managed Albert Takazauckas'
Breaking the Code and Sam
Shepard's *The Late Henry Moss.*

KIMBERLEY JEAN BARRY
(OSF Production Stage
Manager) has worked on 67
productions in 25 years at
OSF, most recently *Daughters*

of the Revolution. Other credits: Backstage Tour Manager (1987-03); stage manager for the 1988-03 Daedalus Project AIDS Benefit Shows; four Festival Tours, including the OSF and Kennedy Center production of *The Magic Fire.*

SUSAN MEDAK

(BRT Managing Director) has served as Berkeley Rep's Managing Director since 1990, during which time she has been responsible for administration and operations of the Theatre. In addition to her work at Berkeley Rep, she currently serves as treasurer of the national service organization Theatre Communications Group (TCG) and is vice-president of the League of Resident Theatres (LORT). She has been a member of that association's national negotiating committee for contracts with Actor's Equity Association, Society of Stage Directors and Choreographers and United Scenic Artists. Ms. Medak has served on the National Endowment for the Arts Theatre Program panel, as well as on Overview, Prescreening, and Creation and Presentation panels. She has chaired panels for the Preservation and Heritage, and Education and Access programs, also serving as an on-site reporter for many years. She has been a site reporter and chaired two theatre panels for the Massachusetts Arts Council. Closer to home, Ms. Medak is Vice President of the Downtown Berkeley Association. She is a commissioner of the Downtown Business Improvement District and is the founding chair of the Berkeley Arts in Education Steering Committee for Berkeley Unified School District and the Berkeley Cultural Trust. She lives in Berkeley with her husband and son. Before coming to Berkeley Rep, Ms. Medak worked at The Guthrie Theater, Milwaukee Repertory Theatre, Northlight Theatre in Evanston, Illinois and The People's Light and Theatre Company in Malvern, Pennsylvania.

LIBBY APPEL

(OSF Artistic Director) is the fourth Artistic Director in the Oregon Shakespeare Festival's 65-year history. At OSF she has directed *Richard II, Macbeth, Saturday, Sunday, Monday, The Trip to Bountiful, Three Sisters,* the world premiere of *The Magic Fire* (also at the Kennedy Center), *Henry V, Hamlet, Henry IV, Part 2, Uncle Vanya, Measure for Measure, King Lear, The Merchant of Venice, The Winter's Tale, Breaking the Silence, Enrico IV (The Emperor)* and *The Seagull.* She served as the Artistic Director of Indiana Repertory Theatre 1991-1995, directing *Molly Sweeney, The Tempest, Miss Ever's Boys, Hamlet, Dancing at Lughnasa,* and many others. She has directed more than 50 plays at more than 20 professional theatre companies throughout the country, including Seattle Repertory Theatre, South Coast Rep, Arizona Theatre

Company, The Goodman, Court Theatre, Syracuse Stage, Repertory Theatre of St. Louis, San Jose Repertory Theatre, and the Utah, Alabama, Colorado and Kern Shakespeare Festivals. A graduate of the University of Michigan with an MFA from Northwestern, she has also served as Dean of the School of Theatre at the California Institute for the Arts. She wrote *Mask Characterization: An Acting Process*, and she created and produced the video, *Inter/Face: The Actor and The Mask*. She co-authored with Michael Flachmann two plays, *Shakespeare's Women* and *Shakespeare's Lovers*.

PAUL NICHOLSON
(OSF Executive Director) became Executive Director of the Oregon Shakespeare Festival in 1995 after serving as General Manager for 16 years. He is responsible for all management aspects of the largest professional theatre in the United States, including strategic planning, budgeting, fund-raising, public relations, marketing, education programs, human resources and Board relations. Prior to joining the Festival he was for six years the Administrative Director of Downstage Theatre, New Zealand's largest and longest-established professional theatre and worked for ten years in the corporate world as a planning manager, management accountant and systems analyst. Mr. Nicholson has been a guest lecturer at Stanford University, Victoria University of Wellington, the New Zealand Department of Trade and Industry, the Oregon Educational Media Association and the B.C. Touring Council for the Performing Arts. He has acted as a management consultant for many arts organizations throughout the United States. He is deeply involved in arts advocacy efforts for the state of Oregon, currently serving as President of the Oregon Cultural Advocacy Coalition. He was a founding faculty member of the Western Arts Management Institute and became an Adjunct Professor at Southern Oregon University in 1984. He has served on many panels for the National Endowment for the Arts and the Theatre Communications Group. Active in community affairs, Mr. Nicholson is Chair of the Ashland Community Hospital Board, is a member and past director of Rotary, served for many years on the board of directors of the Ashland Chamber of Commerce and has participated in many local committees and boards.

Cast
TONY DEBRUNO
(Mitchell Vine/Arnie/Ira/Eddie) is beginning his 30th year as a professional actor. In 12 seasons at the Oregon Shakespeare Festival he has appeared in close to 30 productions, including *The Merchant of Venice, Much Ado About Nothing, Chicago, Saturday, Sunday, Monday, Our Town, Lips Together, Teeth Apart* and *Restoration*. He has also appeared at many theatres across the country, including Seattle Rep, Arizona Theatre Company and Alabama Shakespeare Festival.

MICHELLE DUFFY
(Abby/Beth/Branflake) is honoured to return to Berkeley Rep following her last appearance as Catharine in *Suddenly Last Summer*. Previous Bay Area appearances include Stella in *A Streetcar Named Desire* (A.C.T.), Dot/Marie in *Sunday in the Park with George* (TheatreWorks) and her San Francisco Opera debut in *The Merry Widow*. Some other theatres at which she's worked include the Old Globe Theatre, Pasadena Playhouse, the Goodman, Milwaukee Repertory Theatre, Northlight, the Colony Theatre (company member), ACT Theatre in Tokyo and Vienna's English Theatre. Among her favourite roles: Maggie in *Cat on a Hot Tin Roof*, Hedda in *Hedda Gabler*, Mary in *Our Country's Good*, Vet in *The Boswell Sisters* and Isabel in *My Children! My Africa!*. TV credits include *Family Law* (CBS), *The Huntress* (USA), *Passions* (NBC), *Take My Advice* (Lifetime), *The Untouchables* and *Missing Persons*. Most recently, Michelle appeared as Annie in *The Real Thing* at ITC in Long Beach and in television commercials for Albertson's and Bob Evans. She has been recognized by the Bay Area Theatre Critics Circle, Chicago's Joseph Jefferson Committee, Theatre LA's Ovation Board, Back Stage West and Drama-Logue for performance excellence.

MICHAEL ELICH
(Don D'Avanzo/Bill/Troy/Zee) In ten seasons with the Oregon Shakespeare Festival, Mr. Elich has been seen in roles as varied as Harry Van in *Idiot's Delight*, The Actor in *Enter the Guardsman*, Hotspur and Bardolph in *Henry IV, Parts One and Two*, Torvald in *Nora*, The Conferencier in *Cabaret Verboten*, Moe Axelrod in *Awake and Sing!*, Charles Surface in *The School for Scandal* and Poseidon in *Trojan Women*. Off-Broadway, he has appeared at Playwrights Horizons, The Orpheum and the York Theatre Company. He has played regional theatres including Syracuse Stage, Dallas Theatre Center, Missouri Rep, the Coconut Grove, Capital Rep and the 30th anniversary production of *Inherit the Wind* at the Papermill Playhouse. Film and TV credits include *One Life to Live, Ryan's Hope, Raspberry Heaven* and *Earthbound*. Mr. Elich is a graduate of the Juilliard Theatre Center in NYC.

BILL GEISSLINGER
(Sheldon Vine /Ted/Jimmy/Nighthawk) returns to Berkeley Rep following performances in *Dinner With Friends* and last season's *The House of Blue Leaves*. In 14 seasons at the Oregon Shakespeare Festival, he has appeared in *Continental Divide, Three Sisters, Death of a Salesman, Les Blanc, Nora, Boy Meets Girl, Curse of the Starving Class, Macbeth, Strange Snow, Broadway, An Enemy of the People, Light Up the Sky, The Birthday Party, Buried Child, Twelfth Night, Romersholm, Heathen Valley, Chicago, Lips Together, Teeth Apart, Toys in the Attic, The*

*Marriage of Bette and Boo, The
Iceman Cometh, The Birthday
Party, And a Nightingale Sang*
and *An Enemy of the People*.
At the Old Globe Theatre in
San Diego he performed in
*Strange Snow, Voir Dire, The
Taming of the Shrew, The
Miser, Sun Bearing Down, Moby
Dick Rehearsed, Yankee Wives,
The Sorrows of Stephen* and
The Skin of Our Teeth (also
seen on PBS' *American
Playhouse*). Other credits
include *A Streetcar Named
Desire* and *Bang the Drum
Slowly* at the Huntington
Theatre in Boston, and work at
Intiman Theatre, South Coast
Repertory Theatre, Portland
Center Stage, Virginia Stage
and the Mechanic Theatre.
Film and TV credits include *St.
Elsewhere, Cheers, News
Radio, Nowhere Man, Dead by
Sunset, 1,000 Heroes, Dreamer
of Oz, People Like Us, Ernie
Kovacs: Between Laughter* and
Imaginary Crimes.

MARIELLE HELLER
(Dana/Trina/Aquarius) is
making her Berkeley Rep
debut in *Continental Divide*.
She was last seen in L.A.
playing Ophelia at 2100
Square Feet. She graduated
from U.C.L.A. in theatre and
has studied at the Royal
Academy of Dramatic Art in
London, where she played
Gower in *Pericles*. Other roles
include Hero at Will Geer's
Theatricum Botanicum, a co-
starring role on ABC's *Spin
City* and multiple
performances at U.C.L.A. She
also occupies her time
studying West African Dance.

LORRI HOLT
(Blair Lowe) appeared most
recently as Olga in Carey
Perloff's production of *The
Three Sisters* at A.C.T. this
year. She was the recipient of
a 2003 Bay Area Theatre
Critics Circle award for her
performance in *The Music
Lesson* last fall at Marin
Theatre Company. Ms. Holt was
last seen at Berkeley Rep as
Beth in *Dinner With Friends*;
other productions here include
*Dancing at Lughnasa, Reckless,
Blue Window, Serious Money,
Dream of a Common Language,
Tooth of Crime* and *Our
Country's Good*. Holt has also
worked at San Jose Rep, the
Magic Theatre and the Aurora
Theatre and for ten years was
a company actress with the
Eureka Theatre, where she
first worked with both Tony
Taccone and David Edgar.
Commercial theatre credits
include *The Vagina
Monologues, Top Girls, Cloud
Nine* and *Sister Mary Ignatius
Explains It All For You*. Ms.
Holt works frequently in TV
and radio voiceover, and is a
published fiction writer and
journalist. Her article about
the development of
Continental Divide can be
found in the October 2003
issue of *American Theatre*
magazine.

TERRY LAYMAN
(Michael Bern) recently played
Robert in *Proof* both at Actors
Theater of Louisville and as an
emergency replacement on
Broadway. Other Broadway
credits include *The Ride Down
Mount Morgan* and *The
Rehearsal*. National tours
include *The Royal Family* (with

Eva Le Gallienne) and *Proof*. Off-Broadway shows include *Room Service, Ferocious Kisses, The Butter and Egg Man, A Murder of Crows* and recently standing by for the National Actor's Theatre production of *Arturo Ui* with Al Pacino and Jules Feiffer's *A Bad Friend* at Lincoln Center. Regional work includes: Peck in *How I Learned To Drive* and Big Daddy in *Cat On A Hot Tin Roof* (Buffalo Studio Arena); Atticus in *To Kill a Mockingbird* (Pioneer, Salt Lake City); *Long Day's Journey* (Cincinnati Playhouse); *All My Sons* (the Alliance, Atlanta); *The Royal Family* (McCarter); *Miracle Worker* and *Other People's Money* (George St. Playhouse). He also played in *The Little Foxes* with Geraldine Page and *Trip to Bountiful* with Ellen Burstyn. His Film credits include: *The Patriot*. TV credits include: Guest roles on: *Ed, Law and Order* and *Special Victims Unit*, in addition to most NY soaps. He has also performed and directed for many summers at the Monomoy Theatre on Cape Cod.

CRAIG W. MARKER
(Jack/Darren/Sam/No Shit) was most recently seen as Longaville in *Love's Labour's Lost* with the San Francisco Shakespeare Festival. Bay Area credits include Adam in *The Shape of Things* with the Aurora Theatre Company (Dean Goodman Choice Award), Salerio in *The Merchant of Venice* with Women In Time, Steve in Steven Berkoff's *Decadence* with California State University, Hayward and E.K. Hornbeck in *Inherit the Wind* with Chanticleers Theatre. International credits include Petruchio in *The Taming of the Shrew* at the Edinburgh Festival Fringe and Orestes in *Electra* as part of the International Festival of Ancient Greek Drama at the ITI, Cyprus. Craig can be seen in the forthcoming independent feature film, *Night of Henna* (www.nightofhenna.com). He holds a B.A. in Acting from C.S.U., Hayward.

JACOB MING-TRENT
(Jools/J.C./Rainbow/Bob LeJeune) received his M.F.A. in Acting from the A.C.T. Master of Fine Arts program (2003). Jacob was last seen as Fedotik in *Three Sisters* at A.C.T. (directed by Carey Perloff) and also in A.C.T.'s *A Christmas Carol* as Young Scrooge. He is ecstatic to be working with Berkeley Rep.

ROBYNN RODRIGUEZ
(Connie Vine/Elaine/Ash) is pleased to be back at Berkeley Rep, where she last appeared as Clytemnestra in *The Oresteia*. A veteran of 12 seasons with the Oregon Shakespeare Festival, she has appeared in dozens of productions, including *Pentecost* and *Othello* (both directed by Tony Taccone), *Uncle Vanya, Major Barbara, The Man Who Came to Dinner, The Taming of the Shrew, The Magic Fire* (transferred to The Kennedy Center) and, most recently, the world premiere of *Continental Divide: Mothers*

Against and *Daughters of the Revolution*. Rodriguez has also appeared at the Intiman Theatre, the Denver Center Theatre Company, Portland Center Stage, PCPA/Solvang Theaterfest, Missouri Rep, and the Guthrie Theater, where she played Barbara in the critically acclaimed production of Joan Holden's *Nickel and Dimed*.

SUSANNAH SCHULMAN
(Lorianne Weiner/Firefly) appeared most recently in the Oregon Shakespeare Festival production of *Continental Divide*. She has appeared previously at Berkeley Rep in *The House of Blue Leaves*, and at the California Shakespeare Theatre in *The Seagull, A Midsummer Night's Dream* and *Romeo and Juliet*. South Coast Repertory credits include *The Dazzle, Nostalgia, Six Degrees of Separation, The Taming of the Shrew* and *A Christmas Carol*. Five seasons at Shakespeare Santa Cruz included productions of *Cymbeline, The Tempest, King Lear* and *The Merchant of Venice*. Other credits include *The Two Gentlemen of Verona* at Geva Theatre, *Picnic* at the Marin Theatre Company and the national tour of Steve Martin's *Picasso at the Lapin Agile*.

VILMA SILVA
(Caryl Marquez/Yolande/Kate/ Hoola Hoop) is honoured to make her Berkeley Rep debut with *Continental Divide*. Vilma appeared in the premiere productions of *Mothers Against* and *Daughters of the Revolution* at the Oregon Shakespeare Festival this year, where she has been a company

member since 1995. Some of her credits there include *Julius Caesar, As You Like It, Life is a Dream, Two Sisters and a Piano, Measure for Measure* and *The Magic Fire* (OSF and Kennedy Center Productions). She has also appeared at A.C.T., Actors Theater of Louisville, Dallas Theater Center, San Jose Rep, San Francisco Shakespeare Festival and El Teatro Campesino.

MELISSA SMITH
(Rebecca McKeene) has performed in New York and in regional theatres across the country, including Primary Stages, Soho Rep, the Hangar Theatre, Studio Arena Theatre, American Conservatory Theater and Napa Valley Rep. Past roles include Susan in *Holiday*; Sonia in *Celebration*; Sally in *Lips Together, Teeth Apart*; Dora in *The Hyacinth Macaw*; Fefu in *Fefu and Her Friends*; Laura in *The Glass Menagerie* and a solo piece entitled *The Miller's Daughter*. Smith has been director of the A.C.T. Conservatory since 1995.

DERRICK LEE WEEDEN
(Vincent Baptiste/Kwesi Ntuli) returns to Berkeley Rep following his appearance as Agamemnon and Pylades in *The Oresteia*. In 13 seasons at the Oregon Shakespeare Festival, he has performed the roles of Marcus Brutus in *Julius Caesar*, Aaron in *Titus Andronicus*, Vershinin in *Three Sisters*, Othello in *Othello*, Hedley in *Seven Guitars*, Tshembe Matoseh in *Les Blancs*, Duke in *Measure for Measure*, Edmond in *King Lear*,

Antonio in *Pentecost*, Coriolanus in *Coriolanus*, Bolingbroke in *Richard II*, Leonardo in *Blood Wedding*, Herald Loomis in *Joe Turner's Come and Gone*, Rhodes in *Light in the Village*, Warwick in *The Conclusion of Henry VI*, Pericles in *Pericles Prince of Tyre*, Oberon in *A Midsummer Night's Dream* and Vincent Baptiste and Kwesi Ntuli in the world premiere of *Continental Divide*. Other theatres at which Mr. Weeden has worked include the Great Lakes Theatre Festival, Milwaukee Repertory Theater, Alabama Shakespeare Festival and the Shakespeare Festival of Dallas. He received the Back Stage West Garland award for his performances in *Othello* and *Les Blancs*. Mr. Weeden received his M.F.A. from Southern Methodist University.

CHRISTINE WILLIAMS (Deborah Vine/Ryan/Pat/ Snowbird) most recently appeared in the premiere of *Continental Divide* at the Oregon Shakespeare Festival. Previous OSF season credits include *Who's Afraid of Virginia Woolf, Arcadia, Enter the Guardsman, Night of the Iguana, Julius Caesar, Pericles, The School for Scandal, Love's Labour's Lost* and *The Trojan Women*. Other credits include *How I Learned to Drive* (Arizona Theatre Company), *Our Town* (Utah Shakespeare Festival), *Spring Awakening* (Open Circle Theatre Co.), *EAT TV* (Oregon Cabaret Theatre) and *Present Laughter* (TheatreWorks). Ms. Williams has also performed at the Milwaukee Repertory Theatre, Rogue Music Theatre, Chico City Opera, The Annex in Seattle, the Aspen Opera Theatre Center and American Opera Projects in New York City.

The Actors and Stage Managers employed in this production are members of Actors' Equity Association, the Union of Professional Actors and Stage Managers in the United States.

This production is made possible through the generosity of:

VODAFONE-US FOUNDATION

THE ALLEN FOUNDATION FOR THE ARTS

ROBERTA BIALEK PETER & HELEN BING

NATIONAL ENDOWMENT FOR THE ARTS

O **vodafone**™

Vodafone-US Foundation

CONTINENTAL DIVIDE

Mothers Against
Daughters of the Revolution

These plays can be seen or read in either order

Continental Divide

The idea of writing a pair of plays about the same fictional election – each complete in itself but enriched by seeing the other – came to me three years ago. The concept of each individual play goes way back.

In 1979, I drove across America, talking to people who had been involved in the radical political movements of the 1960s. The most striking thing was the shared biography of so many of the activists I talked to. A large number came from radical, often Communist backgrounds. Unsurprisingly, many of these red diaper babies were Jewish. Because of the anti-Communist witch hunts of the early 1950s, a significant proportion hadn't found out about their parents' political affiliations until they too became caught up in political activism.

Like Presidential politics, the radical mass movements of the '60s had a generational backstory: the children of Senator Joe McCarthy's victims were seeking both to avenge and to outdo their parents. There were other connections between the generations: like the Communists of the '30s and '40s, the New Left in the '60s was particularly concerned with racial discrimination; its politics had a strong cultural element (from folk music to rock and roll); early political success led on to failure, disillusion and reassessment. At its 1962 founding conference in Port Huron, Michigan, Students for a Democratic Society (SDS) declared: 'We regard men as infinitely precious and possessed of unfulfilled capacities for reason, freedom and love.' In 1969, the last SDS convention split into rival Marxist-Leninist and paramilitary factions, leading some of its most dedicated members (again, like the Communists of the 1940s and 1950s) to continue the struggle underground. Both generations had their fair share of defectors, who took the passion and certainty of the radical left into the conservative camp. Finally, both generations faced a massive government campaign of surveillance, infiltration and dirty tricks. I always asked my interviewees if they'd applied for their FBI file – almost all of them had, and were amazed by the level of investigation that was exposed.

I was 20 in 1968, and so I felt a part of the same story. For many years, I'd wanted to write a quest play, in which a former '60s activist would seek to investigate and come to terms with his own past, with all its heroism, passion and betrayal. As the baby-boomer generation began to run for high political office, I realized I could set a play about the legacy of the '60s against the background of a conventional political campaign.

As this idea developed, it was joined by another one. A year after my 1979 trip, I heard the story of an ambitious young congressman pretending to be his former boss, not as part of an amusing office skit, but in order to prepare a Presidential hopeful for a political debate. David Stockman had become disillusioned with Republican primary candidate John Anderson, and so agreed to play Anderson in Ronald Reagan's primary debate rehearsal. Stockman went on to play other Reagan debate opponents (playing Walter Mondale, he so demoralized Reagan that the President lost the real debate). I remained fascinated by the idea of the debate prep grudge match: someone acting somebody they distrusted or disliked, to help someone else wipe the floor with them.

I quickly realized that debate prep had further dramatic possibilities. Prep is a period when all the key players come together to make life-and-death campaign decisions. Often, they do so in the candidate's own home. America has the most dynastic political system of any of the great democracies – the Kennedys, Gores and Bushes in national politics, the Browns in California. Like everyone else, I ached to know what happened in that Texas hotel room in November 2000, as the Bushes senior and junior contemplated the possibility that Jeb might have failed to deliver George W. the state which would avenge their father's defeat eight years before.

So setting a play within a debate prep weekend allowed me to combine a political and a family drama. 'Family' is of course a key concept for the Republicans – it is also a crucial battleground within the party. Most people see the '60s as a period of radical activism for civil rights and against the Vietnam War: on the other side of politics, a parallel movement was forming. In 1960, the Young Americans for Freedom's (YAF) founding statement insisted that political and economic liberty are indivisible; in 1964, many YAF activists cut their teeth campaigning for Barry Goldwater; in 1969, the YAF national convention split down the middle over the issue of the military draft. The divisions that were exposed in the '60s – between traditionalist social conservatives and free-market libertarians, the patrician Republicanism of the northeast and the values voters of the southwest – are fracture-lines that still threaten the Republican Party, despite its current success.

Add to that the difficulty that politicians of all parties have with wayward children, and I felt I had a rich opportunity to combine the most dramatic elements of current politics in a single, climactic weekend.

For a long time, these two ideas were swimming separately round in my head. They came together when Berkeley Repertory Theatre and the Oregon Shakespeare Festival both approached me to write a play for them, and responded enthusiastically to the idea that it should be a joint commission. The result is a cycle of two plays, mapping the inter-generational and inter-party struggle between competing but not always incompatible visions of the American Dream, set on either side of the same election in an imaginary western state.

DAVID EDGAR

MOTHERS AGAINST

Characters

SHELDON VINE, *fifties, candidate*
CONNIE VINE, *fifties, his wife*
DEBORAH VINE, *eighteen, his daughter*
MITCHELL VINE Jr, *sixty, his brother, campaign chair*
DON D'AVANZO, *forties, campaign manager*
VINCENT BAPTISTE, *fifties, political consultant*
LORIANNE WEINER, *thirties, commentator*
CARYL MARQUEZ, *thirties, pollster*

The play is set in a western state in the imminent present.

Notation

A dash (–) means that a character is interrupted. A slash (/) means that the next character to speak starts speaking at that point (what follows the slash need not be completed). An ellipsis (. . .) indicates that a character has interrupted him or herself.

YOUNG AMERICANS FOR FREEDOM: THE SHARON STATEMENT

Adopted in Conference, at Sharon, Connecticut, on September 11, 1960

In this time of moral and political crises, it is the responsibility of the youth of America to affirm certain eternal truths.

We, as young conservatives, believe:

THAT foremost among the transcendent values is the individual's use of his God-given free will, whence derives his right to be free from the restrictions of arbitrary force;

THAT liberty is indivisible, and that political freedom cannot long exist without economic freedom; . . .

THAT the Constitution of the United States is the best arrangement yet devised for empowering government to fulfill its proper role, while restraining it from the concentration and abuse of power; . . .

THAT the market economy, allocating resources by the free play of supply and demand, is the single economic system compatible with the requirements of personal freedom and constitutional government, and that it is at the same time the most productive supplier of human needs;

THAT when government interferes with the work of the market economy, it tends to reduce the moral and physical strength of the nation; that when it takes from one man to bestow on another, it diminishes the incentive of the first, the integrity of the second, and the moral autonomy of both.

STATE CONSTITUTION ARTICLE 2

Voting, Initiative and Referendum, and Recall

SEC. 8. (a) The initiative is the power of the electors to propose statutes and amendments to the Constitution and to adopt or reject them. (b) An initiative measure may be proposed by presenting to the Secretary of State a petition that sets forth the text of the proposed statute or amendment to the Constitution and is certified to have been signed by electors equal in number to 5 percent in the case of a statute, and 8 percent in the case of an amendment to the Constitution, of the votes for all candidates for Governor at the last gubernatorial election. (c) The Secretary of State shall then submit the measure at the next general election held at least 131 days after it qualifies or at any special statewide election held prior to that general election. The Governor may call a special statewide election for the measure.

PROPOSITION 92

Oath of Allegiance
Constitutional Amendment and Statute

Summary: Requires all candidates for elective office, applicants for public employment, current state employees and state beneficiaries, residents of public housing, and new or re-registering voters to affirm loyalty to the United States, its values and its laws in the following terms: 'I do solemnly swear (or affirm) that I will support and defend the United States, against all enemies, foreign and domestic; that I will support its Constitution, uphold its democratic values and observe its laws; that I am not a member or supporter of any organization which pursues its ends by force; and that I take this obligation freely, without any mental reservation or purpose of evasion.'

Debates are to elections what treaties are to wars.
They ratify what has already been accomplished
on the battlefield.

Samuel Popkin
Debate Consultant

I've spoken of the Shining City all my political life ...
a tall, proud city built on rocks stronger than
oceans, windswept, God-blessed, and teeming with
people of all kinds living in harmony and peace; a
city with free ports that hummed with commerce
and creativity. And if there had to be city walls,
the walls had doors and the doors were open to
anyone with the will and the heart to get here.

President Ronald Reagan
Farewell Address, January 1989

Too many people have been beaten because they
tried to substitute substance for style.

Patrick Cadell
to Jimmy Carter

ACT ONE

Scene One

The living room of the country home of the Vine Family, in a wooded area near the Pacific coast. It's a fine Sunday morning in early fall. French windows open out to a terrace on one side. On the other side, there's a door leading to the front hallway. Double doors open out into the rest of the house upstage. There's a large round dining table, and a selection of easy chairs set out around a low table in front of a television and video player. Large black binders are set out on a sideboard; currently there are coffee, newspapers and breakfast pastries on the round table.

CARYL MARQUEZ *is in her thirties. She sits in one of the easy chairs, fast-forwarding and rewinding videos of campaign advertisements to find the correct place for later showing. She's also talking on a cell phone, referring from time to time to two pieces of paper.*

CARYL (*in Spanish*). No, esta bien, Juanita. No, yo te prometí que te iba a leer las preguntas. Si. ¿Estas lista? [No, it's fine, Juanita. No, I promised I'd go through the questions with you. Yes. Are you ready?] What are the colors of the flag of the United States?

A-Plus. La próxima pregunta. [Next question.] What do we celebrate on the fourth of July?

DON D'AVANZO *enters. He's in his forties, the campaign manager. He goes to the table to check the headlines on the newspapers.*

Pues, creo que puedes decir [Well, I guess you could call it] 'liberation from colonial oppression.'

DON *looks quizzically at* CARYL, *who hasn't seen him.*

No, es correcto, en una manera. Ahora [No, it's quite correct, in its way. Now] What is the fundamental belief of the Declaration of Independence?

DON. Good question.

CARYL. Uh . . . Esperate un momento. [Hold on a minute.]

She stands to introduce herself to DON.

Hello.

DON. Hi. I'm Don D'Avanzo.

CARYL. Ah. Right. Gosh. Hello.

DON. And you must be the sub / from Polsby –

CARYL. I'm Caryl Marquez – Polsby, Zuckerman and Lane.

DON. Welcome to boot camp.

CARYL. Mr Vine said I should make myself / at home –

DON. Please. Don't mind me.

CARYL *doesn't really want to carry on in front of* DON. *But as* DON *goes to look at the papers, she allows herself to speak on the phone, lowering her voice a little.*

CARYL. Perdon, ¿si? [I'm sorry, yes?]

She checks one of her pieces of paper:

No. The fundamental belief of the Declaration of Independence is 'All men are created equal.'

DON. Is it now.

CARYL. What is the most important right possessed by US citizens?

DON. Freedom from arbitrary acts of government.

CARYL (*responding to what Juanita has said*). The right to vote, correct. What kind of government do we have in the United States?

DON. Don't get me started.

DON*'s cell phone rings. He goes out.*

CARYL. No, capitalism is the economic system.

El capitalismo es el sistema económico. [Capitalism is the economic system.]

Enter CONNIE VINE. *She is in her fifties, with a patrician air. She carries two vases of flowers.*

No, you could say 'democratic'. But the real answer is 'republican'.

CONNIE. Well, that's what we must hope.

CARYL. Perdóname un momento. Un momento. [Excuse me for a moment. Just a moment.]

CARYL *stands and goes to* CONNIE.

CONNIE. Good morning. I'm Connie Vine.

CARYL. I'm Caryl Marquez. I'm the / substitute –

CONNIE. Ah, you're the stand-in?

CARYL. Well, yes, if you like.

CARYL *puts out her hand to shake.* CONNIE *has to put down at least one vase, does so, and shakes* CARYL*'s hand.*

CONNIE. Big tip. Don't let him bully you. He will interrupt, just before the end of every sentence, as long as he's convinced he'll get away with it. Don't let him.

CARYL. No. Thanks.

CONNIE. It's like with dogs. Don't let them see you're scared.

CARYL. I'll try not to.

CONNIE. But I guess, it isn't really you. So I imagine that's much easier.

CARYL (*baffled*). Uh . . .

Enter VINCENT BAPTISTE. *He's in his fifties, the campaign's policy advisor, African-American.*

VINCENT. Morning.

CONNIE. Vincent. Do you want some coffee?

VINCENT. Please.

CONNIE (*to* CARYL). Please, go on with your call.

CARYL. Uh . . . thank you.

> CONNIE *notices some dying flowers in an existing vase and goes to deal with them.*

CONNIE. It's warm enough to take it on the terrace. It's beautiful and fresh, after the rain.

CARYL. Si, Juanita. Perdóname. No, estas respondiendo bien. [Right, Juanita. Sorry. No, you're doing fine.]

CONNIE (*to* VINCENT). She's the stand-in for McKeene.

VINCENT. Um . . . are you / sure?

CONNIE. You know, she plays her in the mock debate.

CARYL. Yes. Who is the current governor of this state?

CONNIE. Now that she ought to know.

> *Hearing this,* CARYL *turns to see* CONNIE *going out with the dead flowers.* CARYL *sees that* VINCENT *is looking quizzically at her.*

CARYL. Esperate un momento. Espera. [I'm putting you on hold. Hold on.]

> *She stands. To* VINCENT:

Hello.

VINCENT. So what's this, 'phone a friend'?

CARYL (*gesturing to where* CONNIE *departed*). I think there's been a misunderstanding.

VINCENT. Not on my part. You're the sub for Gerry Zuckerman.

CARYL. Correct.

VINCENT. And you're on the phone to somebody who doesn't know who's governor.

CARYL. Yes. Actually / it's my –

VINCENT. Which narrows it right down to half the state.

CARYL. My brother's girlfriend's mother. Taking her
citizenship test tomorrow. I was supposed to be having
lunch with her today.

VINCENT. Then you must continue.

VINCENT takes his coffee and pastry onto the terrace.
CARYL back on the telephone.

CARYL (*continuing*). I'm sorry. Shoot. Perdóname. [Sorry.] So
can you name three articles of the Bill of Rights? Correcto.
No [Correct. No.] that's all the same right as the first right.

DEBORAH has entered from the hallway. She is eighteen.
She wears an expensive if battered overcoat over hippie
attire, and has a backpack. She is also seriously bedraggled.

Freedom of speech, religion, assembly and redress of
grievances.

DEBORAH. Clearly you're not referring to America.

CARYL. Lo siento. Esto se ha sido imposible. Te llamo. Adiós.
[I'm sorry. This has become impossible. I'll call you back.
Goodbye.]

She ends the call, stands and puts her hand out to
DEBORAH.

I'm Caryl Marquez.

DEBORAH. Howdy.

CARYL. I'm a pollster.

DEBORAH. Right.

CARYL. I'm here for the debate prep.

DEBORAH. Oh.

CARYL. Or boot camp.

DEBORAH. Ah.

CARYL. But I'm not the stand-in.

DEBORAH. Obviously.

Slight pause.

CARYL. Um, so, are you . . . ?

DEBORAH. Well, like, you could say, I am from The Other Side.

CARYL. Would you like breakfast?

DEBORAH. No, thanks. So, who else is here?

CARYL. Well, Mr Vine, of course, both Mr Vines, that is, their political advisors, Mrs Vine . . .

DEBORAH. Uh . . .

Suddenly, DEBORAH *is overcome with nausea. There's a wastebasket nearby. She grabs it and throws up in it.*

CARYL. Um, I . . .

DEBORAH. Excuse me. It's been like . . . a heavy day.

She doesn't know what to do with the wastebasket, so she hands it to CARYL.

I'm going to take a shower.

She goes out with her backpack into the rest of the house. CARYL *widens her eyes, breathes deeply.* VINCENT *enters.* CARYL *quickly puts down the wastebasket.*

VINCENT. Hey, the pain au chocolat are good. In fact, I might have just one more.

He goes to get another pastry, assumes CARYL *is not sure whether she should have one, or another one.*

I'm Vincent Baptiste, by the way.

CARYL. Oh? Yes, of course.

VINCENT (*gestures to the pastry*). Go on.

CARYL. No thank you.

VINCENT (*noticing the vomit in the basket*). Ah.

CARYL. Did you say it was nice out?

VINCENT. I didn't. But it sure is.

CARYL. Dandy.

CARYL *picks up the wastebasket and takes it out on to the terrace.* VINCENT *eats another pastry.* CARYL *comes back in, without the basket.*

VINCENT. A little nerve-wracking.

CARYL. Oh, do you think so?

VINCENT. Felt that way when I arrived.

CARYL. Well, gee.

VINCENT. So are you up to speed with the scene around here?

CARYL *tries a nonchalant shrug.* VINCENT *looks quizzical.*

CARYL. I thought I was. Now I'm not so sure.

VINCENT. Have you met the Prince of Darkness?

CARYL. Um – excuse me?

VINCENT. The campaign manager.

CARYL. Sure have.

VINCENT. Then you get your hundred bucks.

CARYL. And this . . . this is the Vine family residence.

VINCENT. Built by Senator Mitch Vine.

CARYL. Gold in them thar Douglas Firs.

VINCENT. And now the residence of Mitchell Junior.

CARYL. Not Sheldon.

VINCENT. No. Why, did you think . . . ?

CARYL. I just assumed that Mrs Vine . . .

VINCENT. I think that Mrs Vine appears to own whatever residence she currently inhabits.

CARYL. Ah. And Mr Mitchell Vine's the campaign chair.

VINCENT. Yes.

CARYL. But not a Prince of Darkness.

VINCENT. More a Lord of Discipline.

CARYL. And is he married?

VINCENT. No, divorced. Why do you / ask?

CARYL. Well, everyone at PZL says that Mr Mitchell should have been the candidate.

Pause.

I mean, he ran his father's last campaign. He took over his father's business when he died. He was the heir apparent. Everybody says so.

Slight pause.

I'm sorry. Is that not the thing to say?

VINCENT. Maybe not to the policy advisor to the actual candidate.

CARYL. I'm such a goof.

VINCENT. No matter.

CARYL. So it's just two brothers?

VINCENT. Now. There was a sister, Deborah.

CARYL. And she . . . ?

VINCENT. Died of pancreatic cancer a quarter of a century ago.

CARYL. Ah. Gee whiz.

Slight pause.

Guess I'm just nosey.

VINCENT. Goes with the job. But in answer to your question, I think it's fair to say that Mitchell Vine is not the candidate *because* he ran the family business and his father's last campaign.

MITCHELL VINE Jr *enters. He is sixty. If he overheard any of the last remark, he shows no sign of it.*

And here he is.

MITCHELL. Vincent. Should my ears be burning?

VINCENT. This is Caryl Marquez.

MITCHELL. Yes, I know.

Gesturing to the videotapes and papers:

Well, you really did get down to it.

CARYL. Yes, I . . . You said . . .

MITCHELL. Of course.

Enter DON.

It's good to see somebody's up and running here.

DON. Even if she thinks that equality is superior to liberty.

CARYL. I didn't write the answers, Mr D'Avanzo.

Pause.

MITCHELL. Hear this. Albert Einstein's secretary comes up to him and says: 'Professor Einstein, you know that test you give your students every Friday? Well, you've given me this week's test to type and I know you're notoriously absent-minded but the questions are the same as last week's and I guess this must be a mistake.' And Einstein says . . .

CARYL. 'I know, it's the answers that are different.'

MITCHELL. Ah . . .

CARYL. Oh gosh, I'm sorry . . .

Difficult pause.

VINCENT (*rescue attempt*). So is Professor Einstein available for consultation?

Slight pause.

MITCHELL. So has anybody seen my brother?

VINCENT. Last seen peddling acrest of the horizon.

Slight pause.

MITCHELL. Goodfriend Baptiste, why not show Miss Marquez around the grounds.

CARYL. Why, thank you.

DON. And if you catch sight of the candidate, give him a holler and tell him to move his butt.

VINCENT. I surely will.

CARYL *allows herself to be led out by* VINCENT.

MITCHELL. So why not Gerry Zuckerman?

DON. Unwell.

MITCHELL. Oh, yes?

DON. My answer is entirely accurate.

MITCHELL. So what's wrong with the question?

DON. The question isn't, 'Why not Gerry?'

MITCHELL. So it must be, 'Why Caryl Marquez?'

DON. You know the news she brings.

MITCHELL. I know it's good.

DON. If we can force a fumble.

Pause.

You've seen the press. The *Post* notes the sudden growth of interest in an obscure ballot proposition about oaths of loyalty. The *Gazette* leads on the DA's excellent if surprising decision not to prosecute a Latino guard for shooting dead an eco-terrorist, caught decapitating genetically-modified poplars at a university. They both point out that the proposition and the shooting may become connected in the public mind. Both use the expression 'lightning rod'.

We debate Rebecca McKeene in fifty-six hours. Sadly, since we lost the pre-debate on moderators, we don't have much control over the questions. That leaves us with the answers.

MITCHELL. Well, you know, on issues, the candidate is hard to move.

DON. Which is why it's so vital to prepare the battlefield.

MITCHELL. So how does the senorita . . . ?

DON. I told Gerry about our little problem. He said he had a junior staffer who could fulfill two roles at once. As an analyst, but also an example.

MITCHELL. I'm not quite sure I understand.

DON. You see . . .

He stops himself, aware that CONNIE *is entering. A 'tell you later' gesture.*

CONNIE. Well, here is the campaign chair and the campaign manager. I've spotted Mr Baptiste and his cute new friend splashing through the puddles around the pool. We are overwhelmed with chiefs. So where's the Indian?

MITCHELL. Apparently he's bicycling.

CONNIE. We must pray he doesn't have a heart attack.

MITCHELL. Well, certainly . . .

CONNIE. I changed the flowers.

MITCHELL (*looking around*). Did you?

CONNIE. They were dead.

CARYL *and* VINCENT *appear from the terrace.*

VINCENT. He's coming up the gulch.

DON (*going to look at the papers again*). 'At last.'

CARYL. He can certainly move on that thing.

CONNIE *returning from the window, passing* CARYL.

CONNIE. Far be it from me to advise you on candidate control, but I'd say you'd have a better morning if Sheldon didn't think that everyone was waiting for his entrance.

DON. Why's that?

CONNIE. I sense that he's a little tigerish today.

Everybody stops looking towards the window.

DON (*reading*). Dune buggies. McKeene's line of the day's dune buggies.

VINCENT. Do we have a position on these things?

DON. We do now.

MITCHELL. And?

DON. We're Republicans. We believe in the inalienable right of all Americans to pursue life, liberty and happiness in any class of powered vehicle they choose.

Most people are surreptitiously glancing towards the window. Overhearing the end of DON's line, SHELDON VINE enters from the front door side, in shorts and a T-shirt, holding up his bicycle with one hand.

SHELDON. I am doing this for three related reasons. One is to demonstrate my extraordinary level of physical preparedness for the trials ahead. Second is to show how light they make these things now. Third is because I was not allowed to bring a bicycle over the front threshold of this house until the age of twenty-nine. And it still gives me a charge.

CONNIE goes to SHELDON and removes his bicycle.

MITCHELL. Hi, Sheldon.

SHELDON. So here we are, incarcerated in our hilltop hideaway, engaged in tense and intense preparations for the make-or-break prime-time debate on Tuesday. Two days without having to see a voter. Two days in which I can ride my bicycle. Why didn't we ask for more of these?

DON. We did.

SHELDON. Two days to remind ourselves that it is indeed life, *liberty* and the pursuit of happiness. Say, Chief, how much change do I have to raise today?

MITCHELL. Same as every day.

SHELDON *sitting to make calls:*

SHELDON. And what's the least number of calls in which I can achieve this?

MITCHELL (*handing him cards with details of donors*). All depends.

DON. The Sixty Kennedy campaign. His father, old Joe, crook and closet Nazi, said that he was happy to buy Jack the presidency, but he was damned if he was buying him a landslide.

SHELDON (*phone*). Ah. Hi there. Is this . . .

Checks card.

Samantha? Great. Hey, is your daddy in?

Hand out to CARYL.

I'm Sheldon Vine. Welcome to Stalag Thirteen.

CARYL. Or boot camp.

SHELDON. Well, exactly. Now, you're . . .

CONNIE. She's the stand-in for the mock.

DON. Um . . .

MITCHELL. What?

CARYL. Um, Mr Vine, I must . . .

SHELDON (*phone*). Oh, hi. That's Harry? Hey, it's Sheldon Vine.

To CARYL:

I like your stuff.

CARYL. Actually, you see . . .

SHELDON. So how's things in the real world?

MITCHELL. Um, when you say 'the stand-in' . . . ?

CONNIE. And when you say her 'stuff'?

SHELDON (*phone*). Now this is the last thing that you need on a fine Sunday morning just back from church, but I've got some good news and some bad news.

CARYL. In fact, I'm not the stand-in, Mrs Vine.

CONNIE. I'm sorry?

SHELDON (*phone*). Yup, you got it.

CARYL. No, I'm the substitute for Gerry Zuckerman, the senior partner in your husband's polling firm, who is sick and sent me in his place.

SHELDON (*phone*). And I'm doing this because like you I'm fed up with the red tape which stops folks like you building affordable homes.

VINCENT. For newlyweds and first-time buyers.

CONNIE. So who is the stand-in?

CARYL. She's upstairs.

DON. She is?

SHELDON (*phone*). And the second piece of bad news is, I'd sure appreciate it if you could mail the check tomorrow.

CARYL. Taking a shower.

MITCHELL. Taking what?

As he speaks, SHELDON *waves to* MITCHELL, *to attract his attention.*

SHELDON (*phone*). Well, that's the third. I'd say what we were hoping for was around . . .

He skywrites the figure twenty, MITCHELL *nods.*

. . . 'round twenty.

CONNIE. Did you say the stand-in is upstairs?

SHELDON (*phone*). Yes, thousand.

CARYL. Yes. I don't think she's very well.

DON. Not very *well*?

SHELDON *gestures 'shhh' before proceeding.*

SHELDON (*phone*). Well, sure, I understand that . . . yuh, sure, anything would be most appreciated . . .

But only, and this is the last piece of bad news, you call up ten people and ask them to do the same.

He gives a thumbs-up sign.

Well, you know how much I value . . . Absolutely. All my best to . . .

The slightest beat as he checks the card.

. . . Barbara and the kids.

He ends the call.

Six grand.

VINCENT. Yo.

CARYL. Hey, neat.

CONNIE. I told you. *Very* tigerish.

MITCHELL. Ninety-four to go.

SHELDON. Harry says he'll make the calls.

DON. Sez he.

SHELDON. Caryl, I think I interrupted you.

CARYL. Actually, Mr Vine / I have to –

SHELDON. My wife will tell you that I interrupt her just before the end of sentences.

CARYL. Yes, but you see, / I'm not . . .

SHELDON. I have to say, that with this pirate band, if I didn't interrupt, I'd never get a word / in edgewise –

CONNIE. Sheldon, apparently, this is not the stand-in.

SHELDON. No?

CONNIE. Miss Marquez is a pollster.

CONNIE*'s noticed another old vase of dying flowers and heading to its rescue, as:*

SHELDON. Ah. What happened to / Gerry –

VINCENT. Gerry Zuckerman is sick.

SHELDON. So . . .

CONNIE. Caryl.

He's making the next call as he speaks.

SHELDON. . . . is here to persuade me to fit my message to the voters, rather than persuade the voters of the virtues of my message.

CARYL. No, sir. I'm just here to report on what we've found.

CONNIE *has taken the flowers out of the vase. She notices the wastebasket has disappeared.*

SHELDON. You want persuasive, you watch this.

His call is answered. Again, he consults his briefing card. Meanwhile, CONNIE *sees that the errant wastebasket is for some reason on the terrace, and heads out for it.*

Hi, Tony? It's Sheldon Vine here. I'm the Republican candidate for governor. So, how's tricks?

DON *looks questioningly.*

MITCHELL. Tony Granito.

DON. The?

MITCHELL *nods.* CONNIE *reenters with the wastebasket.*

CONNIE. While the real stand-in is supposedly / upstairs?

DON. The *real* stand-in?

CONNIE. And apparently, unwell.

She looks to CARYL, *who shrugs weakly, as to confirm that the vomit in the basket is the stand-in's.* SHELDON *gestures for quiet again.*

SHELDON (*phone*). Now, Tony, this is the last thing you need on a sunny Sunday morning with, with Sherry fixing brunch out on the patio, but I've got some good news and some bad news.

CONNIE (*to* CARYL, *quietly*). I must apologize.

DON *looks to* MITCHELL, *who shrugs.*

SHELDON (*phone*). Right on.

CONNIE. We're really not making you feel welcome.

SHELDON (*phone*). No sweat.

CARYL. No, it's dandy. Really.

CONNIE. Really?

SHELDON (*phone*). Well, the kinda ballpark figure folks are going for is kinda in the region of, like, twenty.

CARYL. No, really.

SHELDON (*phone*). Which as coincidence would have it, yuh, is right around the legal limit.

Attention.

Hey man, that's great. But only . . .

Sure, you heard this kind of pitch before. Have a great day.

He puts the phone down.

Perfect, except that Sherry doesn't do the cooking.

ALL. Oh, dear.

SHELDON. Now, hands up how many people see this as humiliating?

No one puts their hand up, though people look at each other.

OK. How many people think the voters see this as humiliating?

A moment. VINCENT *then* CARYL *put their hands up. Then* CONNIE.

So why, as the person who has got to do this, why don't I see this as humiliating?

VINCENT. Because the alternative is public funding.

SHELDON. Oh? Why not spending limits?

DON. Well, if you consult the First Amendment to the Constitution . . .

SHELDON. Then why not cap donations?

MITCHELL. Why are we discussing this?

DON. Because, instead of spending five minutes raising twenty thousand, you spend twenty minutes raising five.

MITCHELL. Plus a lot of time inquiring if your lovely wife, fine son and charming daughter might / chip in as well.

SHELDON. Or you accept, fundraising *is* the process. It's like poker. The money's how you keep score. If your television's good, the checks roll in. I end up in the dumpster Tuesday, nobody returns my calls. And what's Mitch doing when he calls some fat cat Dem and says: 'Do you know what McKeene's energy proposals mean for fuel costs?' He's doing what Don does when he runs a spot saying 'this is what'll happen if you vote McKeene.' It isn't 'buying influence over the democratic process.' It's actually participating in the game.

Slight pause.

How could it be otherwise? We all say – rightly – that we can't be bought. That's why we accept from tobacco companies and gaming interests, to make that very point.

MITCHELL. Well that's part of / the reason.

SHELDON. To say, heck, I take from Colombian Import-Export and Las Vegas Bigger Better Blackjack Inc. *and* the Little Sisters of Eternal Mercy just to show it won't make a bit of difference to what I do in office. But your dollar might – it will – make a difference to whether I get there.

VINCENT. Sir, you're rehearsing.

DON. Yes, sir. Why are you rehearsing?

CARYL. But, you don't take money from the gaming industry?

SHELDON. Sure do. And how does Tony Granito earn his living?

MITCHELL. He publishes *Hot Tips*.

SHELDON. And *Red Hot*. And *Hot Lips*.

CARYL. And you . . .

SHELDON. But because I tell him and the world that I will not allow his donation to affect my actions by one whit, how could it be rational – or even right – to turn him down?

CARYL. Because it's kinda . . . icky?

Pause.

SHELDON. 'Congress shall make no law abridging the freedom of speech or of the press.' I sometimes think that that's the main plank of my platform. Particularly in conjunction with the inalienable right to liberty. Which is why we are discussing it right now.

DON. Miss Marquez, welcome to the House of Fun.

SHELDON. Well, he gave me ten. So what do I have left?

MITCHELL. Eighty-four thousand.

SHELDON. Give me my card.

DON*'s phone rings.*

DON. D'Avanzo.

Simultaneously, MITCHELL *hands over the card.* CARYL *has seen* DEBORAH *enter, wearing a pair of woolly socks and a T-shirt with the slogan 'Trees Are People Too,' currently concealed by the washing she's carrying.*

CARYL. Uh . . .

SHELDON (*phone*). Hi, can I speak to Scott P. Russell please?

MITCHELL. Deborah.

CARYL. Deborah?

DON *concludes his call.*

SHELDON (*phone*). Hey, Scott. Sheldon Vine.

DEBORAH. Well, hi there, all you running dogs.

SHELDON *sees* DEBORAH.

SHELDON (*phone*). Hey, you know what, Scott? I'm going to call you back.

He ends the call. Everyone is looking at DEBORAH.

DEBORAH. Hey, people. Quit looking at me like I'm like a ghost.

CONNIE. I'm sorry. It's just a little bit of a surprise. Caryl, Vincent. Don. This is our daughter.

CARYL. Yes, I see that now.

Slight pause.

DEBORAH. Now, look. I'm sorry, people. But it's been like a kind of fucking nightmare getting here, you know? I mean, profuse apologies and shit for turning up like unannounced but I've been kind of trying to protect the planet from the armed fist of the fascist state.

Slight pause.

MITCHELL. Oh, my God.

DEBORAH. I mean, like defending free speech, free assembly and redress of grievances.

MITCHELL. Uh, when you say 'the state' . . .

SHELDON. My daughter.

Pause.

DEBORAH. Dad. I'm sorry.

SHELDON. Don't be. My daughter Deborah. We disagree on everything. Education, foreign policy. Crime. Economics, just don't go there. She was raised on timber money and she's dedicated her life to bankrupting the industry. But one thing we have in common.

CONNIE. What's that, Sheldon?

SHELDON. We're both rebels with a cause.

Slight pause.

And of course, the first people you rebel against, the people whose job it is to be rebelled against, are the loins from which you sprung.

Slight pause.

Hey, Mitch?

MITCHELL *shrugs.*

And if not fathers, brothers. Say, Vince, you're the younger, right?

VINCENT. By half an hour.

SHELDON. Know how you feel.

Pause.

Now, I still have over eighty thousand bucks to raise. And I'd like to take a shower. Later on we will discuss whether this campaign is salvageable, and if so why. But for five minutes, please, I have to share some matters with my daughter.

DON. Sir, there's a lot to do.

SHELDON. I know. Oh, and Caryl?

CARYL. Yes?

SHELDON. I interrupt. But I never blame the messenger.

As DON, VINCENT, CARYL *and* MITCHELL *go:*

DON. You set up the spots?

CARYL. You betcha.

MITCHELL. Good.

DON (*to* MITCHELL). Got it?

MITCHELL. I got it.

DON. Right.

They've all gone.

CONNIE. This is your laundry?

DEBORAH. I can do it.

CONNIE. Mitchell has a staff.

DEBORAH. I said.

CONNIE *goes to her, takes the laundry.*

CONNIE. Talk to your father.

She might kiss her daughter. But she doesn't, and takes the laundry, exposing DEBORAH's *T-shirt.*

Really?

DEBORAH. Really.

CONNIE *turns to* SHELDON *and explains.*

CONNIE. 'Trees Are People Too.'

CONNIE *leaves.*

SHELDON. It's Mao Tse Tung, right?

DEBORAH. 'Trees Are / People – '?

SHELDON. 'Running dogs'.

DEBORAH. I guess so.

SHELDON. I thought that the phrase was 'paper tigers'.

DEBORAH. They're not mutually exclusive.

SHELDON (*the T-shirt*). Of course, the difference between trees and people . . .

DEBORAH (*continuing an old trope:*) . . . is that trees have roots which bind them to one place, while *people* . . .

SHELDON. . . . are like birds with wings, who come the snows can fly off to the spring.

DEBORAH. Dad, I didn't realize / that this –

SHELDON. You know, we're always here for you.

DEBORAH (*after a beat*). That's why I came.

SHELDON. Do you want a drink?

DEBORAH. Is there, like, peppermint or herbal tea?

SHELDON. Let's look.

There's a little box of teas on the table.

Uh, 'camomile'?

DEBORAH. That's fine.

SHELDON. It's grass.

DEBORAH. It's fine.

SHELDON *fixes the tea.*

SHELDON. You said, you 'didn't realize.'

DEBORAH. I didn't realize that this was, like called boot camp.

SHELDON. Ah. A vital piece of information.

DEBORAH. Why?

SHELDON. What always happens in a boot camp movie?

DEBORAH. I don't know. What always happens in a / boot camp movie?

SHELDON. The recruits rebel.

Slight pause.

DEBORAH. And why do you like have to / rebel –

SHELDON. You know, when I was your age, back before the dawn of time, the great divide between us and the other side was, we knew we were going to lose. That the future, obviously, clearly, was with the left. Which left, that was a question. Great Society or Great Leap Forward. But at least, no one was going to ask any of us folks to run the country.

He takes the tea to his daughter.

DEBORAH. Happy days.

SHELDON. I'm with you there. Drink that.

He hands her the tea.

Is there anything about this fucking nightmare I should know?

Scene Two

Afternoon. The easy chairs are arranged around the television monitors and the videotapes are piled ready for showing. VINCENT alone, waiting for the meeting to begin. CARYL has just entered from the terrace.

CARYL. Well, howdy.

VINCENT. Afternoon.

CARYL (*gestures outside*). Neat kinda day.

VINCENT. It's always lovely after rain.

　　Pause. CARYL sits.

CARYL. Thanks for your help this morning.

VINCENT. You are very welcome.

CARYL. So you're a twin?

VINCENT. Correct.

CARYL. Do you know the theory that everybody has a secret twin and our lives are spent trying to find out who they are?

VINCENT. I know the theory. We're more contradictory than complementary.

　　Enter MITCHELL through the double doors.

CARYL. So are you . . . is your brother, as it were . . . I mean, politically . . . ?

　　MITCHELL *a quizzical look, as SHELDON enters.*

VINCENT. Only our mother can tear us apart.

SHELDON. Good afternoon.

CARYL. Good afternoon, sir.

SHELDON (*the television and the videotapes*). So where's the popcorn?

　　CARYL *sits.* DON *enters, hitting the ground running.*

DON. So, do we have our game faces on?

SHELDON (*sitting down*). We sure do.

DON. Are we ready to rumble?

VINCENT (*sitting*). We sure are.

DON. So let's play ball.

MITCHELL. We're all ready, Dark Master. This is the team.

DON *begins his presentation.*

DON. Then listen up. Ladies and gentlemen, some of this will be familiar but bear with me. Please cast your minds back many moons ago, when the world was young and my opponent planned this year's gubernatorial campaign. Or rather, we planned one on her behalf.

SHELDON. 'Her' is McKeene?

DON. Well, strictly, I meant Blair Lowe, political consultant and cross-pollinator.

CARYL. That's cross-what?

SHELDON. In her youth she took a shine to Mitchell.

CARYL. Gosh.

MITCHELL. Long time ago.

DON. For whom, whatever, we constructed a traditional Democrat campaign – in that it argued for compulsory lesbianism and the forced expropriation of all private property. But it was *un*like a usual campaign in that wc-slash-they planned not just to exhort but to mobilize the electorate. So this campaign we planned for them – which we have good reason to believe they were also planning for themselves – was based on thinking they thought that they'd found the silver bullet.

SHELDON. Which is?

DON. OK. Five years ago, what was the size and voting habits of the non-Anglo populations?

CARYL. Nearly half the population, a third of the citizens eligible to vote, a quarter registered, under a fifth actually voting.

DON. And Latinos?

CARYL. A third underage, a third not citizens, of the remaining third, two-thirds not registered and one in six actually pulls the lever.

DON. And the electorate?

CARYL. Eighty percent white.

DON. What's changed since then?

VINCENT. The Latino vote has doubled.

DON (*reproving*). Vincent.

VINCENT. Sorry.

CARYL. The Latino participation rate has doubled.

DON. And if you are a strategist of the foresight of Ms Lowe, you work out that nobody can take this state with the Anglo vote alone. So to prevent our getting any of it, we – they go for broke on the Hispanic vote. Registration drives. Phone banks. House meetings. Setting up ironing boards outside supermarkets. Vote by mail.

SHELDON. That works for them?

DON. Sure, for Latinos. Anything with a stamp on it. Plus Voter Reg. lays the basis for Vote By Mail which leads straight on to Get Out The Vote and Knock and Drag Out on the day.

SHELDON. Why has no one told me this before?

DON. Because it didn't happen. It's pretend.

SHELDON. Yes, I got that.

DON. And it isn't customary to involve the candidate closely in the imaginary workings of the opposing candidate's campaign.

MITCHELL. Not information he'd use wisely.

DON. But mainly, because after all this work Blair takes a good long look at the real plan and kills it.

VINCENT. Shucks.

SHELDON. Why?

DON. Sure, they run Spanish ads and she appears on Univision in a tablecloth and requires colonic irrigation to dislodge the guava empanadas. But when they – we – cost it out we find they'd need to fundraise till the tricentennial to finance it. That is, if they wanted to run a spot or two as well. So in the cold light of dawn, their tribal elders lay the ancient wisdom on the line.

SHELDON. Which is?

DON. That this isn't '72. That there ain't a McGovern grassroots army out there any more. You're pounding sidewalks when frankly you should be going to cocktail parties to swell the war chest. And having swelled it, you're pissing it away on people two of five of whom won't vote, and that's even if, if they did vote, they'd vote for you. Instead of playing the old game of border warfare for the twenty percent of weak Republicans and soft Democrats who pull that lever every time. So they – we – consigned the whole damn ball of wax to outer darkness.

SHELDON. And were they – you, we – right?

DON. Sure. They were fifteen points ahead. Even if it works, grassroots isn't worth a hill of beans unless you're in a squeaker. And this wasn't even close.

SHELDON. Well, isn't.

DON. Wasn't.

SHELDON. 'Scuse me?

DON. It's close now.

DON *turns to* CARYL.

CARYL. Two weeks ago, we were – actually – twelve points behind. Last weekend we went into the field. Now, sir, we have you six behind among all voters, two point five behind with likely voters.

DON. And thus well within the margin.

SHELDON. Wow.

DON. Your darkest fear.

SHELDON. You said it.

VINCENT. So what, this means they're going to mount a grassroots campaign?

DON. I'd guess so, sure, but that's not the point of this weekend.

MITCHELL. Which is to work out how to use next Tuesday to the maximum advantage.

DON. Particularly as it's one debate in a close race hard up against the wire, and thus likely to be watched by a considerably larger group than the usual sad politicos, parents of loud babies, furniture and pets.

MITCHELL. Presumably you have some recommendations.

VINCENT. Based on sound market research.

DON. And what the good folks out there know of us, and what they don't.

Slight pause.

SHELDON (*suspicious*). Go on.

DON. The story so far. As you know, at the start of this, I'm thinking that Blair's thinking that the race is to the swift and nasty and so I'm all for cutting to the chase and going straight for root canal. But the candidate insists he wants to start out positive, and he writes the checks, and so we introduce him to the populace with 'Values'.

CARYL *shows the first ad –* SHELDON *over stills and footage of his grandfather, pictures of his father's electoral successes,* SHELDON *himself in shirt sleeves in a hi-tech environment, in a school, pictures of him and* CONNIE.

SHELDON. *Hi. I'm Sheldon Vine and I'm running for governor.*

MITCHELL. As is clear to all.

SHELDON *(continuing)*. *Like you I learned my values from my family. My grandfather, who brought a business to this state and made it thrive. My father, who led a life of public service as US senator. Values of hard work, discipline and responsibility . . .*

DON. And helping mom out with the dishes, naturally.

SHELDON *(continuing)*. *. . . which stood me in good stead when I left home to start up a business of my own. Values I want to see passed on to another generation of Americans.*

SHELDON. You remember those kids?

SHELDON *(continuing)*. *Running a business or running for office . . .*

CONNIE *and* SHELDON *on the screen.*

MITCHELL. Who's the plugugly on the right?

SHELDON *(continuing)*. *. . . it's all about the values we all share. I'm Sheldon Vine.*

CARYL *stops the tape. Applause.*

DON. Paid for by Citizens for Puppy Dogs and Long Walks in the Mountains. And to be honest I think they'll think, great, Shel's playing clean, why don't we play mean, and so imagine my surprise when the forces of Beelzebub decide to emulate our lofty tone with 'Desk'.

This McKeene ad has REBECCA *sitting behind desks, striding along State Capitol corridors, chairing committees, speaking to flag-waving crowds and, finally, talking with police and firefighters.*

REBECCA. *Hello, my name's Rebecca McKeene and I'm running on my record. I'm honored to have been chosen by the voters of this state to be an assembly member and twice a state senator. As Chair of the Senate Budget Committee I'm proud to have . . .*

SHELDON (*during the above*). Hand signals.

CARYL. Mixed signals.

VINCENT. Right.

DON gestures to CARYL to fast-forward.

REBECCA. . . . *balanced a budget in the billions –*

CARYL *fast-forwards.* REBECCA *running along corridors, sitting in jerky meetings waving her hands frenetically, as:*

DON. And bayoneting deadbeat dads and flinging widows out into the snow . . .

He gestures CARYL to restart play.

REBECCA. . . . *by firefighters and doctors, taxpayers and businesspeople, prison officers and the police.*

DON. How many in each category, Becca?

That gravelly male VOICE-OVER used in political spots:

VOICE-OVER. *Rebecca McKeene. A record of responsibility.*

CARYL *stops tape and changes it.*

DON. Paid for by Bleeding Hearts for Bankruptcy. And what's the message from the malls?

CARYL *quotes from a paper; looking over her shoulder, DON turns it into a little trope:*

CARYL. Dull.

DON. Boring.

CARYL. Very boring.

DON. Tedious.

CARYL. Though some young female undecideds thought the firefighters were peachy.

DON. And so I'm thinking that they're thinking shit we've sent the state to sleep so they *must* be thinking that we're thinking now's the time to get our second strike in first and introduce the public to the real McKeene. And of course they're on the nail but once again I'm overruled on the grounds of decency and taste, and as I'm but a paid hireling I do as I'm told. Hence 'Vision'.

This ad is set against the sweep of history: sepia stills of loggers and fishermen, construction in the Thirties, airplanes, multi-racial images of energetic entrepreneurship and discovery today. But the main thing is that SHELDON *delivers this incredibly fast.*

SHELDON. *I'm Sheldon Vine, and I'm running for governor. I want to talk to you about my vision for this state.*

CARYL *looks questioningly at* DON, *who gestures for her to fast-forward.*

It's the vision of the people who created it. The fishermen . . .

CARYL *fast-forwards.*

. . . the rich fields of the central valley to the mighty forests . . .

CARYL *fast-forwards again.*

. . . today – from the four corners of the globe – come men and women with the faith that they can realize their dream if no one holds them back. I trust the people of this state, I'm Sheldon Vine.

CARYL *stops the tape. Pause.*

DON. Bu-boom.

CARYL. Gosh.

Pause.

VINCENT. Four corners of the world. Why corners?

Pause.

MITCHELL. How did that seem at the time?

DON. Energetic.

MITCHELL. How does it seem now?

VINCENT. Well . . .

DON. Like he's double-parked, and needs the bathroom.

Pause.

CARYL. It looks good.

DON. It *looks* wonderful. But as it leaves our ass wide open, I don't suspect I *know* Blair knows I know that she knows this is her big chance to bite us in the shorts and bite us big.

MITCHELL. But she doesn't.

DON. Much to my surprise.

MITCHELL. Not mine.

DON. Knowing the lady.

MITCHELL. As you say.

DON. But rather she comes out with what looks like the spot she'd worked out she would have to run if we'd run the spot we would have run had we not been running our campaign on the basis of the leadership techniques of St. Theresa of Lisieux.

REBECCA *talking over location shots of poverty, schools, clearcuts and polluted beaches. She herself appears talking to people and looking concerned.*

REBECCA. *Yes, I'm one of the baby boomers who grew up in the Sixties, and like millions of others felt America wasn't living up to its ideals.*

DON. Did anybody ask?

REBECCA. *I was inspired by leaders like Cesar Chavez, Martin Luther King and Robert Kennedy to work for those ideals in the community. And I ask myself today . . .*

DON. 'Cause no one else is going to.

REBECCA. *. . . . if we still don't have a way to go. In this state, we rank nearly last in the nation for home-ownership . . .*

MITCHELL (*home-ownership*). Whose fault is that?

REBECCA. *. . . . and for per-pupil spending. We continue to pollute the air our kids must breathe . . .*

DON (*pollution*). Hey, let's hear it for the imminent apocalypse.

REBECCA. . . . *and destroy the forests and the seas. Yes I had an ideal then and I have it still today.*

DON. Guess what?

REBECCA. *That ideal is called America. I'm . . .*

Tape switched off.

DON. Financed by Mothers For Cocaine. So, what happened to the figures?

CARYL. Both her negatives and positives went up.

MITCHELL. And how did we respond?

SHELDON. Did we respond / at all?

DON. Well, I'll tell you what we should have aired. It's this.

He nods to CARYL *who plays a dummy tape – roughly put together with* VOICE-OVER *and unflattering still pictures of* REBECCA, *intercut with violent scenes from the Sixties.*

VOICE-OVER. *Since Labor Day, the Democratic candidate for governor has told you two things. She's a responsible legislator, and in her youth she had ideals. As a legislator she's responsible – for a record tax hike. Legislative gridlock. The energy crisis. And her ideals? Supporting foreign and domestic enemies. Then and now. Rebecca McKeene as governor. Responsible? Ideal?*

DON. And why didn't we air that?

SHELDON. I vetoed it.

MITCHELL. 'On principle.'

DON. And I have to tell you at this point I'm on the verge of calling Blair and saying 'heck, let's not bother waiting for November, we'll concede right now.'

SHELDON. Oh, are you?

CARYL. Really?

DON. You bet. When suddenly, mysteriously, and I think inexplicably . . . we start to move.

Slight pause.

A point or two. Well within the margin. No big hoopla. But being a conscientious guy, Gerry Zuckerman decides to assemble a small group of soft Republicans and undecideds, and sticks them in a comfortable room with cold cuts and a two-way mirror and asks them what they think about it all.

VINCENT. When's this?

DON. Three days ago. And what they tell us proves there is a God.

SHELDON. Go on.

DON. Ms Marquez.

CARYL. Well, first, sir, they tell us they like you.

DON. No surprise to me.

CARYL. Then they say that they admire you for not playing dirty.

SHELDON (*glance at* DON). Oh, yes?

CARYL. Nobody has you lower than the upper quadrile on integrity.

SHELDON. Well, that's where I like to be.

CARYL. And then we ask them what you think about the issues.

SHELDON. And?

CARYL. They tell us they don't know.

SHELDON. They don't / *know* what –

DON. And here's the darnedest thing.

CARYL. They still agree with you.

Slight pause.

SHELDON. How can they not know what I think?

DON. Because this has been an exceptionally well-run campaign.

MITCHELL. Take another look at 'Vision'.

VINCENT. And the outcome of an uncontested primary.

DON. So what do they think? That you are anti-crime, anti-environmental, anti-tax.

MITCHELL. Which is all true.

DON. And pro-gun.

VINCENT. Which is also true.

DON. And they assume you're anti-immigration and pro-life . . .

SHELDON. Which in fact I'm not . . .

DON. And tough on drugs, which is also an exaggeration. And they assume these things because Blair didn't want to advertise your positives on choice or draw attention to her negatives on dope. So we find you floating gently upwards on a raft of assumptions about what Republican candidates believe.

CARYL. And, crucially, they're *sure* you'd be / a staunch supporter of security guards –

SHELDON. Where is this heading, please?

During this, CONNIE *enters from the hall with* LORIANNE WEINER, *who is in her mid-thirties, dramatically and provocatively dressed. She is carrying a briefcase.*

DON. In physics there's an experiment, I don't pretend to understand, you make two slits in a piece of cardboard and you shine a light through and guess what, the same particle of light goes through both slits. Which is mysterious enough, light moving in a straight line as we thought it did, otherwise we could see around corners. But what is even odder is – what the light decides to do depends on how and whether and by whom it's looked at.

Pause.

Sir, it seems that you've been firing through both slits at once. By Tuesday evening, we need to know through which you plan to shine.

CONNIE. Um, Sheldon, this is Lorianne / Weiner –

SHELDON. And on what basis / do you think –

DON (*to* CARYL). Where was the single biggest hike in Vine support? In the rate of Vine support.

CARYL. What, in the groups?

DON. The polls.

CARYL. Latino women over thirty.

Pause.

MITCHELL. Ah.

DON. And what are the most important issues to these people?

CARYL. Drugs, education, crime.

SHELDON. Not choice?

CARYL. It's important, it's not that important.

VINCENT. Any Republican who wins more than a third of the Latino vote will be elected.

DON. But only if they look. And if they look, they agree with what they see.

A moment. Then SHELDON *stands, puts his hand out to* LORIANNE.

SHELDON. I'm Sheldon Vine.

LORIANNE (*shakes hands*). Lorianne Weiner.

SHELDON. I met your father.

LORIANNE. Most people to the right of Trotsky have.

SHELDON *turns back to the assembly.*

SHELDON. Ladies and gentlemen, the stand-in has landed.

CONNIE. Sheldon, maybe Lorianne would like to go / and freshen . . .

DON. You move, you're dog meat. Up to speed on the Thoughts of Madame Mao?

DON *goes and brings* LORIANNE *down to the group.*

LORIANNE. More or less.

DON. Done the reading?

LORIANNE (*briefcase*). Most of it.

CONNIE. Don, shouldn't you let / Lorianne go and . . .

DON. Ms McKeene, why the hell should we entrust you with the education of our children?

LORIANNE. Uh . . . Because . . . we're in the last quarter of the nation on education spending and . . . we shouldn't be.

VINCENT. Nearer Mississippi than New York.

LORIANNE. Too right. And I don't think it's right for schools to have to work with textbooks in which Ike is president.

MITCHELL. Good.

LORIANNE. So I'm promising a targeted and focused, costed, monitored . . .

VINCENT. 'Limited.' There must be limited.

LORIANNE. . . . limited spending hike to bring about . . . eternal peace and justice and a new Jerusalem in every classroom served up with apple pie.

CONNIE. Sheldon, do let Lorianne / at least unpack –

SHELDON. While in fact of course any financial increase will go to teachers' salaries rather than class sizes. Unless you're prepared to stand up to the teachers' union.

Slight pause.

As it happens, I'm for the rational solution. Give the money to the customers.

Slight pause.

DON. Who are the *customers*?

SHELDON. The parents.

CARYL. This is vouchers?

MITCHELL. Of the *children*.

VINCENT. Don't we say scholarships?

DON. Anything but 'money'. 'Customers'.

SHELDON. You want me to discuss education without /
    discussing –

DON. 'You want to put a price tag on our kids?'

CARYL. Well, at least if you can go to private school you're
    more likely to get taught to read than how neat it is that
    Heather has two mommies.

DON. Good. Drugs.

LORIANNE. It's . . . a real problem. But frankly I'm less
    bothered with possession. Go for the dealers and the
    growers.

DON. Ever took 'em?

LORIANNE. Pot? Who didn't?

MITCHELL. Has she said that?

VINCENT. Sure. Who hasn't?

CARYL. But hey, whatever happened to / 'just say no . . . '

SHELDON. Hey, you know what? Sure, the growers. But if
    Americans spent whatever it is every year on paper products
    then Colombia would manufacture stationery. So, rationally,
    the money we're donating to the Colombian government to
    fight their civil war might be better spent on drug rehab here
    at home. Caryl, I interrupted you.

CARYL. I was saying – uh – it doesn't matter.

MITCHELL. And crime?

VINCENT. Guns. For older women we are bad on guns.

LORIANNE. Hey, you know what I say? Dealers and
    manufacturers should be liable for crimes committed with
    the guns they make and sell.

SHELDON. So, logically, drug addicts should sue the people
    who make hypodermics?

DON. No.

VINCENT. Drunk drivers suing bartenders? Smokers suing Philip Morris?

DON. No. Still no.

MITCHELL. 'No' to the question or the stance?

DON. I mean 'no' to the stance.

SHELDON. Oh, why?

DON. It's rational.

Slight pause.

SHELDON. What's wrong with rational?

DON. It isn't reasonable. It's logical. It isn't common sense. It's saying actually your kid who drives drunk or smokes a little dope should be responsible for his own actions but the people who provide the wherewithal should not.

CARYL. Which is obviously loopy.

MITCHELL. So how we doing with Latino women so far?

CARYL says nothing.

Which brings us to the real reason why we're moving in the polls.

SHELDON. Which is?

DON nods to CARYL.

CARYL. Well, sir, we have been asking people this. 'Do you agree with the DA that when college security guard Fernando Martinez shot armed GM crops protester Sarah Jane Polowski, he was justified?'

Pause.

SHELDON. Oh, no.

DON. Sooner or later, McKeene has to come out of her hole. Every lizard-licker in the state is screaming for a pronouncement from on high. And when she does, we're ready.

SHELDON. How?

DON. We've tried three spots on groups. They're all ten seconds. They're silent with the text in print, so they may not play so well with high-school graduates. The first is: 'Rebecca McKeene says 'a crime is a crime is a crime'. Unless it's committed by an eco-terrorist.'

DON *gestures to* CARYL *to insert a video, but before she can do so* SHELDON *intervenes:*

SHELDON. No, I'm sorry, there's no point in this.

DON. And I have to say that in every group we ran it by / except for unmarried women –

SHELDON. No, I know where this is going.

MITCHELL. Oh, where's that?

SHELDON. Where you've been trying to take me since day one. The fright wing. Bumper sticker politics. 'Values voters.' Mothers Against Everything. I mean, for Christ's sake, you go on like this, you'll have me endorsing Proposition Ninety-Two.

DON. What's wrong with mothers against things?

Slight pause.

SHELDON. Oh, nothing. 'And unborn babies never have a nice day.' And 'there's no such thing as a good fairy.'

CARYL. And for that matter, what's wrong with Proposition Ninety-Two?

Pause.

I mean, that's what they're asking. Particularly when we talk about the shooting incident at SAU. What they say is, a loyal citizen was doing what he's paid for. He was attacked by a terrorist fanatic with a chainsaw. They think we should be making more of that. They say, we have to do things by the rules. We have to file the forms and take the tests and get the points and pledge allegiance to our country. Why shouldn't everybody else?

And Proposition Ninety-Two. You want the vote, you
commit yourself to the principles of democracy. You don't
join a group which pursues its ends by force. We don't mind
doing this. We're proud to do this. So, a violation of the
First Amendment? I don't think so.

And what's all that about? Sure, dandy. Gay marriage?
Kiddie porn? Everything the same as everything? Nothing
actually right or wrong? Puh-leaze.

Pause.

SHELDON. I see. Don, what's actually wrong with Gerry
Zuckerman?

DON (*to* SHELDON). I don't know, sir. All I know is that he
was fine until he told a group of high propensity
Republicans that you haven't commented on the shooting or
come out for Ninety-Two and your negatives headed off
into the milky way.

SHELDON. Remind me. Is the aim of this weekend to render
my opinions persuasive or to change them to opinions I
don't like? Because having raised quite enough today to
meet the payroll, you should know it's the former that I had
in mind.

DON. Sir, I have lived my life by the simple maxim that the
last thing that you do in a political campaign is tell the
people what you think about the issues. Thus far, Blair
Lowe is of the same opinion. As a result, we have many
options open to us. On drugs, on education, on Prop.
Ninety-Two. But so has she.

Slight pause.

LORIANNE. Um, look . . . Uh, can I ask . . . ?

SHELDON. Yes, what?

Slight pause.

LORIANNE. Is it OK to smoke?

SHELDON *glances to* MITCHELL *who nods.* CONNIE
goes and finds an ashtray.

CONNIE. Just bear in mind the house and grounds and half the county consists of highly flammable material.

SHELDON. And since we skirted around the niceties, this is Ms Weiner who we have engaged to represent the opposition, largely because her stuff on KPOW's a hoot. Lorianne, this is my brother Mitchell, who's my campaign chair. My wife Connie you have met. Mr Baptiste who does the theory and Mr D'Avanzo who does the practice. Miss Marquez who tells me how I'd do if I came out for public executions. The Duke of Wellington said of his troops: 'I don't know about the enemy, but my God they frighten me.'

MITCHELL. Welcome to Planet Ork.

LORIANNE. Well, thanks.

DON. The gates are locked.

SHELDON. Whereas the explorer Vilkjalmer Steffanson took a more proactive view. In the middle of an arctic winter, morale plummeting, everybody at each other's throats . . . he institutes a formal dinner every night. There, in the midst of the ice flows and the tundra. Guys in coats and ties, engaging in polite and witty conversation and remembering that underneath they were fellow human beings after all.

To MITCHELL:

So, Chief, is such a thing conceivable?

MITCHELL. It's not me drawing up the menu.

MITCHELL *looks at* CONNIE.

CONNIE. Yes, of course this is conceivable.

SHELDON. I would like our daughter to be present.

CONNIE. Well, that too.

SHELDON. On the paychecks, I exaggerated. Thus far, only half of you still have a job. I'll make my calls.

He goes out. Pause.

MITCHELL. Alarums and excursions.

CARYL. Well, I guess, if you want to see a rainbow, you gotta stand a little rain.

DON. That's a very helpful thought.

CARYL *suspects that thought is in inverted commas.*

LORIANNE. What's 'alarums'?

VINCENT. Shakespeare.

CARYL. Please excuse me.

She goes out.

DON. Lorianne, remind me, what's your father's one-liner about born-again conservatives?

LORIANNE. What, 'liberals with teenage girls in high school'? But in fact, / I don't –

DON. That's it. You know, there's schools where they insist on teaching Shakespeare, Tchaikovsky and Michelangelo as part of the gay studies course. I'd put that in a spot. But then, I'm just the campaign manager.

He goes out.

CONNIE. Mitchell, why don't you show Lorianne to her room, or offer her a drink, or something.

She goes out.

MITCHELL. I'm sorry. You were saying.

LORIANNE. Nothing. A drink sounds good.

MITCHELL. What can I fix you?

LORIANNE. 'Fix' me? If it's fixing, make mine a Manhattan.

MITCHELL. A Manhattan. Sure.

He goes out.

VINCENT. Well, hi.

LORIANNE. Well, phew. Is it usually this . . .

VINCENT. . . . tempest-tossed? It's been getting more that way.

LORIANNE. And Prop. Ninety-Two's a problem?

VINCENT. Sure.

LORIANNE. You're a new or re-registering voter, you declare you're not a member of a body which pursues its ends by force.

VINCENT. 'A member or supporter.'

LORIANNE. So once the courts get ahold of it, it's in the toilet.

VINCENT. So then why endorse it?

LORIANNE. Because they won't get ahold of it before November 5th.

VINCENT. Two weeks back, this was not on anybody's radar.

LORIANNE. Well, I guess, two weeks ago, an eco-terrorist named Sarah Jane Polowski hadn't tried to slice a patriotic public servant into pieces with a chainsaw.

VINCENT. Plus of course the issue has salience to the wider conflict that you might just have detected lurking beneath the placid surface of this seemingly stress-free campaign.

LORIANNE. Oh, yeah?

VINCENT. Markets versus morals. Liberty versus loyalty.

LORIANNE. Oh, that old thing.

VINCENT. If we want to keep the state out of the boardroom, does it have any business in the bedroom.

LORIANNE. The circle that my father's spent a decade trying to square.

VINCENT. Trying and succeeding, some say.

LORIANNE. He would be delighted.

VINCENT. So what did you really want to know?

LORIANNE. When?

VINCENT. When you changed your mind, and asked if you could smoke a cigarette.

LORIANNE. What do you think I meant?

VINCENT. 'Why am I here?'

Pause.

I've listened to your stuff.

LORIANNE. I'm pleased.

VINCENT. Not just the comedy.

LORIANNE. I'm even pleaseder.

VINCENT. From which it's clear to me you think the best way to achieve the good society is to let the market rip.

LORIANNE. Correct.

VINCENT. So does the candidate.

LORIANNE. I can't quite see the problem.

VINCENT. Not everyone agrees.

LORIANNE. Who writes the checks?

VINCENT. Have you heard of the battle of Gallipoli?

LORIANNE. No, but I can name the capital, bird, song and reptile of each and every state.

VINCENT. Gallipoli was Sir Winston Churchill's mission to invade Germany from the south in World War One. It fails disastrously, and so Churchill spends much of World War Two trying to engineer the opportunity to prove that had he had the ships and men he asked for it'd all have been just fine.

LORIANNE. Well, mercy, you learn something / new –

VINCENT. In 1990, Mitchell Vine ran his father's last campaign. He was severely wounded in the primary by an ocean-bed Republican from the religious right but wouldn't fight back till it was too late. Then in the general he lost out to a liberal Democrat who was able to point out how much he'd flipped and flopped since June. Mitchell thinks that if he'd served up raw meat from the get-go he'd have won. And though Sheldon is a very different politician from his father, that is essentially the battle that is being refought this weekend.

LORIANNE. So where do you stand on these weighty questions?

VINCENT. Why do you ask?

LORIANNE. Because the other option is to ask you what *you're* doing here.

VINCENT. What, 'as a black conservative'?

LORIANNE. Not particularly, but if you like.

Slight pause.

With a brother who's an unrepentant hero of the people's struggle. With you receiving the Alexis de Toqueville award for the promotion of traditional values in the American Academy. What did 'The Nation' call you? Vincent Oreo?

VINCENT. Yes, you know, it amazes me, the people who've read *Freud for Dummies* and assume this all comes down to sibling rivalry.

LORIANNE. But big brother was a Panther, right?

VINCENT. And that the normal course for a smart young educated middle-class American is to buy a gun, move to Oakland and join a guerrilla army.

LORIANNE. Well, you tell me.

VINCENT. Our father was a teacher. He took the view you judge a man by three things: the state of his lawn, his car and his shoes. He didn't go out and march for civil rights, though he gave money – in fact it was important that professional people didn't lose their jobs, so that people could stand bail. Just as importantly, he insisted his children learn their ABCs, backed up sometimes with a switch broken off the willow tree. Not a particularly bookish household but we knew how to use a library and to share books with our friends. For us, a place at Louisiana State or Jackson would have been a triumph of perseverance over prejudice. But then we moved out west and I got a place at a university beyond my parents' wildest dreams. And I knew that I was sitting down in class with kids who looked at me and thought – we got here climbing up a ladder but this guy rode the escalator instead.

So who put me in that position? Well, here's the thing. It turns out to be the same people who denied me and my folks the vote. It was the same folks stood on steps and said there'd never be a black man at the University of Alabama. It was the governors and legislators and boards of regents of each and every state who saw fit first to deny me rights and then take away my pride. So you won't find me pandering to the authority of government.

LORIANNE. So what d'they say to *that* down there in Lweesyanna?

VINCENT. I'll tell you what I say. Imagine this. There's a group of people in a country, who were first enslaved and then excluded. When through their collective efforts they level out the playing field, they discover that as individuals they can make it in the same world as the people who excluded them, that praise the lord they're not inferior at all. And what's their response to this discovery? It's to insist in fact they are inferior, that they're not qualified to join the club that now accepts them as a member. And whatever they might say, I'd say: these are folks who are clinging desperately to their enslavement. And I think the senator was right to stand up against the politics of tribal trauma, and I think his son's right too.

LORIANNE. That's kind of tough to say to people who think you're a traitor to your race.

VINCENT. My brother changed his name, to Kwesi something. I'm proud to share my father's name. But that doesn't mean I have to follow in his footsteps.

LORIANNE. Ditto.

Enter CONNIE *with* LORIANNE's *drink.*

CONNIE. Your drink. I'm sorry that it took so long.

LORIANNE (*taking it*). It's fine, thanks.

CONNIE. Men can't be trusted to fix cocktails any more. If I hadn't stepped in, you'd have had a shot of angostura bitters, if not lemonade.

Hiatus. LORIANNE *sips her drink.*

So what have you young people been discussing?

LORIANNE (*with a glance at* VINCENT). Job descriptions.

CONNIE. Ah.

Hiatus.

Vincent, I think Big Chief would like a pow-wow in the den.

VINCENT. I'm there.

VINCENT *goes out. Hiatus.*

LORIANNE. It's a great place you have / here . . .

CONNIE. It must be odd.

LORIANNE. What?

CONNIE. Being hired to lose.

LORIANNE. I plan to go down fighting.

CONNIE. So what's the deal?

LORIANNE. What deal?

CONNIE. You're a reporter. Presumably this is something worth reporting.

LORIANNE. I'm not really a reporter.

CONNIE. No?

LORIANNE. The term of art's 'pundette'.

CONNIE. As of course you haven't actually been hired to lose.

LORIANNE. I must check my contract.

CONNIE. You've been brought here to enable him to win.

LORIANNE. Well, we're on the same page there.

CONNIE. But there are differing views on how to bring that end about.

LORIANNE. I think I picked that up.

CONNIE. I want my husband to win, but in a manner he feels to be right.

LORIANNE. I'm sold.

CONNIE. There has been enough dishonor in this great place we have here.

Slight pause.

LORIANNE. Um, anything that I / should know –

CONNIE. Or more accurately, this place that Mitchell has. Or that Mitchell has here now.

She goes to the windows.

Time was the family owned everything the eye could see.

Slight pause.

But then the senator lost his seat, and died, and left the running of the business to his son, who decided that it too needed dragging into the brave new world of post-Reaganite America. Unfortunately, some gentlemen from Phoenix had already worked out that the stock price bore no relation to the assets and so made Mitch an offer it wasn't in his nature to refuse.

LORIANNE. Ah. Right.

CONNIE *still looking out of the window.*

But I don't quite understand . . . If you lost the company . . .

CONNIE. They let Mitch keep the house. Sentimental reasons.

LORIANNE. Sentimental reasons?

CONNIE. Though in fact, for sedimental reasons, my daughter tells me, if they go on razing everything above us to the ground, the Cougar breaks its banks and we become beach-front property.

She turns back to LORIANNE*:*

Like old Joe Kennedy, the gentlemen from Phoenix didn't care to buy a landslide.

CONNIE *sees* MITCHELL *enter.*

MITCHELL. Connie.

CONNIE. Ah, Mitch.

MITCHELL. I've just seen Vincent.

CONNIE. Oh?

MITCHELL. He said you said I asked to see him in the den.

CONNIE. Oh, yes?

MITCHELL. I didn't.

CONNIE. Ah.

MITCHELL. But Don would like to see Lorianne. And he *is* in the den.

LORIANNE (*relieved*). I'm there.

LORIANNE *goes quickly out.*

CONNIE. Well, what a dish.

MITCHELL. We had a deal.

CONNIE. I know.

MITCHELL. I don't think you've accepted it.

CONNIE. I know *you've* not accepted it.

Slight pause.

I didn't want you involved in this campaign. For reasons you well know. I particularly didn't want to spend a weekend here.

MITCHELL. Connie, I've done my best / to make it feel –

CONNIE. But even I didn't think you'd deliberately set out to sabotage it.

Pause.

MITCHELL. No, Connie. It's not sabotage. It's the opposite. Now there's a chance that he can win this. A real chance. And I'm not prepared to let him piss it all away.

CONNIE. Oh?

MITCHELL. And if you really wanted to help us win it, then you'd talk to the two people who really are a threat to this campaign.

CONNIE. And who might they be?

MITCHELL. Well, it would be good to know what your daughter means by 'the armed might of the fascist state.'

CONNIE. And the second?

MITCHELL. Connie, I'm sure that Don D'Avanzo offends your sensibilities, as he does some of mine. But he knows his job. And he tells me that our biggest problem currently is a candidate who doesn't want to win.

CONNIE. Why ever not?

MITCHELL. Because, deep down, he prefers the other side.

LORIANNE *has reentered.*

LORIANNE. I'm sorry. I forgot my bag.

She finds it. She turns to go.

CONNIE. Miss Weiner, you'll have learnt that in order to repel the Phoenix raiding party, some sacrifices were made. Many of them were very tall and very old and to be found in forests. Others were a little younger, but still loyal and longstanding assets to the company.

MITCHELL. Oh, Connie.

CONNIE. One was my father. Which was why I swore I'd never set foot in this house again.

She turns to MITCHELL.

Don't worry, Chief. I'm there.

She goes out. LORIANNE *and* MITCHELL *look at each other.*

Scene Three

Evening. Towards the end of the formal meal. Not everybody
is in a coat and tie, but there has been some effort. Currently,
DON, VINCENT, CARYL, MITCHELL and SHELDON are
at the table. There are places for three others – one of which
(DEBORAH's) has not been used. DON and CARYL may
have drunk a little more than they should. DON is currently
master of ceremonies.

CARYL. North Carolina.

DON. Nixon Carter.

SHELDON. Wisconsin?

DON. Reagan Nixon Carter Clinton.

CARYL. Idaho.

CONNIE and LORIANNE enter with coffee and desserts
which they put on a sideboard near the easy chairs.

DON. Oh, come on. There's a logic to this. You're just picking
state names from the air.

CONNIE. What's going on?

MITCHELL. We're trying to guess the most consistent voting
state in presidential politics in the postwar era.

CONNIE. Well, my. Here's coffee.

LORIANNE. The answer has to be more interesting than the
question.

DON. You don't have to guess.

Slight pause.

SHELDON. Where's Debs?

CONNIE. She's still asleep.

Slight pause.

VINCENT. Presumably, it has to be a state that went the wrong
way in a landslide.

DON. Yo.

MITCHELL. Massachusctts.

DON. Reagan.

CARYL. Excuse me?

DON. Weird but true.

VINCENT. Minnesota.

DON. Nixon, '72. When Massachusetts . . .

SHELDON. So it's a GOP state.

DON. *Yes.*

VINCENT. So it's a state that went Republican in '64.

DON. This guy really should be running something.

MITCHELL. Who voted Goldwater?

DON. More people than you think.

VINCENT. The south . . .

SHELDON. Which also voted Carter, Reagan . . .

LORIANNE. Wallace.

VINCENT. So it must be Barry Goldwater's home state.

DON. Right *on.*

MITCHELL. It's Arizona.

DON. Which voted GOP from 1948 till in a moment of aberration it went Clinton against Dole.

VINCENT. So what's the state bird?

DON. Sorry?

VINCENT. The Arizona state bird, flower and reptile.

Enter DEBORAH.

LORIANNE. Arizona? Well, the cactus wren's the bird, not sure about the flower. But the reptile is the ridge-nosed rattlesnake.

CONNIE. Is there a very pressing need / to know this . . . ?

VINCENT. It's Ms Weiner's party piece. She knows the emblems of all fifty states.

DEBORAH. Boy, am I just in time.

SHELDON. Debs.

He kisses her.

Do you want some dinner?

DEBORAH. Presumably it consists of some dead animal.

CONNIE. There's cheese.

DEBORAH. Which consists of some live animal. Please don't let me interrupt. What's the state fish of Hawaii?

LORIANNE. It's the humuhumunukunukuapaua'a.

CONNIE. Now, oddly, that *is* interesting. Did you know / that there's a –

SHELDON. In fact, we were discussing Barry Goldwater.

DEBORAH. Barry Goldwater the fascist.

DON. No, he's not a fascist.

DEBORAH. What, 'extremism in the defense of liberty is no vice'?

SHELDON. You see, my daughter affects fashionable ignorance / but actually . . .

VINCENT. But also . . . 'Freedom balanced, so that order, lacking liberty, will not become the slavery of the prison cell.'

MITCHELL. But balanced, also . . .

LORIANNE. '. . . so that liberty, lacking order, will not become the license of the mob and of the jungle.'

Slight pause. MITCHELL *smiles.* LORIANNE *explains:*

It's my father's favorite quotation.

CARYL. Beg pardon, what from?

MITCHELL. Barry Goldwater's acceptance speech.

LORIANNE. Squaring the circle.

SHELDON. Yes. Wonder what happens when liberty and order collide?

MITCHELL. Well, I guess, you call upon the democratic process.

CONNIE. Which you did with such success in 1990.

Pause.

DON. Hey, you know what? There were twice as many volunteers for Goldwater as Johnson. Sixty thousand people gave to Kennedy, a *million* gave to Goldwater. *And* he was Jew. How far outside the fucking charmed circle do you want to get?

To DEBORAH, *mock helpful:*

That's the fascist, Barry Goldwater.

CARYL. I couldn't do it.

SHELDON. Do what?

CARYL. Ask strangers for their money.

VINCENT. Come on, you ask for their opinions.

MITCHELL. Dad used to say the real problem was meeting people in the street who thank you for a letter. It's heartfelt, clearly you've done something good. But was your letter congratulating on achievement or condolence for a loss? So he came up with the perfect sentence to fit all eventualities.

CARYL. Yes?

MITCHELL. 'I felt it was the least that I could do.'

SHELDON. He also said that a politician is a man judged on the basis of his worst mistake.

CARYL. And what's that?

SHELDON. What, my father's worst mistake?

CARYL. No, actually, I meant . . . I'm sorry.

SHELDON *demurs. Pause.*

DON. Hey, you know what? If you'll pardon me for saying this, your father's big mistake was not biting back when the Dems were obviously handing over their research to the Bible-thumper in the primary.

CARYL. They did that?

DON. Sure. I mean you've got to hand it to those schmucks. Time after time, they turn tricks if we'd done them we'd be shish-kebabbed and they come out smelling sweetly every time.

DEBORAH. Watergate?

DON. Exactly.

He picks up that DEBORAH *was presenting a counter-example.*

No, exactly. Watergate was a liberal coup d'état. Nixon creams McGovern in the vote and so they use the courts to chuck him out. 'By any means necessary.' Hey, why can't we be like them?

LORIANNE. Gallipoli.

VINCENT. Gallipoli.

DON. Hey, wasn't that a movie with Australians?

Pause.

CONNIE. So Mitch, was that your worst call?

MITCHELL. What?

CONNIE. The primary. Would you say that was your worst mistake?

MITCHELL. Oh, Connie. Please.

CONNIE. Or was that what happened afterwards, when you let your father's firm be snaffled up by Global Reach Incorporated, Phoenix Arizona?

SHELDON. OK. Now here's the thing. In the greatest movie ever made, which is not *The Godfather* nor *Star Wars* but one made by Orson Welles in 1940, the basic plot device is this. A man writes out a pledge. He publishes it on the front page of his newspaper. His best friend pockets the original. And years later when all dreams have turned to dust, he produces it and says to Kane, 'Well, what became of *that*.'

He taps the dining table.

In this house the equivalent to that piece of paper is right here.

MITCHELL. Sheldon, what does this / have to do with –

SHELDON. This table. Mitchell, what's its history?

Slight pause.

MITCHELL. Well, Sheldon, as you know, it was fashioned in the 1940s.

SHELDON. Off it, we ate Christmas and Thanksgiving dinners.

MITCHEL, Certainly. And on it, birthday gifts were piled.

SHELDON. And around it, we sat silently when Deborah and our father died.

Slight pause.

MITCHELL. Yes.

SHELDON. When we pledged that whatever we might think of his defeat, between us we'd take up the standard he had borne and carry on.

MITCHELL. We did.

SHELDON. And it was here that you and I decided – for better or for worse – that it was me who should assume his mantle and ride forth.

Pause.

CARYL. It is . . . it's very beautiful.

CONNIE. Isn't this right, it was actually fashioned from a single cut across an old-growth redwood?

DEBORAH. Yuh, Dad, like it's not so great to say, 'we spent our happy childhood sitting around a corpse.'

MITCHELL. No, Deborah, it's not a corpse. It's a cut of wood.

DEBORAH. Yuh, well, that's the mindset that's / killed off –

MITCHELL. One of the thousand upon thousand of such cuts of timber which financed your upbringing and education.

DEBORAH. So I'm expected to feel good / about that?

DON. Hey, you know what . . .

MITCHELL. No I don't expect it. There is absolutely nothing that you've said or done since arriving here which indicates that you feel any gratitude for what your family has done for you.

DEBORAH. What?

CONNIE. Mitchell, please don't shout at Deborah.

MITCHELL. I'm not. But you know what I think you should ask her. And demand she answer, fully, truthfully, in front of everyone, and now.

Pause.

CONNIE. Mitchell, are you serious?

MITCHELL. Oh, absolutely.

DEBORAH. Huh . . .

CARYL. Um . . .

DON. Maybe . . .

He gestures vaguely.

Lorianne . . .

CONNIE. Please. Please, anything but the Idaho state mushroom.

MITCHELL. Well?

DEBORAH. I'm so way not a part of this.

She makes to go out.

SHELDON. Hey, Debs.

She stops, turns to him.

Hey. Debs.

DEBORAH. Yes, Dad?

SHELDON. What was the game we used to play?

MITCHELL. What's this?

DEBORAH. Like, which . . .

SHELDON. It was – kind of 'truth or dare.' But our version was much longer.

DON. Well, surprise, surprise.

SHELDON. It was 'Truth, dare, kiss, demand or promise.'

Pause.

DEBORAH. It was like, 'command.'

CONNIE. And I think we made it 'truth dare *wish.*'

CARYL. At college we used to spin a bottle.

SHELDON. So did we.

He picks up a nearly empty wine bottle, pours it into a glass and picks it up. To DEBORAH:

I can't remember, do you drink wine?

DEBORAH. Depends whose glass.

SHELDON. Your mother's.

DEBORAH *takes the glass.*

SHELDON. Now, remind me, it's the fat end asks the question and the thin end answers?

DEBORAH. Yuh, but like you have to spin the bottle first, and the person who gets pointed at like / gets to choose –

SHELDON (*pointing the wine bottle at* DEBORAH). Debs, as I asked you this morning. Were you involved in any way with this . . . action against GM poplars at the university?

Beat.

DEBORAH. No I wasn't.

MITCHELL. Was anyone you know involved?

DEBORAH. Not that I know of.

SHELDON. Fine.

MITCHELL. And do you or anyone you know support this action?

SHELDON. Yes. Excuse me. Do you or anyone you know support this action?

Slight pause.

DEBORAH. So can you ask me that?

SHELDON. I can ask you. Under the terms of the Constitution of the United States as it stands presently, you don't have to answer. Even if you choose to vote, move, or, should you wish to, enter into state employment.

DEBORAH. Good.

SHELDON. Well, I think that settles it, don't you?

MITCHELL. Well, that's all very rational.

SHELDON. I thought you wanted her to tell the truth.

DEBORAH. So can I / go now?

MITCHELL. The full truth.

SHELDON (*pointing the bottle at* MITCHELL). What, you want the *full* truth, Mitchell? Really?

He's gone too far. He points the bottle around to the others. DEBORAH *sips her wine.*

Or hey, someone else. Wish? Dare?

CARYL (*concerned with the rules*). Um, actually, the person with the bottle doesn't get to / choose which actual question . . .

SHELDON. Command?

LORIANNE. I think I speak for all the non-Vine group / in saying . . .

SHELDON. But, hey, I'm just the candidate.

LORIANNE. . . . that I wish I knew / what's going on . . .

SHELDON. Hey. Promise.

He points the bottle at DON.

Don.

DON *waves, demurring.*

Hey, come on. You're the master of the dark arts. Promises are what you do.

Pause.

DON. Well, I can't promise you'll be governor at noon on January 6th.

SHELDON. But you'll do your damnedest.

DON. Yes.

SHELDON. I sense a hanging 'but'.

DON. It's a hanging 'if'.

SHELDON. Then spit it out.

DON *looks to* MITCHELL *who shrugs 'why not.'*

DON. If you promise that you want me to.

Slight pause.

SHELDON. Why do you think I don't?

DON. Because . . .

He gestures vaguely.

CONNIE. Because he thinks you want the other side to win.

Pause.

SHELDON. Oh, really?

DON. Yes.

SHELDON. Why? Full truth, now.

DON. Because you admire the other side more than your own.

Pause.

VINCENT (*quoting* DON). 'Hey, why can't we be like them?'

DON. I'm not the candidate.

SHELDON. No. And I am. And I owe it to you all to be so in full heart and soul.

Pause.

VINCENT. Sir, everybody's listening.

SHELDON. There was another meeting around this table. It was in 1969, and I'd just returned from the convention of the Young Americans for Freedom in St. Louis, which turned out to be a very boisterous affair: traditionalists versus what were called the laissez-fairies, the trads chanting 'sock it to the left' and the laissez-fairies 'sock it to the state,' and when a guy gets up and burns his draft card half the hall cheers and the other tries to lynch him. Well, a little more than half, which is why I end up being purged from the executive for nihilism, and as my colleagues head off on their journey to the Reagan White House or the 97th Congress, I hitch a ride home with the daughter of an up-and-coming manager in my daddy's lumber company. And we get back in the middle of the night, and we open up a bottle and sit around this table, and we map a glowing future for our country and the world.

A gathering of friends would come together, raise a million bucks, and buy a piece of land, which we would deed to God, so nobody could sell it. I think – I fear – we planned to call it Jefferson. And on this land, on Jefferson, we would make anarchy in action. And as the wine flowed, and who knows other things as well, we moved on to a wider vision: great cities seceding from the state, and states seceding from the union, and within these new utopias the abolition of all taxes, the institution of a voluntary tithe for the public good, the provision of asylum for people fleeing drug enforcement laws and military conscription, the creation of a haven in which individual genius could flourish, freed from the fetters of the state . . . I guess, before that phrase got tarnished, a shining city on a hill.

I'm not jealous of the other side. I'm furious with us for abdicating territory that should be ours. I was hounded out of the Young Americans for Freedom for opposing a section of the draft law which deemed it a criminal offence to aid, abet or counsel young men to resist involuntary military servitude. How did the left – the people who want to conscript everybody, how the fuck did they get ahold of *that*?

But, still, it seems these guys still claim an exclusive franchise on the future.

Look around. The most extraordinary experiment in human history is occurring, conducted not by governments or armies, but in fact by people on their own. People cutting off the strings that bind them to the social status, the economic conditions, certainly the place, often the beliefs, that they've inherited. And that's the real divide. Not left or right, or coast or center, free or good. But between the people who stay home and the people who fly free.

And it's happening most right here. Here, we are reinventing genetics, gender, generation. Ways of being. Who and what we are. We could be anything. The possibilities are infinite. So why, when we can invent ourselves in any way we please, do we scurry back to our ancient Gods, our dead traditions, and the petty hierarchies, narrow jealousies and closed horizons of the family?

MITCHELL. You mean, like this one?

SHELDON *looks at* MITCHELL.

SHELDON. Of course I'm thrilled with the idea that we might win this thing. Of course I'm proud to carry on the family standard. But I made a promise to myself, to do the thing that everyone agrees you can't do, which is to run a principled Republican campaign, which doesn't sell out to the country club Republicans on economics nor the paleos on values. And happily, we have here a group so brilliant that it will find a strategy to win this thing on the platform Vincent drafted and we all agreed on, without requiring me to lie.

DON. Is that a command?

SHELDON. No, it's a dare.

He goes out.

DON. Well, we all danced away with *that*.

CONNIE. What do you mean?

DON. It doesn't matter what I mean.

VINCENT. He means that the candidate has decided that he wants to win on his own terms.

DON. Yup.

CONNIE. Well, Chief, looks like you're running, what?

MITCHELL (*wryly*). A tiger.

CONNIE. Told you so.

DEBORAH *raps the table, as applause.*

DON. Hey – respect the dead.

DEBORAH. Oh for Christ's sake.

DEBORAH *stands and goes out.* CARYL *stands and starts to clear dishes.*

CARYL. Now, look, why don't we . . .

CONNIE. Oh please. Mitchell has a perfectly well-documented Filipino maid who will clear this in the morning.

CARYL *stops.*

By any means necessary. Goodnight.

CONNIE *goes out.* CARYL *sits.*

MITCHELL. Vincent, do you have questions version three?

VINCENT. Four. Yup. I did them before dinner. They're in the den.

DON. And the revised McKeene notes?

VINCENT. As requested.

MITCHELL. Thank you.

VINCENT realizes he's being asked to go and get the notes. A moment, then he goes out.

DON. You're a good man, Charlie Brown.

MITCHELL. Caryl, if I may say so, you are an advertisement for beauty sleep.

CARYL. Well, mercy, Mr Vine.

DON stares at CARYL. She gets the hint.

Ah. I'll see you gentlemen tomorrow.

She goes out. MITCHELL goes to the bar cart.

MITCHELL. Drink, anyone?

LORIANNE. I'll have a . . . bourbon.

MITCHELL. Anything in that?

LORIANNE. Just rocks.

MITCHELL. Don?

DON. The same.

To LORIANNE:

You'll be bored with this, but I met your father in the early Eighties.

LORIANNE smiles politely. MITCHELL is fixing drinks.

And he told me he'd been part of the anti-Nixon witch hunt, 'demeaning the great office,' all that snake oil, but now he wanted to apologize. He realized now it had been what we said it was. And my father was a prisoner of war.

LORIANNE. Your father?

MITCHEL. Anthony Angelis D'Avanzo served six months in an open prison for obstructing justice.

LORIANNE. That's right?

DON. Over now.

As MITCHELL *gives* LORIANNE *her bourbon,* VINCENT *reenters with the notes.*

VINCENT. So are you planning anything?

MITCHELL. What can you mean?

VINCENT. Are you planning to redraft any of the questions?

VINCENT *gives one document to* MITCHELL *and the other to* LORIANNE.

MITCHELL. I think we should run through the game plan with Lorianne.

Slight pause. LORIANNE *is looking at her folder.*

VINCENT. You mean 'the strategy we all agreed'?

MITCHELL. Yes, Vince, the strategy we all agreed.

DON (*the documents*). Hey, thanks.

VINCENT. Um, I . . . You're welcome.

VINCENT *goes out.*

DON. Well, you see the problem.

LORIANNE. With Charlie?

Slight pause.

MITCHELL. No, with the candidate.

LORIANNE. He's committed to a winning game.

DON. And to a losing strategy.

LORIANNE. Oh, yes?

DON. You got the picture. On economics, voodoo-heavy. On social stuff, Rebecca-lite.

LORIANNE. And that's unwinnable?

DON. Let's be polite and call it 'maverick'.

LORIANNE. Oh, do we have to be polite?

DON. Then, sure, unwinnable, unreasonable and wrong.

MITCHELL. And I think we have to say that this evening has not improved our chances of persuading him of the virtues of our chosen strategy.

LORIANNE. Which is to hammer home McKeene's political backstory, in order to imply that once in power she'd emerge as a Big-Governing ACLU-supporting gay-righting tax-and-spending double-dipping loony tooner.

MITCHELL (*surprised*). Yes.

LORIANNE. I read the briefing book.

DON. We call the strategy 'True Colors'.

LORIANNE. But your problem is that Sheldon won't pursue it because actually he agrees with some of her more extra-terrestrial opinions, like on gays and drugs he's actually closer to some things she used to say than what she's saying now.

DON. We'd spotted that. But, thanks.

LORIANNE. As of course am I.

DON. Excuse me?

LORIANNE. I mean, not entirely. I wouldn't legalize hard drugs and I think that gays have all the rights they need, thank you kindly. But I'm not too enamored of the draft, and I can do without the federal government in between my sheets, and actually I find all that 'Puff the Magic Dragon' stuff he came out with pretty damn inspiring.

MITCHELL. Well, do you now.

LORIANNE. So, were my opinion to be courted, I'd say what you need / to do –

MITCHELL. No, I don't think so.

LORIANNE. Uh – I hadn't really finished.

MITCHELL. Yes I know. But I don't recall proposing we *debate* the strategy, Lorianne.

Pause.

LORIANNE. Then I seemingly misheard. I thought you asked me to contribute.

MITCHELL. I'm perfectly happy for you to contribute.

LORIANNE. As long as it's what you think my father would advise the candidate to say.

Slight pause.

Elegant. Restrained. Prudent on the economics. Culturally conservative. The words of traditional raw meat Republicanism, set to Mozart.

MITCHELL. Well, if we thought that, we were wrong.

LORIANNE. So why are you keeping C.B. off the team?

MITCHELL. Because, as must be obvious, Vincent aids, abets and counsels Sheldon in the articulation of his maverick opinions.

He makes to go.

Let me know if there's anything that you don't follow.

LORIANNE. Hey, you know, she doesn't speak like you've got her in the books. Like she has five basic tropes and you don't use any of them.

MITCHELL. Lorianne. That's what she says. How she says it is entirely up to you.

LORIANNE. And I guess you've delved into her murky past. 'Cause if you had a smoking gun, presumably / you wouldn't have to –

MITCHELL. Lorianne, we've done our opp. research.

DON. That's where we got the quotes.

LORIANNE. But you haven't got her running a Vietcong flag up the flagpole of a ROTC building.

DON. No, nor being on the Ten Most Wanted List or living with the Manson family.

LORIANNE. The difference being, that the flag is true.

Pause.

MITCHELL. How do you know that?

LORIANNE. The guy I live with is a former student revolutionary.

MITCHELL. Well, we're all glad he saw the light.

LORIANNE. He also saw her do it.

DON. And did he have a camera?

LORIANNE. No. But surely somebody / must have –

MITCHELL. Yes, thanks, Lorianne.

LORIANNE. A college campus in broad daylight.

MITCHELL. Sure. We'll set our people on it right away.

LORIANNE. The cops, a campus newspaper, the FBI . . .

MITCHELL. Lorianne. It would be very nice. But in the unlikely event of our not finding anything by Tuesday, let's stick with Plan A.

He goes out. A moment.

DON. It's simple. Move or lose. That's the means, and it is necessary. If it wasn't, I would be delighted. But it is.

LORIANNE. So what's 'the full truth'?

DON. What?

LORIANNE. Sheldon said there was a 'full truth' about Mitchell.

DON. Well, he dated Blair Lowe in the early Seventies.

LORIANNE. What, McKeene's consultant?

DON. Yes.

LORIANNE. Well, that's a skeleton.

DON. You think so? I'd say it shows hidden depths.

LORIANNE. Speaking of youthful indiscretions, you realize of course there's a way to make 'True Colors' work.

DON (*weary*). Uh, Lorianne . . .

LORIANNE. You change it to 'Two-Faced'.

Pause.

DON. This is my second bourbon.

LORIANNE. What has the media campaign achieved?

DON. You tell me.

LORIANNE. Or preserved.

DON. Our candidate's moral integrity.

LORIANNE. Well, there you are.

DON *waves her on.*

'Two-Faced' attacks her flip-flopping. It doesn't matter what the flip is, so long as there's a flop. Who cares what Sheldon thinks about it? Hey, you don't even have to know.

Pause.

DON. You mean . . .

LORIANNE. I mean, is there a topic on which McKeene hasn't changed her mind? Welfare? Quotas? Mind-expanding substances?

DON. Death penalty.

LORIANNE. I mean, you can't trust anything she says.

DON. Her negatives confirm his positives.

LORIANNE. Her negatives *increase* his positives.

DON. His positives increase her negatives.

LORIANNE. 'Cause however loopy his opinions, at least Shel's straight.

DON *stands, stands to walk about, planning.*

DON. OK. Take this down.

LORIANNE. Excuse me?

DON. It's an expression. The mock begins. Sheldon wins one, hey, he needs to know he can get it up, this is about the guy's morale. Then on question two, he has a chance to cream her on the yawning gap between her current and her previous opinions on . . . taxes, single mothers or pornography, but he omits to do so, and he ends up on the floor. Then gradually we demonstrate that if he points out what McKeene said then and stops – *she*'s on the mat. Again. Again. Again.

Slight pause.

Well, stranger things have worked. Look at 'Senator, you're no Jack Kennedy.'

LORIANNE. Look at 'there you go again.'

DON. I'll talk to Mitch.

LORIANNE. You'll 'talk to Mitch.'

DON. The campaign chair.

LORIANNE. And you tell him that McKeene is skunked.

DON. And that the stand-in's back on board the team.

Pause.

LORIANNE. Sure I'm on board. Hey, it's my strategy.

DON. Even though like any strategy it may need to bend a little in the wind.

LORIANNE. Of course.

DON. And even though there's one thing that won't work this way.

LORIANNE. What's that?

DON. Prop. Ninety-Two.

LORIANNE. That easy, huh?

DON. That easy?

LORIANNE. It's the same. You turn it back on her.

Slight pause.

DON. Please demonstrate.

LORIANNE. It's kind of nearly sort of what he said.

DON. That helps.

LORIANNE. It's the big lie that's behind the little lies.

DON. I'm sold so far.

LORIANNE. It was told by communists in the 1930s and
radicals in the 1960s and the liberals are still telling it today.

DON. And so, 'the lie' . . . ?

LORIANNE. Is this. Oppression is the worst thing in the
world, but the oppressed are best. Sure, the poor have more
than their fair share of inadequates and psychopaths, but
that's the Big O. talkin' and when they throw it off they'll
all emerge as – Beethoven and Einstein, or at least as people
Just Like Us. But as it comes clear that's the last thing that
is going to happen, we just spin it around. The oppressed
are best, let's live like them.

And the consequences of this lie. My father's actually quite
pleased to have gotten out of a tough neighborhood in
Brooklyn to Columbia, but they tell him it was white
chauvinist and worse uncool and he ought to drop out and
become a hobo. And of course a smart young kid like my
guy in the Sixties wants to read the best that has been
written, so the Maoists have to patiently explain that college
is a white-skin privilege, it's trash or be trashed, so he
trashes it or else he's out. And guess what, when I get to
college, which is now run by the only people left who still
buy this shit, I'm told that if I don't think M.C. Hammer's
preferable to Keats, or that some people might be naturally
smarter than some others, or that, hey, if black folks don't
do well at school it might be that they spend too little time
book reading and too much time with their nose in
something else . . . they run you outta town.

So d'you know what I'd say? I'd say what he said. It's the
left tells other people what's permissible to say. It's the left
which guilt-trips and gut-checks. It's the left who want to
force you to salute and sign oaths and make declarations,

because what they say ain't true. Shel's right. Our vision is the best, because it promises you can transform yourself and it delivers. Its wish is your command. All you have to do is dare. And, yes, the liberals stole that vision off of us and it's time we took it back. And, lo, the light shall be divided from the darkness, and behold God saw that it was good.

Slight pause.

Hey, I haven't hit a riff like that for quite a while. You'll tell Mitch?

DON. Sure.

LORIANNE. Hey – thanks.

She goes out.

DON. I felt it was the least that I could do.

End of Act One.

ACT TWO

Scene One

Monday morning. The garage of the Vine house is set up as a television studio for the mock debate, with two miked podiums facing the single chair and desk of the moderator. Video cameras are set up to record the rehearsal. There are two decks – one recording the entire event, the other there to stop and rewind, to view a particular section on monitors. There are chairs and tables for staff. CONNIE has brought in a tray of coffee and cookies. DEBORAH has entered. She is dressed like she was when she arrived – though her clothes are now clean. She carries her backpack.

CONNIE. You're on your way?

DEBORAH. Yuh.

CONNIE. Right.

DEBORAH. Uh, thanks for letting me . . .

CONNIE. Well, I'm sure your uncle felt . . .

DEBORAH. 'It was the least that he could do.'

There is almost a shared smile between the two women – for both, it turns into a wry, ironical gesture.

CONNIE. Where are you going?

Slight pause.

DEBORAH. Back.

Slight pause.

CONNIE. Back being . . . ?

DEBORAH. Kind of where I came from.

CONNIE. Do you want some coffee, before you go?

DEBORAH. Is there . . . hey, why not.

She puts down her backpack, pours herself coffee and takes a cookie. She looks on the tray for something.

CONNIE. So what did . . . Oh, did I forget the milk?

DEBORAH. I don't drink milk. Like I usually take sugar.

CONNIE makes to go.

Mom, it's OK.

CONNIE. So what *did* you tell your father?

DEBORAH. What, about GM poplars thing?

CONNIE. Of course.

DEBORAH. Just what I said last night.

CONNIE. I see.

Pause.

DEBORAH. So was last night a set-up?

CONNIE. What can you mean?

DEBORAH. Did you like wind Mitch up so he'd go for me so Dad turns into the alpha dog?

CONNIE. Now why would I do that?

DEBORAH. My question. Seeing as I guess that on the issues you're much nearer Uncle Mitch. Like on thinking Phyllis Schlafly's basically sound, just a little soft on sodomy.

CONNIE. Well, I'm all for honesty within the family.

DEBORAH. Oh, yuh?

CONNIE. As long as it's a two-way street.

Pause.

Of course I set out to provoke your uncle.

DEBORAH. I guess I've got a good idea who did the GM poplar thing.

Pause.

CONNIE. Yes.

DEBORAH. I mean, like what they look like, not their legal names and shit, or where they are now. But I guess like I'm notionally complicit in the commission of a felony.

CONNIE. Why don't you know their names?

DEBORAH. Like we all have forest names.

CONNIE. So none of them know who you are?

Slight pause.

DEBORAH. I trust them.

CONNIE. I repeat the question.

DEBORAH. I repeat the answer. They're my tribe.

CONNIE. Your tribe?

DEBORAH. Yeah, you know, like a family.

CONNIE. And you're convinced that none of them . . .

DEBORAH. Not unless we're infiltrated.

CONNIE. Oh, and are you?

DEBORAH (*after a very slight beat*). No.

CONNIE. Why did you lie to father?

DEBORAH. Hello? He knows, he's asked, what does he say?

CONNIE. That's right. Well done.

DEBORAH. 'Well done'?

CONNIE. That's remarkably perceptive.

DEBORAH. *Mom.*

CONNIE. So what's your forest name?

DEBORAH. It's secret. It's an alias.

CONNIE. Known only to 'the tribe'.

Slight pause.

DEBORAH. 'Fraid so. But hey, you know, like this is cool.

CONNIE. In what way?

DEBORAH. It's a real conversation.

CONNIE. Oh yes. For as we know, no parents ever / talk to –

DEBORAH. So their kids like end up sitting in the tops of trees.

Pause.

CONNIE. Yes, I've always wondered . . . how . . .

DEBORAH. A garbage-bag in a bucket. Then you tie it up and rope it down.

CONNIE. I see.

Slight pause.

It was always my fundamental reservation about summer camp. Which accounts in fact . . .

DEBORAH. What's up?

CONNIE. Oh, it doesn't matter.

Slight pause.

DEBORAH. What is it?

CONNIE. I shouldn't bring it up.

DEBORAH. Oh, come on, mom.

CONNIE. It's about my name. It's really not . . .

DEBORAH. Do you want to see my nipple ring?

CONNIE. They called me Miss Contrary.

DEBORAH. What?

Slight pause.

CONNIE. Which got shortened naturally to 'Con.' There was a family joke, 'Pacific Con,' which is what I absolutely wasn't. And having been contracted, Con could be conveniently expanded into Connie.

DEBORAH. So what's your real name?

CONNIE. Patricia. I haven't told that to anyone for thirty years.

DEBORAH. No shit.

CONNIE. So I'll thank you to preserve the confidence.

DEBORAH. Done deal. And thanks.

CONNIE. Thanks? Why?

DEBORAH. Thanks for telling that to me.

Pause.

I never knew that stuff – about the Young Americans. And Jefferson. I'd vote for *that*.

CONNIE. Well, some of it was nearly accurate.

DEBORAH. Oh, *mom*.

CONNIE. Why, what?

DEBORAH. Why is there like nothing in your life that isn't 'nearly'? Why isn't there anything that's like 'absolutely'?

CONNIE. Is that really true?

Pause.

DEBORAH. You tell me.

Slight pause.

CONNIE. Did I ever tell you where I learned to swim?

DEBORAH *shakes her head.*

Well, it was a lake, about half a mile from the place we used to vacation in the summer. I would go there every day. And local lore maintained that it had an Indian name, which comes out as approximately Chargoggagoggmanchauggaug-gagoggchaubunagungamaugg. Which I learnt to say as a party trick, just like that woman of your uncle's and the state fish of Hawaii. And which translates very roughly as 'we fish our side, you fish your side, and no one fishes in the middle.' Which as my father used to say, gave rise to the ancient and venerable Nipmuk saying, 'the fish are always

greener on the other side of the Chargoggagoggmanchaug-
gauggagoggchaubunagungamaug.' The locals call it 'Webster'.

Which while one understands one does regret. Because
Chargoggagoggmanchauggauggagoggchaubunagungamaugg
clearly is a place. While Webster's just a name.

And the first thing I remember thinking when I got here was
that people didn't really have a place. Everybody was on
wheels. Big wheels and little wheels. And thinking, don't
these people ever feel the need for something to hold on to?
And then I thought of us, our lives, how we were torn up
from our roots and blown like leaves across the continent.
And as my father said, once you're here, the only place to
go's out of your mind . . . And in the Sixties, all those
cracks and fissures in the crust. And is it any wonder people
want to feel at home. Even if 'home' slid off into the ocean
long ago.

DEBORAH. There's trees that started growing long before
Columbus.

CONNIE. I think you'll find there's trees that started growing
before Christ. You better go and find your father.

DEBORAH. Mom. I told another lie.

CONNIE. Oh, yes?

DEBORAH. I told him I came here because I was in trouble
and I knew you guys were here.

CONNIE. And didn't you?

DEBORAH. It was just the closest place I knew.

Slight pause.

CONNIE. I see.

Pause.

He's sequestered with his policy advisor. You just had to go.

DEBORAH. OK. I'll leave a . . .

CONNIE *turns to go, turns back.*

CONNIE. Of course, the real plotting coup in *Citizen Kane* is when you realize that Rosebud, the thing that he loved most of all, was the thing he had to leave behind.

DEBORAH. The sled.

CONNIE. The sled. For him, the sled was Jefferson.

DEBORAH. And for you, I guess, it's Chargoggagog . . .

CONNIE. Well, absolutely.

> CONNIE *goes out.* DEBORAH *finds a piece of paper and writes a note. She leaves it on the podium. Enter* LORIANNE. *She's dressed up to look a little like Rebecca McKeene.* DEBORAH *leaves the note, goes to her backpack.*

LORIANNE. Last minute tips?

> DEBORAH *sees* LORIANNE *and picks up what she means.*

DEBORAH. It's just a good luck note for Dad.

LORIANNE. That's not his podium.

DEBORAH. Oh, right.

> LORIANNE*'s nearer her podium than* DEBORAH *so she gets to the note first.*

LORIANNE. It was a deal-breaker in the pre-debate I'm told. Ms McKeene was most concerned that the public sees her better side. Which begs the question, obviously.

> *Glancing at the note.*

'Stick to your guns.' Well, there's no doubt about that.

DEBORAH (*gets the double meaning*). Oh, like I didn't mean . . .

LORIANNE. No. But he does. And in the next five minutes, I have to work out how to shoot him down.

DEBORAH. But still – really – I mean, why you're here and shit – you want to shoot her down.

LORIANNE. You got it.

DEBORAH. Why?

LORIANNE. What, apart from her being somebody who believes in state regulation of all activities except for incest and illegal immigration?

DEBORAH. Yes, and you being like I guess supposed to be some kind of like, objective . . .

LORIANNE. Well, it's not that often anyone accuses me of being *that*.

DEBORAH. As opposed to being a hired gun for a partisan political campaign.

Slight pause.

LORIANNE. You're presumably named Deborah after your aunt.

DEBORAH. Uh, yeah?

LORIANNE. Who died in her twenties, right?

DEBORAH. Yes, of cancer.

LORIANNE. Well, imagine this. She didn't die of cancer. She was shot. One evening, in her home. And a politician running in a liberal district comes out against the death penalty for her murderer, because of course all human life is sacred, unless it's in its mother's womb. And then let's imagine this same politician changes her opinion on this question, maybe just before she decides to run for governor. And let's say you share a home with the murdered woman's father and you get the chance to show the politician up, in her true colors, as cynical, hypocritical, and two-faced. I'd say, objectively, you'd do it. Hired or otherwise.

Pause.

DEBORAH. Yeah, well.

LORIANNE. Yeah, well.

DEBORAH. Hey, did you know that fourteen teenagers are killed by handguns every day?

LORIANNE. Uh . . . I, why . . . ?

DEBORAH (*picking up her backpack*). Just thought, like, it might help.

DEBORAH hurries out, leaving LORIANNE alone. LORIANNE goes to her podium, stands there, breathing heavily, calming herself down.

LORIANNE (*to herself*). OK. Yeah. Sure.

During this, SHELDON enters at the other end of the room, with a file. LORIANNE, testing an answer:

'Fourteen teenagers are killed by handguns every day.' 'So is the literal reading of a two-hundred-year-old document worth the cost of so many young lives?'

Or . . . How many kids are killed by handguns every day? Fourteen. That's one approximately every hundred minutes. How many of those fourteen is Mr Vine prepared to sacrifice to a narrow, suspect and – uh, OK – over-literal reading of the Second Amendment?

So, hey, guess what? Ban on kitchen table dealing? Yes. Trigger locks? You bet. One gun-a-month rule? Sure. And this junks the Bill of Rights? Oh, please.

SHELDON. Give us a break.

LORIANNE. I know.

SHELDON. No, that was a suggestion.

LORIANNE. Ah. Oh, yes. Hey you know, you shouldn't really / be listening –

SHELDON. Hey, do you know, two thousand / women . . .

LORIANNE. Two thousand what?

SHELDON (*thinking better of it*). But, as you say.

Hearing others coming, SHELDON goes to the side to check over last-minute notes. Enter DON and CARYL, followed by MITCHELL and CONNIE, with a sugar bowl. LORIANNE leaves the podium.

DON. No, what you do, say your opponent has a zipper problem, you don't say, 'Senator, how do you square your

line on reasserting family values with the fact you hump
your secretary?'

CARYL *looks a little alarmed,* CONNIE *askance.*
MITCHELL *places a folder on the moderator's desk, as:*

No, you take another question, say on taxes, and you say,
now as my opponent will be well aware, his secretary . . .
pause . . . pays more in tax than Boeing and you wonder if
he thinks that's right. So you hint you're going to drop the
shoe, but then you don't. But now he knows you know. And
knows that you still might.

CONNIE. What's this?

MITCHELL. I think the campaign manager's raising the
smoking bimbo issue good and early.

CONNIE. The smoking bimbo?

CARYL (*with a whiff of distaste*). As in smoking gun.

CONNIE. Yes, I understand that.

SHELDON. Excuse me, there's a smoking bimbo?

MITCHELL. No, Sheldon, there is no smoking bimbo.

SHELDON. If there is, I'd like to be the first to know.

A slight pause.

MITCHELL. And so where's . . .

SHELDON. Vincent and I have had a most productive
breakfast. We've come up with some formulations which we
think will wow the populace.

MITCHELL. Tomorrow evening.

DON. Um, when you say 'come up with'?

SHELDON. No experiments, but much 'innovation'. No roll-
backs, much 'reform'. No cuts, for sure, but a whole pile of
'relief'.

CONNIE. What are you saying, Sheldon?

CARYL. It's the good words v. the bad words.

MITCHELL (*to* DON, *quietly*). He hasn't seen the questions?

DON. No.

SHELDON. And a cornucopia of 'ity' words.

CARYL (*to* CONNIE). Responsibility. Integrity. Prosperity.

SHELDON *opening his black ring file.*

SHELDON. Though generally we feel we might cut down on the assonance.

DON. The what?

SHELDON. 'From the shirkers to the workers.' 'From the desk-bound to the upward-bound.'

DON. You don't go for 'upward-bound'?

SHELDON. We felt it made me sound like Jesse Jackson.

CONNIE. Excuse me?

MITCHELL. Heaven forefend.

DON. He's right. 'From Charity to Parity, from aid to trade . . . '

Enter VINCENT.

CARYL. Hey. Will someone tell me something? Why is it that police mugshots, you know, the composites they put together on computers, why they always look like Jesse Jackson?

Everyone else has seen VINCENT.

MITCHELL. Good morning Vincent.

CARYL *catches up.*

VINCENT. Well, I sure hope nobody thinks I'd take offense at that.

He goes to the moderator's desk.

Unless you think all mugshots look like me.

MITCHELL. Vince, good morning.

Other 'good mornings' and 'hi theres'.

VINCENT. Good morning.

VINCENT opens the folder on the desk and sees that it contains new questions.

DON. OK. Don's golden rules.

SHELDON. Hard answers short, easy answers long.

VINCENT. Hey, are these new questions?

DON (*to* SHELDON). Two.

SHELDON. Hey, what's up?

DON. Two?

MITCHELL. We had some research just in on our moderator, Bob Lejeune. He's just bought a beach-front property. So we reckon he'll be little bent out of shape by offshore oil.

DON. And his wife's just been admitted to Betty Ford.

MITCHELL. So we don't think he'll be big on prescription drugs.

VINCENT. Yes, but . . .

DON. And we've shifted some of them around.

Pause.

VINCENT. Why's that?

MITCHELL. Well, as I say.

DON (*to* SHELDON). Two.

SHELDON. Don't repeat your opponent's charges.

VINCENT sits.

DON. Nor apologize. So, three:

SHELDON. The first two sentences of any answer's all that anyone remembers.

DON. Four.

SHELDON. Remind me.

DON. Never commit yourself to numerated answers.

SHELDON. Give me five good reasons.

DON. But most of all, if you're feeling good, your plates are spinning, that little heart is thumpin' and those arteries are pumpin', then . . .

MOST EVERYONE. Slow Down.

DON. Do you want to see the bounce?

SHELDON. I do so want to see the bounce.

CONNIE. What is the bounce?

DON *goes to* SHELDON*'s podium. As* DON *demonstrates the bounce, people watch on the screens.*

DON. The bounce is how the experienced debater moves his or her head from one side of the frame to the other. This is what happens normally. 'I am happy to give a complete assurance that I spent the whole of my idyllic adolescence . . . '

He turns his head the other way.

'. . . in a structured program of cold showers, musical appreciation, helping mom and bicycling.'

MITCHELL. Shifty.

CARYL. *Very* shifty.

DON. On the other hand . . . 'Believe me, or the evidence of observation, probability or common logic?'

This time he takes his eyes down to the desk en route from one side to the other.

'It is for the people to decide.'

LORIANNE. Open.

CONNIE. Transparent.

MITCHELL. Honest.

CARYL. And possessing of a quiet dignity.

DON. You people. So do we want to get this pop stand on the road?

DON *leaves the lectern;* SHELDON *and* LORIANNE *to their lecterns.*

SHELDON. That is exactly where we want to get it.

MITCHELL. Connie, do you want to sit here?

CONNIE. No, I'm fine. I'll stand.

SHELDON. Remind me of my stopgaps.

CARYL. What's a stopgap?

DON. 'So let me give a categorical assurance.'

MITCHELL. Things to fill in while he's thinking of the answer.

DON. 'Well, it's interesting you say that.' 'Let me put it this way.' 'Well, Bob, I've thought about this matter, as you would expect . . . '

CONNIE. It's the confidence that is so reassuring.

MITCHELL. Try and see it as insurance, Connie.

DON. Like 'You know what I say? I say this.'

SHELDON *sees the note on his podium.*

LORIANNE. No, he can't have that, it's mine.

DON. I know.

CARYL. Hey, can I ask one question before we begin?

A little concern.

DON. Yuh, sure.

CARYL (*to* SHELDON). What's written on your pad?

Pause.

SHELDON. Three words. I have to say, my guiding principles. 'Duplicity.' 'Profanity.' 'Velocity.'

DON. Let's *go.*

Everyone sorts themselves out to watch the mock.

MITCHELL. Connie, be careful of the sightlines.

CARYL (*for asking about the pad*). Uh . . . I'm sorry.

VINCENT. Good evening. If there was justice in the world, I would be Robert W. Lejeune, welcoming you to tonight's live gubernatorial debate, between Sheldon B. Vine for the Republicans and Rebecca J. McKeene the Democratic candidate. The format agreed upon between the candidates . . .

MITCHELL. Eventually.

DON. And grudgingly.

VINCENT. . . . . is that I will ask one candidate a question, and she or he will have two minutes to respond.

DON. At a reasonable pace.

VINCENT. I will then invite the other candidate to question the first candidate, again for up to two minutes of discussion. Then we reverse. A prior coin toss would have determined which candidate goes first but it seems that's already been decided. First question, Ms McKeene. There's one thing everyone agrees on. That education should be above politics. But improving public schools has a tendency to be placed in the file marked 'vital but intractable.' So what's the plan?

LORIANNE. Well, yes, you see, everybody thinks this can't be solved, which is why I'm keen to lock this down right from the get-go.

A glance at MITCHELL *and* DON.

Thirty years ago our schools were the best funded in the nation. Now they're in the last quarter on everything from buildings to books to text scores. And it's worth remembering which party was in the governor's mansion while all this was happening. But you and I owe it to the people of this state to be straight with them about my program. Yes of course we look at basic skills. Sure, we need to get the balance right between class sizes and teachers' salaries. But a quality, creative experience in the classroom is important too. And you know, I was in a classroom somewhere folksy just the other day with dripping ceilings and kids doubled up at desks and Atlases with two Vietnams if not one Korea. And so I would propose a targeted, and focused, monitored and limited spending hike to bring the . . . expenditure-per-child up to the national average.

VINCENT. Mr Vine, do you want to come back on that.

SHELDON. Well, I'm glad Ms McKeene went partisan good and early, because I want to do it too. I do think there's a choice between teacher salaries and class sizes. Class sizes for the children. I think there's a huge curriculum issue . . .

DON. Yih-hah!

SHELDON. . . . around bilingual education, which studies show to be deleterious for *children*.

MITCHELL. Delewhat?

SHELDON. And on the money, we agree there should be more, it's just we don't agree on how. So can I ask why she won't support my proposal for Opportunity scholarships to allow *parents* to choose the best school for their *child*?

LORIANNE. Oh, why? Guess what. Because Opportunity scholarships aren't Opportunity scholarships.

SHELDON. Oh, what are they?

LORIANNE. They are vouchers.

SHELDON. Vouchers?

LORIANNE. Vouchers.

SHELDON. Yes they are.

Slight pause.

It's a pretty term for vouchers. You're quite right. And I'm in favor of them, for the reasons I've outlined.

Pause.

LORIANNE. Yes, well, I think my views on vouchers are well known. On the other issue that you mentioned . . . uh, the right for Hispanic children to learn their mother tongue . . . the evidence as you know is quite ambiguous.

SHELDON. No it is not.

LORIANNE. It is.

SHELDON. The studies are conclusive.

LORIANNE. The studies are selective.

SHELDON. They're conclusive in the areas selected.

LORIANNE. I just think we have to get beyond the idea that if people speak one language there's a law says they can't speak another one.

SHELDON. Yes, wouldn't it be nice if Americans were like the Dutch? (*In Finnish, phonetically:*) KOO-aw-uh-SOO-AH-men NO-kyee-ee-nen PREZ-ee-dent-ih? [Who is the current President of Finland?]

LORIANNE. Excuse me?

DON. Vouchers.

VINCENT. Overrun.

DON. Allow it.

LORIANNE. Vouchers. So what do I say? I say this. The voucher problem's what it's always been. You strap the cash to the backs of kids instead of schools so they can take it from poor schools to rich ones.

SHELDON. Except that it isn't strapping, what it is is trapping, you are trapping smart poor kids in ghetto schools, while the middle class can choose. In fact, the two issues are the same. You're trapping kids in schools where they won't learn and you're teaching them in a language they won't need. You're denying them the education *our* kids get and the words they speak. I call that discrimination on the grounds of income and let's be honest that means race. I'm for the civil rights of kids. Money is power. Knowledge is power. I'm for giving power to the people.

VINCENT. Time!

SHELDON. Huh? Hey?

CARYL. That's *neat*.

SHELDON. You *bet*.

DON. Fifteen-love.

MITCHELL (*to himself*). 'Power to the People'?

CONNIE. Well done, dear.

DON. But take care of the ping-pong.

LORIANNE. Ping-pong?

MITCHELL. 'No it isn't, yes it is.'

SHELDON. It's hard.

DON. So what's with the fucking Tagalog?

SHELDON. It was Finnish.

DON. I repeat the question.

SHELDON *gestures to* VINCENT.

VINCENT. 'Who is the current President of Finland?'

DON. And who is it?

VINCENT. I have no idea.

Slight pause.

MITCHELL. Vincent.

VINCENT. So this is . . . this is the next question. Mr Vine, I don't know if you've recently had occasion to visit the Arthur Hopwood Gallery at UPE, which is of course owned and supported by the regents of the university and thus bankrolled by the taxpayer. As you may have read or seen, there's an exhibition there called 'Contrary Perspectives,' containing what might be called a sculpture of a naked woman with our country's flag between her legs, with the title 'My Country 'Tis Of Thee.'

CARYL. Ugh.

VINCENT. Would that be there under a McKeene, sorry a Vine governorship?

SHELDON. Well, I haven't seen the exhibition as in the closing days of this campaign I've decided to devote the majority of my free time to shaving.

He waits for a response, which comes, albeit politely. He gives a 'jury's out' gesture.

But I can say that this exhibit would not be subsidized, because a Vine administration would not be using your tax dollars to subsidize the pleasures of the rich. It would only be there if the gallery could persuade enough people to pay a market cost to see it. And if they did, then it's not my business to stop them.

VINCENT. That's it?

SHELDON. I don't think it's very hard, but I'm answering short anyway.

MITCHELL (*to* DON). Didn't we . . . we've prepped this?

DON. Yes.

VINCENT. Ms McKeene?

LORIANNE. Well. The first thing to say is that of course I am opposed to censorship of any kind, unlike many members of my opponent's party. But because you don't believe in banning something doesn't mean you have to like it, and from how this object's been described to me it seems to be gratuitously offensive to just about everybody. And if I single out the fact that it's pornographic it's because women have had to put up for too long with propaganda for hate crimes disguised as art.

VINCENT. Do you want come back, Mr Vine?

SHELDON. No, thanks.

DON. Why not?

SHELDON. Because I've nothing to add to my first answer.

DON. What, having let her scoop up coastal feminazis and Mothers For Leviticus in one fell swoop?

DON *rewinding the show-tape during this:*

SHELDON. Did she do that?

DON. Caryl, do we have anything on this?

CARYL. Sixty-nine percent of likely voters. Seventy-six percent of over-forties, and eighty-two percent of those in inland counties.

DON. Did what?

CARYL. Said that it's a scandal.

SHELDON. It's a scandal that it's subsidized.

DON. It's a scandal that it's *shown*.

He's found the place he wants.

At the very least, let's make it a little harder for her.

He plays the tape:

SHELDON. . . . *using your tax dollars to subsidize the pleasures of the rich.*

DON *freezes frame.*

DON. 'I use the word 'pleasure' loosely in this case.'

Plays:

SHELDON. *It would only be there if the gallery could persuade enough people to pay a market cost to see it.*

DON. 'Which I doubt.'

Freeze. Plays:

SHELDON. *And if they did, then it's not my business to stop them.*

DON *stops the tape.*

DON. 'Whatever I might personally want to do.' And then after she says, what she said, what do you come back with?

SHELDON. I have to come back?

MITCHELL. It's the purpose of the exercise.

SHELDON. It's a free speech issue. Pornography's not a hate crime. I don't know what a hate crime is.

DON. Oh, well in that case, please, no, don't come back.

SHELDON. And I suppose I could say that fifteen years ago, she picketed some City Hall or other in defense of an exhibition of explicit gay and lesbian photography. Involving I've no doubt an affront to taste and basic hygiene.

DON. Involving a black guy's fist up another / guy's ass.

SHELDON. And then she changed her mind.

DON. And then she changed her *line*.

CARYL. Which is good for you sir, as we have you very high among the same groups for consistency.

SHELDON. Oh, great. Next question?

MITCHELL. Shel, it's fifteen all.

SHELDON. Oh, you cannot be ser-i-ous.

Pause.

VINCENT. Ms McKeene, the Constitution is quite clear. The right of the people to keep and bear arms shall not be infringed. So why do you plan on infringing it?

LORIANNE. Hey, Bob, guess what? Let's not be disingenuous. Like, nobody thinks the people have a right to march down Rodeo Drive at lunchtime with an M-16. We're talking reasonable here. And my position is quite clear on this. Ban private ownership of guns? No, clearly not. Make sure the guns are in the right hands? Obviously yes. So I'm in favor of a ban on kitchen table sales, while Mr Vine is not, I'm in favor of a ban on sales at state and county shows, he's not, I'm certainly for trigger-locks and a one-gun-a-month rule and national registration and I don't think stopping young dudes swaggering around with lethal weapons purchased by their girlfriends undermines one comma of the Constitution.

VINCENT. Mr / Vine –

LORIANNE. Oh, and does he know how many kids are killed by handguns every day? Fourteen. How many of those fourteen is Mr Vine prepared to sacrifice to a suspect and perverse interpretation of the Bill of Rights?

SHELDON. But you don't really think that's enough.

LORIANNE. What's enough, the fourteen?

SHELDON. No, the proposals you've described.

LORIANNE. Well, mercy, it's a start.

SHELDON. Well, exactly. It's a stepping stone.

LORIANNE. I didn't say that.

SHELDON. 'For a start' implies 'for now'.

LORIANNE. Not necessarily.

SHELDON. You really think guns should be banned.

LORIANNE. Mr Vine, please don't tell me what I think.

SHELDON. But don't you?

LORIANNE. No I don't.

SHELDON. I don't believe you.

LORIANNE. Well, I can't help that.

DON. Ping-pong!

CONNIE. I would say, game set and match.

MITCHELL. You need to change the subject.

SHELDON. No, I'm trying something else. 'You actually think they should be banned.'

LORIANNE. 'Don't . . . tell me what I think.'

SHELDON. You know . . .

LORIANNE. Don't tell me what I know.

SHELDON. D'you know that two thousand women are killed by their husbands or their boyfriends every year?

This is one of the new formulations SHELDON *worked out with* VINCENT.

We know what we mean by 'make my day.' We think of a dark stranger invading our domestic hearth. But for those two thousand women, it's the hearth that is the problem.

Slight pause.

That's over six a day. Let's call it a good day. That's –

Looks at his watch.

– five down, one to go, this very day.

DON (*although he doesn't want* SHELDON *to win this question*). Hey *right*.

SHELDON. Gun clubs know that. Like me, they think that women have put up with male violence for too long. That's why they're giving free tuition so when women are attacked they have a chance. Which is why, yes, I think the founding fathers were correct when they sought to guarantee that people had the right to own the means to protect themselves from being killed.

LORIANNE. Um, hey, I . . . uh, well, let me put it this way . . .

Unable to counter SHELDON*'s answer, she mimes shooting herself in the head with a handgun.* DON, VINCENT *and* CARYL *laugh.*

CONNIE. Thirty-fifteen.

DON *nods to* MITCHELL *to cover, and goes and leans over* VINCENT, *changing the order of the questions.*

MITCHELL. Speaking of great Republican debaters, what were the three worst years of Dan Quayle's life?

SHELDON. Second grade.

MITCHELL *does his 'someone's stolen my punch line' gesture.*

CONNIE (*to* CARYL). You see . . .

CARYL. Don't even go there, Mrs Vine.

DON. Next question.

SHELDON. I am bent back like a bow.

VINCENT. Ms McKeene.

SHELDON. In fact, it's my question.

DON. Trust me.

SHELDON. Why?

For a moment, that's real. Then DON *turns into a joke, laughing.*

DON. In *serious* revolt mode. Vincent, nail these good people to the mat.

VINCENT. You want this now?

DON. Go for it.

VINCENT. Ms McKeene. We're hitting a recession. As you say, schools are overcrowded. We have simultaneous crises in water and electricity supply. There's a housing shortage and you're not too sold on urban sprawl. Can we afford the level of illegal immigration we have now?

LORIANNE. Hey, look. There's two simple lines on this. One, from the demagogues who try to use this issue to inflame prejudice and hatred. On the other side there are people who appear not to be bothered about people's genuine concerns. I think the only responsible position is to accept there is a problem but to be sensitive about solving it. Fiscally, we can't support expanding welfare costs and Medicaid. Environmentally, resources are finite. For labor, I'm against employers using immigration as a form of cost control. In agriculture *or* dotcom. So, a fair policy? Yes. Streamline and clarify procedures? Sure. Welcome? Every time. Borders wide open? Give us a break.

SHELDON. Well, Bob, I'm intrigued by that, because when Ms McKeene was running for the state assembly – in a heavily Latino district – she was for a blanket amnesty for illegal immigrants. What's changed?

CARYL. Hear hear.

DON gestures CARYL *not to support* SHELDON – *he wants him to go on.*

SHELDON. But, you know what?

CARYL (*to* DON). Shouldn't he . . . 'hard answers short'?

DON *shakes his head.*

SHELDON. Unlike my opponent I've not bent to the prevailing wind.

He leaves a challenging pause.

This country was built on the energy and enterprise of people who came here to make better lives for themselves and their children. Immigration policy has been a mess. I'm for a clean-slate amnesty, on one condition: that not a penny of your tax dollars goes to support the people who we welcome here.

Slight pause.

I think that's 'whom'.

LORIANNE. So, let me lock this down. You're for opening the floodgates, undercutting American workers, *and* putting undocumented moms in jail for sending kids to school?

MITCHELL. Or turning them away from hospitals.

SHELDON. No, I'm not for sending moms to jail, that is a travesty of my / position –

DON. Sir, at least, please don't repeat the charges. Let's leave that there.

SHELDON. What, we're leaving that at her point?

DON. Well, we'll come back to that. Now this next one *is* for you.

SHELDON. But in that case . . . never mind. Next question.

Pause. VINCENT*'s got the strategy.*

MITCHELL. Vincent.

A moment.

VINCENT. Yes. I see. OK. Mr Vine, last week a group of protesters broke into an agricultural research faculty . . . excuse me, that must be facility . . . at one of our universities, in order to cut down genetically-mutilated trees that were being grown there for experimental purposes. As we all know, this led to the death of a young woman, which the District Attorney has ruled to be justifiable homicide. On the issue of the right of protest . . .

He decides to recast the question.

So, aside from the specific issue, this has raised the general question of environmental activism, and the thorny question of scientific research into areas which cause environmental, social and religious concern.

MITCHELL *instinctively wants to challenge this rewrite of the question.* DON *gestures to him not to intervene, which will do more harm than good.* VINCENT *has continued:*

I'm thinking of stem-cell research, and / animal testing . . .

SHELDON. Well, it's interesting you put it that way, Bob, and I'm glad you're not asking me to comment on a case that neither I nor my opponent knows the whole truth about, so I don't propose to comment on it one way or the other.

A challenging look at DON *and* MITCHELL, *implying he thinks that was an effective answer.*

But I want to talk about, what aren't genetically-mutilated, but actually genetically-manipulated crops.

VINCENT *acknowledges his mistake.*

Whose purpose is to produce not – I don't mean manipulated I mean modified, damn it – whose purpose is to produce cheap and plentiful new sources of, in this case, timber, but also food, to feed our families and those of other countries, cheaply.

Slight pause.

Which, far from rejecting on the grounds of dangers which have not been proved, we should embrace and welcome just as we embraced and welcomed penicillin and the other great leap forwards of the . . . um . . .

He realizes he's dug himself into a hole.

With due safeguards obviously and without . . . the cheap food thing.

Slight pause.

And 'great leap forward' really is the Little Red Book, right?

DON. Sir, I understand what you're up to here, but do you really want to screw the farmers and the frog fuckers and the Catholics *at the same time*?

SHELDON. OK. So what . . .

CARYL. And what happens if she goes back to the DA and the shooting?

DON. Good.

MITCHELL. Assuming Bob Lejeune doesn't let her off the hook / so easily.

LORIANNE. Do we have McKeene on this?

DON. Well, she was on cable yesterday reiterating her condemnation of political violence from whatever source.

MITCHELL. That's interesting.

DON. Why?

MITCHELL *takes a videotape from his briefcase.*

MITCHELL. Because of this.

SHELDON. What's that?

MITCHELL (*with a glance at* LORIANNE). Oh, just something our ground people FedExed up today.

He plays an amateur videotaping of REBECCA McKEENE *speaking to a small fundraising brunch, in a back yard near the ocean. We just see* REBECCA. *We hear the voice of a* HECKLER *intervening:*

HECKLER *So hey, is anybody going to mention Sarah Jane Polowski?*

REBECCA. *I'm sorry?*

HECKLER *This is the twenty-one-year-old shot dead while protesting the contamination of the planet.*

SHELDON. So what's this?

MITCHELL. A fundraiser.

REBECCA. *Yes, I know who she is and what she was doing.*

HECKLER *But I guess this didn't happen in the Sixties.*

DON. Hey.

REBECCA. *And while I'm on the record against tolerance for– terrorism, / I have also said . . .*

HECKLER *Oh, so protesting GM crops makes you a / terrorist –*

REBECCA. . . . *I don't think it's the time to exploit . . .*

A VOICE *from the side:*

SAM. *Hey, folks, the food's congealing.*

REBECCA. . . . *a family's grief.*

HECKLER *OK. Forget about it. Let's go eat.*

VINCENT. When was this?

MITCHELL (*looks at the tape cover*). Saturday.

REBECCA. *I'm not forgetting it. I'm just not commenting / on it right now.*

HECKLER *I mean, like one way of helping out that family might be for the Democratic candidate to say her killer should be charged with killing her. But, then, this is the Democrat who won't come out against Prop. Ninety-Two, / so I guess –*

DON *looks to* MITCHELL *in surprise.* MITCHELL *looks pleased with himself.*

REBECCA (*stung*). *OK. What do I say? I say this. Do I respect her motivations? Yes. Do I have serious reservations about GM crops? I do. Do I intend to make a snap judgment on a tragic accident without knowing all the facts? No I do not.*

SAM. *And the food is on / the porch.*

REBECCA. *But if you – or anybody else – feels it's inappropriate to continue with this fundraiser then I'm quite happy to go home.*

MITCHELL *stops the tape.*

VINCENT. So where did you get that?

MITCHELL (*with a glance at* LORIANNE). Oh, just our inadequate opposition research.

SHELDON. So, what . . .

DON. Oh, I'd guess, something like . . . 'I would like to echo my opponent's sympathy with all those touched by this tragic event. I was impressed by her commitment to non-violence expressed so eloquently on Sunday morning. But, Rebecca, I must ask you why, three days ago, you said you respected someone who breaks into and then vandalizes private property. Particularly when you're not prepared to back the judgment of the DA in this case.'

General approval. CARYL *applauds.*

SHELDON. And then I can talk about the wider issues.

DON. No, I'd leave it there.

SHELDON. But Vincent's question . . .

DON. Hey, when did the six o'clock news show the question?

LORIANNE. And it's good for me. In the sense of bad for me. In that I'm thinking, hey fuck, they got that, what else they got?

DON. And she flails around waiting for the other shoe to drop.

Pause.

SHELDON. All right. Next question.

DON *goes to the show-tape, starts rewinding.*

DON. Hey, while we've stopped, why don't we go back to immigration.

SHELDON. Why?

DON. Trust me.

He plays:

LORIANNE. *– agriculture or dotcom. So, a fair policy? Yes. Streamline and clarify procedures? Sure. Welcome? Every time. Borders wide open? Give us a break.*

SHELDON. *Well, Bob, I'm intrigued by that, because when Ms McKeene was running for the state assembly – in a heavily Latino district – she was for a blanket amnesty for illegal immigrants. What's changed?*

CARYL *Hear hear.*

DON *stops the tape.*

DON. 'Hear hear.' Caryl's right.

SHELDON. What are you saying?

MITCHELL. First two sentences.

CARYL. Hard answers short.

DON. Quit while you're winning.

SHELDON. And I guess that would apply to gay and lesbian pornography.

DON. Yes, I guess it would.

SHELDON. Point out she's flip-flopped, leave it there.

DON. That's right.

SHELDON *leaves the podium and goes to* LORIANNE*'s podium and looks through her mock brief.*

MITCHELL. Uh, Sheldon . . .

CONNIE. That is kind of cheating, dear.

SHELDON. So on preferences, I say my piece and she says she's down on quotas, she favors affirmative access or some other weasel term. And I quote her stout defense of quotas to the 1993 Western Convention of the N.double-A.C.P. On drugs she says that as governor she'd make it a priority to get the dealers and rather than pointing out the war on drugs has failed, I point out that she smoked a little dope at college and when she's asked about cocaine she tends to change the subject. On guns, maybe there's grainy footage of her at a rally saying young men in the ghettoes have every right to defend themselves against the fascist insect. And if as you say it's a cynical and calculated flip-flop, then I'm implying that that she still believes in an immigration amnesty and legalising drugs and black self-defense and the beneficial influence of gay and lesbian pornography.

He goes and sits in the body of the room.

Which I think lets her off the hook because all she has to do is go, 'that was then, I've changed my mind,' and if I say 'no you haven't' she says 'I have too.'

DON. Sir, it's the purpose of this exercise to / find a way –

SHELDON. But I don't think that's actually the point. I think what this does is to imply that I disagree with what she said when she was young. So although I don't actually say what I think, because I stop before I get there, it sure *sounds* like I'm anti-preferences – which I am – and that I'm for censorship and tougher drug laws and building a Berlin Wall across our southern border, which I'm not. It's a two-slit trick. It looks as if I'm shining light on her hypocrisy but in fact I'm concealing what I actually believe.

DON. Yes, sir, you're absolutely right.

SHELDON. I am?

DON. We're busted.

SHELDON. Good. So, can we drop this and proceed / to work out –

DON. But I want to point out two things to you.

Slight pause.

SHELDON. Yes?

DON. We're twenty minutes in. Apart from threatening to flood us with illegal aliens, you've said remarkably little to alarm the populace. And yet you haven't had to lie.

Slight pause.

Wasn't that the deal?

SHELDON. So what's the second thing?

MITCHELL. You know that.

SHELDON. I do?

MITCHELL. It's the one thing you can't slip away from.

SHELDON. Not Indian gaming or dune buggies.

MITCHELL. No.

SHELDON. Yes. No.

Slight pause.

No, I do not endorse Proposition Ninety-Two. Three reasons. It's unconstitutional, it's discriminatory between one citizen and another. We know it will cause religious difficulty for the Amish, the Jehovah's Witnesses, the Mennonites and Quakers. Four – excuse me – it will cause political difficulties for members or supporters of groups who advocate the use of force.

MITCHELL. Like?

SHELDON. The Aryan Alliance, American Restitution, the Convocation of Militias of America . . .

MITCHELL. And?

SHELDON. Yes, Wildfire, the Gaia Fellowship and People United for the Liberation of the Planet.

MITCHELL. Deborah.

SHELDON. Deborah.

Slight pause.

I won't condemn it. I'll keep quiet about it. But all else being equal, I'm not inclined to endorse a proposition that is unconstitutional, unworkable and will criminalize my daughter.

LORIANNE. But, sir, you don't have to.

MITCHELL. Doesn't he?

LORIANNE. No, sir. You say you've never doubted the commitment of Americans, both old and new, to the principles of democracy. It's an insult to these people to insist that they declare an oath affirming something that's so obviously right. Sure, the liberals ban books and rip down pictures and impose language codes, because they're liberals and they think they know best on all questions. We're not like that. We don't care to tell folks what they can or cannot say. Mostly because, unlike the liberals, we trust them.

Pause. To DON, *a challenge for him to come to her support:*

Huh?

DON. Caryl, what d'you think?

LORIANNE. Caryl?

DON. How would that line play?

CARYL. I guess that people might say, gee, if you're so convinced it's right, why not stand up and say so?

DON. I see.

Slight pause. LORIANNE *thrown by* DON*'s response.*

LORIANNE. Well, then, you do what Sheldon said. You just keep quiet about it.

DON. Caryl?

CARYL. We did ask people what they thought of no stance.

DON. And?

CARYL. They thought it sounded kind of shifty.

Slight pause.

DON. Right.

LORIANNE. OK. You pursue the strategy. You point out what she's said about this in the past. I mean, for fuck's sake, you guys must be able to come up with McKeene saying something against *loyalty*.

DON. Yuh, sure. But that's not quite the problem in his case.

SHELDON. Why not?

DON. Because it's not about her.

SHELDON. In what way?

DON *going to* SHELDON*'s podium.*

DON. OK, McKeene, what's your line on Ninety-Two?

Slight pause.

MITCHELL. Lorianne.

LORIANNE. Um, I . . . ?

DON. Lorianne, your line is 'I endorse.'

Thrown, LORIANNE *goes back to her podium. Then she reacts:*

LORIANNE. Is that remotely possible?

MITCHELL. If it isn't possible, why hasn't she come out against it?

LORIANNE. Well, OK. I've thought about this as you would expect, and after due consideration I've decided to endorse it.

Slight pause.

DON. 'Oh. Right. Well, in that case . . . hey you know what? I guess I might as well endorse it too.' Or else, as you suggest, she declines to state.

LORIANNE. Um . . . I guess, despite the superficial popularity of this . . . whatever, I do share the concerns of those who view this as unconstitutional and it would be irresponsible for me to endorse it before the judicial arm has had its say.

DON. 'Oh, right. Well having remained silent on this issue thus far, now and only now you've decided not to check the box, I've decided that I'm going to listen to my base and say yea after all.' Does everybody get this?

LORIANNE. You're saying, she goes first, we're fucked.

During this, DON *leaves the podium.*

DON. Yes, but it's worse than that. We're first. 'Well, Bob, I've thought about this matter, obviously, as you would imagine, and although I'm just as loyal as the next guy I've decided it's ill-drafted, ill-thought out and almost certainly illegal and I propose to stick it where the sun don't shine.' And she responds: 'Well that's odd, Bob, because I've decided that despite my opponent's carping caveats, I'm not going to impugn the motives of the fine Americans who drafted this and so I'm pleased to take this opportunity to unconditionally endorse this fine and patriotic proposition.' So, no, it's not just first is fucked. If we don't endorse, we're still fucked, either way. Unless she comes out, at the top, before you've spoken on the question, and condemns the thing outright.

SHELDON. In which case, I can say, while I respect the motivations / of the patriotic people . . .

DON. But, sir, it isn't going to happen.

SHELDON. Why?

MITCHELL Because they've done this exercise as well.

Pause.

SHELDON. So what you're saying is, that I / can't actually –

MITCHELL. What Don's saying is, we can smoke and mirror you on drugs and immigration. Even crime. But there's no escape on Ninety-Two. Unless you can guarantee – can *guarantee* – that she'll come out against it, then it's endorse or die. As Don has just so ably demonstrated.

SHELDON. Well, in that case, it appears, we're dead.

He stands and makes to go.

DON. Why?

LORIANNE. This is so unnecessary.

MITCHELL. Lorianne, it *really* isn't helpful / now for you . . .

SHELDON. Oh, and speaking of things being dead, you know, Don's right, I shouldn't duck the Sarah Jane Polowski thing.

DON. Well, good.

SHELDON. 'Cause on this one I'm with McKeene.

DON. You're what?

SHELDON. I mean, I disagree with what Polowski thought and what she did, but I can still respect her *motivations*.

MITCHELL. Oh, Sheldon . . .

VINCENT. Uh . . . Excuse me. Can I ask a question here?

SHELDON. Of course.

VINCENT (*to* MITCHELL). I just want to get this straight.

MITCHELL. Please, go ahead.

VINCENT. Exactly when was this thing planned?

Pause.

MITCHELL. This 'thing'?

VINCENT. 'Cause it's clear you guys sat down and said – hey, there's this strategy and there's this game plan that's been worked up here, but we don't agree with it . . .

DON. Or we find the voters don't / agree with it –

VINCENT. We don't agree with it, because we don't think it'll work, or because it's wrong, whatever, but we don't want to discuss it, so we'll meet in secret corners . . .

LORIANNE. In the wee small hours . . .

VINCENT. And we'll bring out tapes that have miraculously appeared this morning, in which a heckler who is obviously a plant conveniently clamps the right to bear and use arms to Prop. Ninety-Two. And we'll wait till it's too late to properly debate our new proposals, we'll just have him junk his strategy and adopt ours. Have I got that roughly right?

LORIANNE. I'd say you've hit the nail right on the head.

MITCHELL. Busted again.

VINCENT. I'd say, that's dealing from the bottom of the deck.

LORIANNE. Particularly if you thought you'd cut a deal.

Pause.

SHELDON. What deal?

MITCHELL. I think Lorianne's referring to a conversation, in the wee small hours, when she and Don discussed the strategy.

LORIANNE. When we *agreed* on the strategy.

MITCHELL. Among some other things.

SHELDON. What other things?

MITCHELL. Oh, I don't think I should say.

CONNIE. Why ever not?

MITCHELL. Well, apparently, Lorianne is of the view that it's absurd to think of rap as poetry, and the reason African-Americans don't do so well at school is because they're doped-out or they're dumb.

LORIANNE. That's not . . . I didn't mean . . .

DON. Oh, no?

LORIANNE. No. I . . .

MITCHELL. But as she says, it's the liberals who tell us what we can or cannot say.

VINCENT. I see.

VINCENT *stands and gathers his papers.*

You know, they say two things. Back home in Lweesyanna. One falls under the general heading of house nigger. 'They'll use you. You will be manipulated. They will ask for your opinion but they won't actually listen because that isn't really what they want you for.' And you say, no, that is a stereotype, this is profiling. This is defining people by the class and race and culture in which they were born.

MITCHELL. Vincent, I wonder whether it's the time / for this . . .

VINCENT. The other thing they say is this. Whatever they are saying, watch their hands. You may think that you've quit one club and been accepted in another. But listen to the bass

line. Alien flooding. 'Genuine concerns.' Young men
swaggering around with weapons of destruction. Young –
dark – strangers preying on your hearth and home. Who's
'you'? Who's 'me'?

Dark, doped and dumb.

And you know, you think, shit man, will there come a day
when they stop *treating* you like Charlie Brown.

He goes out. Pause.

LORIANNE. That is . . . a travesty of what I said.

SHELDON. But not I think a travesty of what was done.

DON doesn't reply. LORIANNE *goes to pick up her
papers, realizes there isn't much point in doing that. From
the lectern, she turns back to* SHELDON.

LORIANNE. So are you going to say that? About respecting
Sarah Jane Polowski?

SHELDON. In fact, I'd go a little further. I've been looking
at the papers, and I'm not convinced the DA's got it right.
I mean, the right to bear arms doesn't mean you have the
right to empty one into a scared kid trying to operate a
chainsaw. So if Don here keeps his promise, then the first
thing I'll do January 6th, apart from sending Ninety-Two
straight up into the state supreme court, is have Vince check
out how we open this thing up and get Polowski's family
some justice here.

LORIANNE. Well, good.

MITCHELL. Well, if you do say that, there'd be very little
danger of / your having to do anything on –

LORIANNE. Sir, your daughter asked me why I came to
work for you this weekend. And I told her than unlike the
Democrat you weren't prepared to bend to the prevailing
wind. Which made you, in my eyes, in these benighted
times, some kind of hero.

MITCHELL *gives a slight snort.*

Hope I got that right.

LORIANNE *goes out.*

DON. Well, I guess that loses us / the stand-in vote –

CONNIE (*interrupts*). So, Mitch, what happens now?

MITCHELL. I think what happens is, we have a conversation.

CONNIE. Oh, aren't we / having one now?

MITCHELL. Just the three of us.

CONNIE. What, en famille?

MITCHELL. Exactly.

Slight pause.

I think that is the least that we can do.

DON. Well. Yeah.

He nods to CARYL.

CARYL. Mr Vine, may I say something?

SHELDON. Please.

CARYL. It's clear to me you have a choice.

SHELDON. Tell me about it.

CARYL. I just ask you to remember, that it isn't just you, sir.
It's the people who have worked for you and supported you
and fought for you. It's the future of the party and if it
doesn't sound too tacky, it's the future of the state. And
I think that makes it pretty obvious, I mean as a choice,
don't you?

Slight pause.

SHELDON. Well, no, I don't.

Slight pause.

But thank you, anyway.

CARYL. I'll . . . give your best to Mr Zuckerman.

CARYL *goes.*

DON. Responsibility. Reality.

DON *goes.* SHELDON, CONNIE *and* MITCHELL *left there.*

CONNIE. So I declare this session of the tribal council open.

SHELDON. So what's this, Mitch?

MITCHELL. Well, certainly, we need to delve a little into tribal memory.

CONNIE. How?

MITCHELL. Sheldon, remind us why you're carrying the family flag?

SHELDON. Oh, right. We're back to that.

MITCHELL. Remind me of your argument.

SHELDON. Well, of course, it wasn't so much an argument.

MITCHELL. No, more a threat.

CONNIE. Do we really need to / go over –

SHELDON. I pointed out some obvious realities.

MITCHELL. You said . . .

SHELDON. I said that if you ran for governor you would be vulnerable.

MITCHELL. Oh, why?

SHELDON Well . . . because of what had happened to the company.

MITCHELL. You mean – you meant – what I did to try and save it.

SHELDON. Yes.

MITCHELL. Remember how you put it?

CONNIE. He put it like it was. A company that for half a century stewards its vast resources wisely, harvesting its natural assets so that they may be naturally renewed, balancing ancient growths with vigorous new seedlings, protecting the mesh of elements necessary for the whole to thrive. Then, suddenly, deciding that to save itself from some mythical apocalyptic threat / reverses –

MITCHELL. Oh, the threat was real.

CONNIE. Reverses everything, consigns its traditional supporters to the wilderness, brings in mercenaries whose only interest is money, and duly sets about to destroy its natural inheritance.

Oh, while providing its executives with golden parachutes to break their fall.

I'd say that's not so much a threat. It's more a paradigm.

MITCHELL. Of what?

CONNIE. The party Caryl Marquez is so eager to preserve.

SHELDON. I said – I made the point that all they'd have to do is interview a laid-off logger standing in a clearcut, and point out who fired him, and at what loss to himself. And before you say it, yes, I know the golden parachutes were there to make the company a bigger pill to swallow, standard anti-raider operating practice. And yes, no doubt I would have done the same.

CONNIE. You would?

MITCHELL. I'm glad you say that.

SHELDON. So I had to say that if you still felt you should run, I'd back you.

CONNIE. Oh, did you?

SHELDON. Yes.

MITCHELL. And then you offered me the chairmanship of your campaign.

CONNIE. Why, I've never understood.

MITCHELL. In the hope that I might change my mind. And so you wouldn't have to say what you knew you'd have to say if I refused.

Slight pause.

CONNIE. I beg your pardon?

MITCHELL. And so you wouldn't have to say / what you knew . . .

CONNIE. You mean, there was something else?

SHELDON. Yes.

Pause. MITCHELL *smiling, a wry little gesture, indicating to* SHELDON *that the ball is in his court now.*

CONNIE. Not – not your divorce.

SHELDON. Connie, Reagan was divorced.

CONNIE. Not the affair you had with Lowe?

SHELDON. I wish.

MITCHELL. We'd be all over *People* magazine.

CONNIE. So, what . . . ?

MITCHELL. No, the contradiction between what I think and what I am was a bit more serious than that.

CONNIE. I'm afraid you're going to have to spell it out.

MITCHELL. When you're on the side that's calling other people 'laissez fairies'. When you're not interested in playing victim, when your – sexuality doesn't feel like your identity. When it's more like an occasional and unwelcome interruption to a life of wholesome chastity.

CONNIE. I see. But how . . .

MITCHELL. And you think you're over it. You meet 'the Right Girl'. Even if she happens to be a fully paid-up liberal Democrat. Which works and then it doesn't work. And you meet, well not the wrong girl, but a kind of sweet, kind, ordinary person and you marry her and you think you've got it beat. And apart from the rarest of occasions, actually, you have.

CONNIE (*to* SHELDON). And this is how . . .

SHELDON. Yes, Connie. That is how. And the only thing that justifies it is that on this occasion I was right.

MITCHELL. Oh, you were *right*?

SHELDON. Look, here's the awful irony. If it had been me, as a good old-fashioned let-it-hang-out do-your-own-thing libertarian, I might have ridden out the storm. But ten years ago, Mitch, you made a pact you couldn't break. With Mothers Against Everything. You didn't have to, but you did. And as I said, it just takes one young man to turn on the television and say: 'Hey, I recognize that guy.'

Pause.

MITCHELL. So you're saying you were *right* / to use this –

SHELDON. And, yes, sure, you can say that I'm in no position to leap up on a high horse of moral principle and righteous indignation. And you can see it as an act of family betrayal, and I'd understand that. I mean, for God's sake, I only knew because you told me. But still.

MITCHELL. But still.

Pause.

SHELDON. And of course I'd understand if you decided that / you didn't want –

MITCHELL. But still, you're still set against endorsing Ninety-Two?

SHELDON. Of course I am.

MITCHELL. But still I'm going to save you.

Slight pause.

SHELDON. How?

MITCHELL. I'm going to take what you said last evening at face value. I am going to assume you really want to win. There is a way for you to do that, without compromising what you think and what you say.

SHELDON. What's that?

MITCHELL. In the early Seventies, Rebecca McKeene occupied a ROTC building on a university campus.

SHELDON. Yes, like a million other / students –

MITCHELL. She was in possession of a flag.

SHELDON. Hey, as far as I'm concerned it's just a piece of cloth.

MITCHELL. She didn't burn it.

SHELDON. So what did she do with it?

MITCHELL. She ran it up the flagpole of the building.

SHELDON. So?

MITCHELL. It was the flag of the people who we were at war with at the time.

Slight pause.

It's quite clear that it's her.

CONNIE. You mean . . .

MITCHELL. I mean, yes, in the photograph. I'd say the Vietcong was a body which pursued its ends by force, wouldn't you?

Slight pause.

SHELDON. Why didn't you . . . ?

MITCHELL. You'd have let Don use it?

SHELDON. No.

MITCHELL. 'On principle.'

CONNIE. So, what do you propose?

MITCHELL. I'm going to go to Blair. And I'll tell that if they don't do the one thing that we know they won't do, which is to come out against the proposition, at the top, first answer, we'll reveal it.

SHELDON. You mean you'll blackmail her.

MITCHELL. In defiance of your every principle of proper conduct. And if it works, it's off the table and the playing field is level and you can commit yourself to selling off the Board of Education to MacDonalds and declare Sarah Jane Polowski's birthday a state holiday. But if it doesn't work, and McKeene endorses, then you endorse. And as we know that that won't be enough, you do the rest. You are reasonable not rational. You are socially as well as fiscally conservative. You hold Sarah Jane Polowski's motives in contempt. And you say these things in the debate, and afterwards, right up until the polls close. You promise me you'll run exactly the campaign I want you to.

CONNIE. But surely, if they won't agree, you use the photograph.

MITCHELL. No I'm not prepared to do that, Connie. That's my point. I'll tell her what I know. But if she calls our bluff, then Sheldon does it my way. It's a risk he'll have to take.

SHELDON. So let me get this straight. You're asking me to choose between my principles of conduct and my political beliefs.

MITCHELL. I'm asking you to do to her exactly what you did to me.

He looks at his watch.

I imagine you'll want two minutes with your wife.

MITCHELL *goes out.*

CONNIE. Sheldon –

SHELDON. Connie, it wasn't my secret to reveal.

CONNIE. No, I understand that.

SHELDON. Thank you.

CONNIE. What I find hard to get my mind around is the notion that if you'd been in Mitchell's shoes you'd have done the same thing with the company.

SHELDON. You mean, would I have fired your father?

CONNIE. Yes.

SHELDON. Connie, Mitch thinks I'm sacrificing this campaign for Deborah.

CONNIE. Is that a no?

SHELDON. Of course.

Pause.

CONNIE. We had a conversation.

SHELDON. You and Mitch?

CONNIE. No, me and Deborah.

SHELDON. What d'she say?

CONNIE. I'm not allowed to tell you.

SHELDON. Why?

CONNIE. Well, I'd like to say, 'because it's not my secret to reveal.' But in fact, it was something that she wanted you to know but she couldn't tell you because if you knew it could damage your campaign. I told her that that was remarkably astute of her and she took umbrage at the word 'remarkable'.

SHELDON. As well she might.

CONNIE. Well yes.

SHELDON. She said they all have 'forest names'.

CONNIE. She told me that.

SHELDON. But still, they might know who she is.

CONNIE. She said that too. But that she trusted them. Because they were her tribe. Just like the family.

SHELDON. And you don't trust that?

CONNIE. Oh, I trust it. But then, I've always trusted families. So it's no surprise to me that when push comes to shove, our daughter is prepared to do the politically pragmatic thing. Whatever she might think of what you think. Because deep down, her roots mean more to her than her wings.

SHELDON. Oh, really?

CONNIE. Yes.

Reenter MITCHELL.

MITCHELL. So what have you decided?

SHELDON. You know, Dad thought like me. He talked about
the journey west. The sense of liberation, at the point where
there was nowhere left to go. The relief of knowing every
morning that he'd open up his window and however dark
the day he wouldn't see Connecticut. The chance to reinvent
ourselves, to free us from the fetters of the past, to spread
our wings and fly. But then of course, he got seduced, by
the golf links and the paneled clubrooms, and eventually the
US Senate, and Connecticut became a rosy memory of a
forgotten gilded age.

MITCHELL. So is that a 'yes'?

SHELDON. I didn't take this on to emulate my father. Nor
even to avenge him. I took it on because he got it wrong
and I made a promise to myself to get it right.

MITCHELL. I repeat the question.

Pause.

CONNIE. I think that Sheldon's been reminded that you don't
betray your tribe.

SHELDON *looks at* CONNIE, *then* MITCHELL. *Then he
looks at his watch.*

SHELDON. I've still got thirty seconds.

He goes out.

CONNIE. Well, Mitchell.

MITCHELL. Please, don't tell me that you look on me with
unexpected sympathy.

CONNIE. Oh, no. This makes no difference to my view that
the male line of your family consists entirely of assholes.
Except for Sheldon, obviously.

MITCHELL. But you don't betray your tribe.

CONNIE. So will it work?

MITCHELL. It relies on the idea that when push comes to
shove, people will always act in their individual self-
interest.

CONNIE. Well that's all right then.

MITCHELL. Even Sheldon, obviously.

CONNIE *smiles, a smile which goes quizzical. She's about to go when something strikes her.*

CONNIE. Thought. If you're not going to leak the photograph, how do we know you showed it?

MITCHELL. Oh, you'll just have to trust me, Connie.

CONNIE. Right.

She turns and goes out. MITCHELL *smiles.* DON *enters.*

DON. What's up?

MITCHELL. I've explained to Sheldon why and how McKeene is going to come out against Prop. Ninety-Two.

DON. And how precisely / is that –

MITCHELL. Because the alternative is publication of a photograph of her running a Vietcong flag up the flagpole of a ROTC building.

DON. But, there is no such photograph.

MITCHELL. No, but we know they know there could be. And they know the only way we'd know that's if there was.

DON. Yeah, but . . . ?

MITCHELL. Don, as you never tire of saying, I have some knowledge of Blair Lowe. And I assure you, if Shel agrees to what I have proposed, then she will do exactly what I want her to.

DON. And will he agree to it?

MITCHELL. Oh, I think we have a deal.

DON. And he'll stick to it?

MITCHELL. Of course. My brother is a man of principle.

He goes out.

DON. And they call me 'Prince of Darkness'.

Blackout. In the change, we hear a TV ANCHOR:

TV ANCHOR. Here's how it looks this election night
November 5th. With forty percent of precincts reporting,
this year's nail-biter of a governor's contest seems set for a
photo-finish. Meanwhile, exit polls are encouraging to
supporters of a controversial proposition to require all new
and re-registering voters . . .

Scene Two

It's the evening of election day. The debate prep room is empty.
DEBORAH *enters – again with her backpack, dressed
aggressively unsuitably for an election night appearance with
her father. She sees there is a script on* SHELDON'*s podium.
She starts to read it.*

DEBORAH. 'Good evening. My name's Sheldon Vine, and
I'm speaking to you on this election night from the home
my grandfather built, which I grew up in, and from which
Senator Mitchell Vine acknowledged many victories and
conceded one defeat.

Like any politician, Dad knew that in the heat of battle
many things are said and done. One hopes that all of them
are honorably meant. But inevitably there's fine judgments
and close calls. How could it not be so. The stakes are high.
This is about the leadership of a great state.

But now the battle's over, it is possible, it's proper to look
back on the campaign and honestly assess how it was
fought. This is something politicians ought to do, and often
do. But usually . . .

SHELDON *has appeared, in his dark politician's suit and
necktie.*

SHELDON. . . . . in the privacy of their own homes.'

DEBORAH. 'I can't speak for my opponent. But I faced some
tough choices.'

SHELDON. Go on.

DEBORAH. 'Knowing the hardest choice is not between two wrongs but between two rights.'

SHELDON. 'The right to security, or the right to liberty.'

DEBORAH. 'The wider good . . .

SHELDON. . . . against the loyalty you owe the people nearest you.'

DEBORAH. 'The choice you sometimes face, between your political beliefs, and the principles of conduct on which those beliefs are founded.'

SHELDON. And the question that you ask yourself, the only question you can ask yourself, is 'If I do this, can I live with it hereafter?'

DEBORAH. You mean, in the debate.

Slight pause.

SHELDON. I made two promises. One promise to your uncle, one to me.

DEBORAH. And you kept one of them.

SHELDON. And the result?

DEBORAH. Well. I'd say – victory.

CONNIE *has entered.*

CONNIE. Sheldon, I'm told, unless you do this now, then the networks switch to the Senate race in Utah.

SHELDON. Right.

Pause. CONNIE *realizes she is being dismissed.*

CONNIE. One minute.

She turns and goes. SHELDON *turns to* DEBORAH.

SHELDON. So do I get a hug?

DEBORAH. Of course you get a hug.

She goes and hugs him.

DEBORAH. Hey, Dad –

SHELDON. Hey, Debs. Live like the better part of me.

DEBORAH. What's that?

SHELDON. The part I handed on to you.

Pause. DEBORAH *leaves her father.*

CONNIE (*from off*). Sheldon!

SHELDON. I'm coming!

DEBORAH. Snowbird. My name is Snowbird.

SHELDON. Is it?

DEBORAH. Hey. Running Tiger. Go.

SHELDON *picks up his script and goes out to deliver his speech.* DEBORAH *picks up her backpack and goes out the other way.*

End of Play.

DAUGHTERS OF THE REVOLUTION

Characters

Daughters of the Revolution is written for a cast of 15.

MICHAEL BERN, *fifty-five, Community College professor*
ABBY, *mid-thirties, graphic designer*
BLAIR LOWE, *fifties, consultant*
REBECCA McKEENE, *fifty, Democratic candidate for Governor*
KWESI NTULI, *fifties, former Black Panther, now community activist*
LORIANNE WEINER, *thirties, columnist*
IRA KIRSCHENBAUM, *sixty, writer*
TROY PRACTICE, *fifties, donor*
ASH, *mid-fifties, fugitive woman*

The Party
ARNIE, *early fifties, lawyer, Michael's best friend*
ELAINE, *fifties, Arnie's wife*
BILL, *forties, Michael's brother*
TED, *fifties, Michael's college friend*
KATE, *forties, Michael's colleague*
DANA, *young, Michael's niece*
RYAN, *young, graduate student*
JOOLS, *young, actor*

The Campaign
PAT, *thirties, campaign assistant*
STUDIO AIDES *and* TECHNICIANS
SAM SOMERVILLE, *twenties*
HECKLER
BRUNCHERS

The Community
YOLANDE
EDDIE, *old beatnik*

JIMMY, *Vietnam vet*
BETH, *lady in her fifties*
TRINA, *young*
DARREN, *young*
J.C., *young*

The Past
JACK SAND, *twenty-two, revolutionary*
CLAUDIA PEROWNE, *twenty-five, revolutionary*
SONNY CRANE, *twenties, Black Panther*

The Forest
NO SHIT, *twenties, man*
SNOWBIRD, *eighteen, woman*
AQUARIUS, *twenty, woman*
RAINBOW, *twenties, man*
FIREFLY, *late twenties, woman*
ZEE, *older man*
HULA HOOP, *forties, woman*
BRANFLAKE, *late twenties, woman*
NIGHTHAWK, *fifties, security guard*

The Debate
MITCHELL VINE, *Republican campaign*
DON D'AVANZO, *Republican campaign*
SHELDON VINE, *Republican candidate*
CONNIE, *Sheldon's wife*
1st REPORTER
2nd REPORTER
BOB LEJEUNE, *moderator*

Notation

A dash (–) means that a character is interrupted. A slash (/) means that the next character to speak starts speaking at that point (what follows the slash need not be completed). An ellipsis (. . .) indicates that a character has interrupted him or herself.

STUDENTS FOR A DEMOCRATIC SOCIETY: PORT HURON STATEMENT

*Adopted at the SDS National Convention
in Port Huron, Michigan, on June 15, 1962*

We regard men as infinitely precious and possessed of unfulfilled capacities for reason, freedom, and love. Men have unrealized potential for self-cultivation, self- direction, self-understanding, and creativity. It is this potential that we regard as crucial and to which we appeal, not to the human potentiality for violence, unreason, and submission to authority.

In a participatory democracy, the political life would be based in several root principles:

THAT decision-making of basic social consequence be carried on by public groupings;

THAT politics be seen positively, as the art of collectively creating an acceptable pattern of social relations;

THAT politics has the function of bringing people out of isolation and into community, thus being a necessary, though not sufficient, means of finding meaning in personal life; . . .

THAT work should involve incentives worthier than money or survival. It should be educative, not stultifying; creative, not mechanical; self-directed, not manipulated, encouraging independence, a respect for others, a sense of dignity, and a willingness to accept social responsibility, . . .

THAT the economic experience is so personally decisive that the individual must share in its full determination.

"PLEDGE"   :30 secs TV
(Client: Citizens for the American Way)

1. *Scroll of great national documents and monuments, mixed with footage of new citizens taking the pledge of allegiance.*

> ANNOUNCER
> On November 5, you can vote not just for your party but your country.

2. *A picture of a* HISPANIC MAN *making the pledge of allegiance. We pan back to see that this is a framed print that the* MAN *is holding proudly in front of himself:*

> HISPANIC MAN
> It was the proudest moment of my life.

> ANNOUNCER
> There's a proposition on the ballot which will allow all new and re-registering voters to declare their allegiance to democracy.

3. ASIAN WOMAN *speaks to camera:*

> ASIAN WOMAN
> I really felt, now I'm an American.

> ANNOUNCER
> Every year thousands of new Americans make this pledge. Now it can be a privilege for all our citizens.

4. *An* AMERICAN MAN *stands outside his house, next to his flag:*

> AMERICAN MAN
> Hey, these new guys get to say the oath. So why can't I?

> ANNOUNCER
> One flag. One pledge. One nation. One America. Vote Yes on Ninety-Two.

Recent events taking place on college campuses illustrate the growing trend towards anarchy which is overtaking our nation. It is important that the Bureau, as a result of these events, redouble its efforts in penetrating these groups which have spearheaded the attacks on our established institutions . . .

J. Edgar Hoover,
Director, Federal Bureau of Investigations,
memo of 16 May 1968

The people of Berkeley must increase their combative-ness; develop, tighten, and toughen their organizations; and transcend their middle-class, ego-centered life styles . . . We shall create a genuine community and control it to serve our material and spiritual needs. We shall develop new forms of democratic participation and new, more humane styles of work and play. In solidarity with other revolutionary centers and movements, our Berkeley will permanently challenge the present system and act as one of many training grounds for the liberation of the planet. We will make Telegraph Avenue and the South Campus a strategic free territory for revolution.

From the 1969 manifesto of the
Berkeley Liberation Program

Earth First! is not just a conservation movement, it is also a social change movement . . . It doesn't make sense to bemoan the destruction of nature while supporting the system that is destroying it.

Judi Bari
Timber Wars (*Common Courage Press, 1994*)

ACT ONE

Scene One: The Agitator Index

*The living room of MICHAEL and ABBY's house in a small
city near the Pacific coast. It is early evening on a fine fall
day. The house betrays the different histories and tastes of its
inhabitants: MICHAEL a fifty-five-year-old former student
radical; ABBY a graphic designer in her thirties. There are
easy chairs and a sofa. Double doors open into the dining
room / kitchen beyond. There is an exit heading to the yard
on one side and to the street on the other.*

*At the start, MICHAEL stands in his cycling helmet, wind-
breaker and bicycle clips, holding his bicycle. ABBY sits in an
armchair, a book open before her, affecting casual nonchalance.
She is dressed as a hippie. A Forties-style soft hat lies osten-
tatiously on the sofa.*

MICHAEL. Hi, hon.

ABBY. Hi, hon.

> MICHAEL *takes off his helmet and puts it down. As he does
> so, a* YOUNG AFRICAN-AMERICAN MAN *in a suit
> shoots across the aperture of the open doorway.*

MICHAEL. How was your day?

ABBY. My day was fine.

> *Pause.* MICHAEL *takes his bike to its home, just offstage,
> towards the yard. As he does so, a* YOUNG WOMAN
> *crawls round from behind the sofa so as not to be seen by*
> MICHAEL *from his current angle. The* YOUNG WOMAN
> *is dressed in dark clothes. She sees the hat and waves at it.*

MICHAEL (*calls*). Did the people come and see the house?

ABBY (*calls*). Uh-huh.

ABBY *goes for the hat, but it's too late, as* MICHAEL *has reentered, unexpectedly fast. Lightly and nonchalantly,* ABBY *sits back.*

MICHAEL. Are they still here?

ABBY (*bemusement at this absurd idea*). Huh-uh.

MICHAEL *goes and picks up the hat, then looks back at* ABBY.

MICHAEL. Why are you dressed like Grace Slick?

ABBY *stands, takes the hat from* MICHAEL.

ABBY. Mikey, I'm sorry.

The AFRICAN-AMERICAN, JOOLS, *appears through from the yard side with a handgun pointed at* MICHAEL.

JOOLS. Michael Bern?

MICHAEL. Oh, no.

A white woman in her fifties, ELAINE, *comes through the double doors, also with a gun pointing at* MICHAEL. *Like the* YOUNG WOMAN *she is in dark clothes.*

ELAINE. Also known as Benjamin Michael Bern?

MICHAEL. What's this?

The YOUNG WOMAN, RYAN, *stands up, pointing a gun at* MICHAEL. *Like the other two, she has a loose-leaf script with her which she consults when necessary. As this unfolds, other people enter from the other room. They are all dressed in approximations of late Sixties costumes.*

RYAN. Also known as Ben Bern, Benjamin M. Bern . . .

JOOLS. And Benjie Bern.

TED *is a college lecturer in his fifties.*

TED. *Benjie* Bern?

MICHAEL. Only by my mother. Hey, guys . . .

ELAINE. Also known as Walter Wojcieckowski?

MICHAEL. Hey . . .

RYAN. And believed to be identical with . . .

Checks script.

. . . Mike or Michael Bern . . .

MICHAEL. Hey, how . . .

JOOLS. Consider yourself busted.

MICHAEL. *What?*

By now, TED *has been followed out by* ARNIE, *a lawyer in his fifties; Michael's brother* BILL, *in his forties;* KATE, *in her forties, associate professor; Michael's young niece* DANA. *They stand around watching the show.*

ELAINE. You have the right to remain silent . . .

ABBY *is leading* MICHAEL *to her chair, from which he is to watch the show.*

ABBY. He has the obligation to remain silent.

RYAN (*reading*). But anything you say will certainly be held against you if not in a court of law then before the court of your peers.

JOOLS. In other words . . .

RYAN. Benjamin Michael Bern . . .

They wave their scripts.

ALL THREE. This Is Your File.

Cheers from the 'audience'. ABBY *tosses the slouch hat to* RYAN *who puts it on.*

MICHAEL. How . . .

ELAINE. So how indeed did a respected member of the faculty of a major educational facility . . .

KATE. Well, I'd drop the 'major'.

ABBY. Now about to move on to even higher things . . .

BILL. Hey, go the *man.*

TED. Depending on your point of view.

ELAINE. . . . become a person deemed to pose a serious and immediate threat to the security of the United States?

MICHAEL. This is my FBI file.

JOOLS. So let's meet Special Agent in Charge BLANK BLANK.

MICHAEL. How the fuck d'you get my file?

In the hat, RYAN *is playing an FBI Special Agent in Charge.*

RYAN (*reading*). My name is SAC BLANK BLANK and on February 28, 1968 I received a communication from Bureau Headquarters . . .

DANA. This is the *FBI*?

BILL. Sure is.

DANA. Wow.

RYAN (*continues reading*). . . . intimating that in view of the election of Benjamin Michael Bern as Vice President . . .

MICHAEL (*to* ARNIE). Arnie, this is a crime, right?

RYAN (*continues reading*). . . . of the BLANK chapter of Students for a Democratic Society . . .

ARNIE (*shrug*). Technically it's a misdemeanor.

RYAN. . . . an investigation be conducted for the purpose of making a determination . . .

ARNIE. I'd kick back and enjoy it. You can visit her in jail.

RYAN. . . . as to whether his activities are such to justify a full security investigation.

ELAINE. And were they such?

RYAN. You bet.

TED. Hey.

DANA. Cool.

BILL. Right on.

RYAN *tosses the hat to* JOOLS.

RYAN. According to a source who has furnished reliable information in the past . . .

ABBY. Come on in, hitherto reliable source . . .

JOOLS (*puts the hat on, all of this read out*). . . . . the subject was observed attending a meeting in support of US policy in Vietnam.

BILL. Huh? Michael?

KATE. Some mistake here surely.

TED. So when is this?

JOOLS. Which was subject to disruption by a group of beatnik-style protesters identified as members of the self-styled Concerned Honkies Against Foreign Wars.

BILL. All is revealed.

JOOLS. . . . including a young Caucasian male . . .

KATE. Don't tell me, let me speculate.

JOOLS. . . . also of particularly unkempt, hippie-style appearance.

TED. That's our boy.

JOOLS. . . . identified by sources as –

ALL THREE. – The Subject!

JOOLS *tosses the hat, mistakenly, to* RYAN, *who tosses it, correctly, to* ELAINE.

TED. All *right*.

ARNIE. Whoo-hoo.

ELAINE (*reads*). Who seized the microphone and proceeded to harangue the audience with anti-patriotic sentiments.

She throws the hat to RYAN.

TED. Making our *move*.

RYAN. . . . concluding by explaining to the platform speakers that 'we're not expletive going to fight your criminal expletive fascist war go fight it your expletive self.'

ARNIE. Yih-hah.

DANA. Hey, this is Uncle Michael?

BILL. Right the expletive on.

RYAN. In view of which it is apparent that the subject can be categorized as having attracted sufficient attention . . .

Hat to JOOLS.

JOOLS. . . . to warrant immediate inclusion on . . .

ALL THREE. . . . . the Agitator Index!

BILL / OTHERS. Yo!

DANA. Awesome.

TED. You go, brother.

MICHAEL. Now, guys . . .

ABBY. But this is not end of story surely?

ELAINE. It certainly was not.

MICHAEL. That's what I / feared –

ELAINE. As in subsequent months the subject was observed by established sources affiliated to BLANK University addressing rallies in support of the struggles of the Negro people . . .

JOOLS. Seize the Time!

RYAN. Leading a group of approximately thirty individuals to the Headquarters of the SAPD to sing protest songs, set to well-known tunes . . .

ELAINE. At least one of which the subject will now sing to us.

MICHAEL. Like hell he will.

ELAINE. Hey, Ted, how did that thing go? 'On the twelfth day of Christmas my true love sent to me . . . '

TED. 'Twelve jailers jailing . . . '

MICHAEL. Ted.

ELAINE. 'Eleven bondsmen bailing . . . '

MICHAEL. Absolutely / not.

ELAINE (*as she gestures to* RYAN *to continue*). Chicken.

RYAN. And was noted in attendance at a meeting of a body strangely titled Running Dogs Against US Imperialism . . .

BILL. By another previously reliable source no doubt.

DANA. Uh, running whats?

KATE. It's Chairman Mao.

MICHAEL. It was that or 'paper tigers'.

ELAINE. At which meeting the subject advertised two buttons he had produced for sale, one reading:

RYAN. 'I am not yet convinced the Dean's an asshole.'

ELAINE. And the other reading:

JOOLS. 'Now I Am.'

DANA. That is so cool.

ABBY. And then . . .

TED. There's more?

ELAINE. He graduated.

ALL. Oh!

RYAN. Entered employment as teaching assistant in the sociology department at BLANK grad school.

General disappointment and shaking of heads.

TED. Oh, heck.

RYAN. And accordingly . . .

ELAINE. . . . as of approximately ten two nineteen-seventy-one . . .

JOOLS. . . . it is recommended that the subject be deleted from the Agitator Index.

ALL. Oh!

BILL. No *shit*.

DANA. Oh my God.

TED. Hey . . .

KATE. Mike, I am – so – sorry.

Led by ABBY, *the company sings the opening lines of 'Yesterday'.*

ABBY. Until, that is . . .

BILL. Aha.

TED. Don't say we Spoke Too Soon.

ELAINE. . . . an informant who-has-furnished-reliable-etcetera has advised that after a period of political inactivity . . .

BILL. Buying the Bug.

TED. Wasn't there a marriage?

KATE. Well, we know what happened to *that*.

As ELAINE *begins her next speech.*

ARNIE (*to* ABBY, *graciously*). Landed on his feet.

ABBY. Too kind.

KATE. Too true.

ELAINE. . . . the subject is now actively involved in a small revolutionary organization entitled the Bad Moon Rising Revolutionary Collective . . .

Response. BILL *sings a phrase from 'Bad Moon Rising'.*

DANA. Heavy duty.

RYAN. . . . an organization of approximately two hundred individuals organized in so-called modules led by a group colloquially known as Ground Control.

DANA. Modules?

KATE. This will be lunar-speak, I'm guessing.

MICHAEL *gestures wearily.*

TED. Cute.

RYAN. Members of this group include blank blank, blank blank-blank, blank-blank-blank blank, blank-blank blank, blank, blank blank.

ARNIE. *Blank*? Blank was in Blank?

TED. Yeah, whatever happened to old Blank?

MICHAEL. Good question.

RYAN. Blank-blank, blank blank-blank, Michael Bern.

BILL. Keeping the best till last, I'm sure.

RYAN. The aim of this organization is to incite insurrectionary activity particularly in furtherance of the rights of the Negro population which is regarded under Marxist-Leninistic ideology as a revolutionary vanguard along with women, youth and other dropouts from society.

MICHAEL. Approximately.

ELAINE. In pursuit of which objectives the organization is involved with planning missions in collaboration with other revolutionary groups, including . . .

JOOLS. Disruption of the Selective Service System in order to undermine the war effort in Vietnam!

Supportive cheers.

BILL. Hey, go the man!

RYAN. Blocking the approaches to courthouses and the disruption of trials of persons characterized as revolutionary fighters!

Cheers, perhaps a little less robust.

ELAINE. Mob action against police and military targets, and actions in collaboration with militant Negro organizations!

More cheers, a little muted.

KATE. Phew.

JOOLS. Including –

RYAN. – according to a source whose intelligence is known to be reliable –

JOOLS. – securing the release of specified Negro militants awaiting trial, targeting leading Republicans, and the / planning of a plot to –

MICHAEL *stands.*

MICHAEL. Look, excuse me, can I see that, please?

JOOLS. Uh, sorry?

MICHAEL. Can I please see that document?

ARNIE. Uh, Mike . . .

MICHAEL *takes the script from* JOOLS.

RYAN. It's just the script.

TED. Is something wrong?

MICHAEL (*looks at the script*). And do you . . . does anyone have the original?

RYAN *looks at* ABBY.

KATE. There's something wrong.

TED. Hey, pal . . .

MICHAEL. The file. The actual document you wrote this from. Presumably there is the actual file.

JOOLS *and* RYAN *look blankly at him.*

ABBY. Yes. Yes, I have the actual file.

ABBY *goes and gets a wrapped present, and brings it to* MICHAEL, *as:*

BILL. Mike.

MICHAEL. Look, I'm sorry, but . . .

DANA. What's happening?

ELAINE. Abby, it's OK.

ABBY. Well, clearly not. But there we are.

TED. Should we maybe . . .

ABBY No, it's fine.

OK. This was the plan. To mark this fearfully anticipated, God I'm fifty-five and where-has-it-all-gone-to birthday. Even though, in fact, you're actually off to run a primo state commission vital to our future. Hence of course much wailing, hair-tearing, and am-I-selling-outing. And remembering that you'd never got your FBI file, for fear it wouldn't have you down as a serious and urgent threat to national security, I sent off for it on the off-chance that it might. So. Happy birthday.

She hands the present over.

MICHAEL. Yeah.

Slight pause.

BILL. Mike, open it.

MICHAEL. Yes, right.

He opens the parcel. It's full of loose photocopied sheets, which fall and spread across the floor.

Oh, shit.

This is too much for ABBY.

ABBY. Yeah, right. Dumb plan. I'm sorry.

She hurries out through the double doors.

ELAINE. Oh, Michael.

ELAINE *goes out after* ABBY. *Pause.*

DANA. Hey. Uncle Mike.

RYAN. So – this is where we light the candles?

ARNIE. Yeah. Candles would be good. And drinks. Drinks would be cool as well. Through there.

JOOLS. Exeunt severally.

ARNIE. Correct.

BILL. Let's hear it for the cabaret?

ARNIE. Why, surely. But just now . . .

DANA. Get the expletive outta here.

ARNIE. You got it.

KATE. Fine.

> KATE, DANA, BILL, JOOLS, *and* RYAN *go out.*
> MICHAEL *and* ARNIE *are left alone in a sea of paper.*

MICHAEL. Who wrote it, Arnie?

ARNIE. She did. With Elaine. That is if you mean the skit. The
file appears to have been written by a series of thick black
lines.

MICHAEL (*picking up pages and reading them*). My parents.
They investigate my folks. 'Discreet inquiries at a
brownstone block on 7th north of 83rd.'

As he searches on:

ARNIE. And Walter – Wu . . .

MICHAEL. After Bad Moon, I spent a thankfully short period
in a group called Proletarian Advance, who sent me off to
foment the revolution in a tuna-canning factory. Aha. I seem
to have run naked through a Board of Regents Meeting in
support of divestment from South Africa. 'A source whose
intelligence has proved reliable.'

ARNIE. Though not on this occasion.

MICHAEL flipping on through the pages.

MICHAEL. 'An established source, conceal identity by
request.'

Another sheet.

'Which if divulged could jeopardize this informant's
subsequent effectiveness, and thus adversely affect . . . '
Ah, here it is.

He reads.

'Including, according to a source whose intelligence is known to be reliable, securing the release of specified Negro militants awaiting trial, targeting leading Republicans, and the planning of a plot to kidnap politicians allegedly associated with the white establishment.'

Pause.

ARNIE. Uh . . . did this happen?

MICHAEL. No. And it wasn't actually a politician. And it never got beyond the paper stage.

ARNIE. Good.

MICHAEL. So how did she . . .

ARNIE. Simple. You submit an application. You declare under penalty of perjury that the details of the letter are correct. It helps if you live in the same house as 'the subject' and he goes to work before the mail arrives.

MICHAEL. And you?

ARNIE. As I said. I am technically complicit in a conspiracy to commit a federal misdemeanor.

MICHAEL. As was I. And not just technically.

ARNIE. And not just a misdemeanor.

MICHAEL (*reading from the file*). 'It is believed that if the university authorities are acquainted with this information, the subject's contract is unlikely to be renewed.'

ARNIE. Yes?

MICHAEL. My department chair informed me I'd been kicked off tenure track in April of '73.

ARNIE. And you think this was because . . .

MICHAEL. You see, I remember the meeting where the mission to secure the release of 'a specific Negro militant' was planned. And where it was and when it was. And the eight people who were there.

He stops himself as ABBY *and* ELAINE *reenter.*

ELAINE. We decided to assist. Though you don't deserve it.

Slight pause.

MICHAEL. Thanks.

ELAINE. 'Abby, I'm sorry.'

MICHAEL. Abby –

ABBY. Let's clean up.

They begin to clear up.

ELAINE. So, what was in / the file?

ARNIE. So, Abby, how's the wild and wacky world of statewide politics?

ELAINE. Excuse me?

ARNIE. Abby's been hired to do direct mail for McKeene for Governor.

ELAINE. Missed me.

ABBY. It's targeted. You know, like outer-directed fiscally conservative pro-choice Latino females.

ELAINE. Well, that explains it.

ARNIE. And how are such people swung? Graphically speaking?

ABBY. Well, you'd think it would be color. But actually it's typeface.

ELAINE. What, Times New Roman is inherently reactionary?

ABBY. Hey, don't knock it. Univers for high achievers, Garamond for girls. Judiciously insert a serif embellishment, hey presto, you've transformed a hyper-liberal, duck-squeezing, Chablis-quaffing bleeding-heart into Donald Rumsfeld.

ELAINE. Or vice versa, hopefully.

ARNIE. Hey, Mikey, didn't you once take a tumble with McKeene?

MICHAEL. A very tiny tumble.

ELAINE. What?

MICHAEL. When Abby here . . .

ABBY. . . . was five.

ARNIE. Bowled over doubtless by his unkempt, hippie-style / appearance –

ELAINE. And giving no hint she'd go on to become a hotshot liberal lawyer, legislator and now / favorite for governor.

ARNIE. Now facing us with a tantalizing choice between a Republican who wants to sell the state parks to the nuclear waste dumping industry, and a Democrat who's not too sure about universal suffrage.

ABBY. Uh, did I miss . . .

ARNIE (*spoofing a line from a campaign ad*). 'I really felt, now I'm an American.'

MICHAEL. Proposition Ninety-Two.

ABBY. Which she's not endorsed.

ARNIE. Which she's not condemned.

ELAINE. And isn't this the woman who put Mike up for his hot new job?

ARNIE. For which he's / eminently qualified.

ELAINE. Thereby releasing him from the clammy grip of entry-level sociology?

ARNIE. Well, that and a piece of groundbreaking / research –

MICHAEL. Elaine, I'm a dean. I haven't actually taught a class since 1993.

ELAINE. Well, we've established that all deans are assholes.

This is too much. A moment, then MICHAEL *decides to make light of it.*

MICHAEL. So wasn't there a party?

ARNIE (*sensing that* MICHAEL *wants a private word with* ABBY). The whereabouts of which my lovely wife and I will now check out.

ARNIE *and* ELAINE *leave.*

MICHAEL. Abs, I'm sorry.

ABBY. So you should be. As should I.

MICHAEL. What for?

ABBY *gives an 'obvious' gesture to the file.*

No, this was good.

ABBY. Oh, why?

MICHAEL. Because in nineteen days' time I appear before a state committee charged with approving my appointment. And if someone knows what happened at a meeting I attended in January of 1972, then I'd rather know that now than to have it come up then.

ABBY. But you said they'd done an FBI check.

MICHAEL. The FBI file doesn't say I was at the meeting.

ABBY. Well, good.

MICHAEL. So they may not know.

ABBY. Well, even better.

MICHAEL. But the informer does.

ABBY. Well, they've kept pretty quiet about it for the last, what, thirty / years –

MICHAEL. While I've been working in a community college in the boondocks no one's ever heard of.

Pause. ABBY *gets what* MICHAEL *is saying.*

ABBY. Mikey, we've put earnest money on a house.

MICHAEL. I know.

ABBY. I'm pretty much signed up with Cain and Klonsky.

MICHAEL. Yes.

ABBY. As of Monday, you are unemployed.

MICHAEL. I could withdraw my / resignation –

ABBY. No.

Pause.

MICHAEL. Abby, you get this?

ABBY. Yes, I get this.

MICHAEL. So you / understand –

ABBY. And this is all about a meeting?

MICHAEL. Yes.

ABBY. Where some important 'action' was discussed.

MICHAEL. Important and illegal.

ABBY. Attended by, what…

MICHAEL. As I remember it, eight people.

ABBY. And do you remember who was there?

MICHAEL. Oh, yes. In fact / one of them –

ABBY. Then presumably you're going to try and find them.

MICHAEL. What, and ask them if they snitched on me to the FBI?

ABBY. As your other option's dumping a six-figure job you'd do like gangbusters and staying back here in the boondocks with your memories.

ARNIE *is leading* ELAINE, BILL, TED, KATE, DANA, RYAN *and* JOOLS *back into the room, with bottles, glasses and a cunning but probably painful manual corkscrew.*

MICHAEL. You mean . . .

ABBY. I mean, the new job was a kind of promise, Michael.

ARNIE (*to draw attention*). Ready or not, here we come.

The rest of the company is back in.

TED. Enter the feast, left.

ELAINE (*fanfare*). Du-dah, du-dar.

JOOLS. With alarums and excursions.

ARNIE (*to* MICHAEL). And a few carefully chosen words.

KATE (*alarums*). That expression's always baffled me.

MICHAEL. Um, guys. A moment if you please.

Everyone turns to MICHAEL, *some in mock freeze.*

First of all, let's hear it for the cabaret.

People applaud.

Then for Abby.

Cheers. Amid:

BILL. Yo!

JOOLS. All right.

KATE. You go girl!

MICHAEL. Mostly because I'm told she's guilty of a federal misdemeanor, so this maybe is the last time for some time . . .

Laughter and:

DANA. Go for it.

MICHAEL *cracks up at the sight of everybody.*

MICHAEL. Hey, you people.

Recovering.

Now of course a birthday is a time to look back and assess one's past achievements and mistakes . . . I just didn't think I'd be hearing all my craziest decisions clamped quite so close together.

Laughter.

And I guess we all wonder how we would respond if our past self walked in on us. What would I say? Would I see him as a threat? Or an embarrassment? And how would he see me?

TED. He'd mistake you for a burglar.

MICHAEL. So, before I finally . . . throw in my lot with the running dogs of liberal reformism . . .

ABBY. Oh –

ELAINE. Michael.

MICHAEL. . . . . I guess I need to ask him . . . me, some questions. And some other folks as well.

Slight hiatus. BILL *does suspense, 'Dragnet' music.*

(*To recover.*) But, hey. All this goes to prove the adage I have lived my life by. Just because you're paranoid, it doesn't mean . . .

MOST PEOPLE (*variously*). They aren't out to get you / they're not going to get you / the bastards aren't out to get you.

MICHAEL *raises his glass. An afterthought:*

MICHAEL. Oh, and it was 'twelve mayors proclaiming.'

ELAINE. What?

MICHAEL. 'Twelve mayors proclaiming.' Then 'eleven jailers jailing.'

TED (*sings*). 'Ten bondsmen bailing.'

ELAINE. 'Nine tanks a-rolling?'

KATE. Please. Not the whole descent.

TED. 'Four billy clubs,

MICHAEL. 'Three cattle prods, two . . .

ELAINE. 'Tear gas bombs, and –

ALL THREE. ' – A Smith and Wesson from the armory!'

They slap hands. Then MICHAEL *raises his glass again.*

MICHAEL. And so – Lochayim.

KATE. Michael, you're the only person with a drink.

MICHAEL. You haven't started *drinking*?

KATE. Nobody can work your corkscrew.

MICHAEL. What?

DANA. And is the stuff on oval plates all vegan?

ABBY. Yes.

ARNIE. Is there a man's drink?

ELAINE. Arnie.

> ARNIE *goes out.*

MICHAEL (*takes the corkscrew*). I can't believe you couldn't work the corkscrew.

TED. The one we have at home's electric.

ABBY. I bet you guys all shop at Sharper Image.

RYAN. And I bet they all drive SUVs.

> ABBY*'s going to* MICHAEL *as he opens the bottle.*

BILL (*to* TED). Are there no drugs? I was assured there would be drugs.

DANA. Hey, *Uncle Billy.*

> MICHAEL *pulls the cork.*

ABBY (*to* MICHAEL). So, what, you're going to . . .

MICHAEL. I didn't see the other option as an option.

> ABBY *kisses him and turns to go.*

> Abs, I'll need your boss's cell.

ABBY. You need to call McKeene?

MICHAEL. No, I mean her manager.

ABBY. Why?

MICHAEL. She was at the meeting.

> ARNIE *appears, waving an empty tumbler, disconsolately.*

> Hey, can we find a scotch for Arnie?

ABBY *goes.* MICHAEL *goes to pick up his file. Behind him, a young, male* REVOLUTIONARY *enters. He is dressed in the style of the early Seventies so initially he looks like someone late for the party.*

REVOLUTIONARY. Hey, brother.

MICHAEL. Brother.

REVOLUTIONARY. So what gives?

MICHAEL. What about?

REVOLUTIONARY. 'A primo state commission.'

MICHAEL. I've been appointed executive director of a select committee of the state assembly, investigating why kids from community colleges don't go on to a university.

REVOLUTIONARY. Right on. Why you?

MICHAEL. I did a piece of mildly groundbreaking research into this topic at my place of work.

REVOLUTIONARY No doubt you laid the blame at the door of an inherently oppressive social system?

MICHAEL. Not exactly.

REVOLUTIONARY (*the room*). Well, that figures.

MICHAEL. It's more what we've identified as a lack of integrative cultural skills.

REVOLUTIONARY. What, black kids don't do jack at school because their mama didn't take 'em to the opera?

MICHAEL. Or the library. Or teach them how to fill in forms and use the phone.

REVOLUTIONARY. Hey, dig it, man. You're blown off tenure track. You work your ass off in the school from hell for a quarter of a century. Now at last you get a job you're wired for. And who comes back to fuck it up?

MICHAEL *looks ruefully at the* REVOLUTIONARY.

A linking sequence on high screens: consisting of a montage of political advertisements and – later – television news and

archive footage, backed by snatches from MICHAEL*'s
telephone calls and flashbacks from the January 1972
meeting. The full texts of the Vine and McKeene spots are in*
Mothers Against*; the text of the Proposition 92 spot forms
the frontispiece to* Daughters of the Revolution.

OPERATOR. Hi, you've reached McKeene for Governor. If
you want to make a contribution, please press one.

SHELDON (*Vine spot*). *Hi. I'm Sheldon Vine and I'm running
for governor. Like you I learned my values from my family.*

REBECCA (*McKeene spot*). *Hello, my name's Rebecca
McKeene and I'm running on my record.*

VOICE-OVER (*Proposition 92 spot*). *On November 5, you can
vote not just for your party, but for your country.*

HISPANIC MAN (*Proposition 92 spot*). *It was the proudest
moment of my life.*

BLAIR (*young, at the 1972 meeting*). I'm sorry. Fuck, like I . . .
Hey. Michael, sorry.

BLAIR (*now, on the phone*). Michael? I shall be at suite one
five zero, seven two three five Nebraska, nearest junction
Twelfth, at fourteen hundred hours on Tuesday nine
seventeen.

Scene Two: Ideals

*A small television studio. Upstage, the studio itself, where the
candidate,* REBECCA McKEENE, *is recording a TV ad in
Spanish. With her are* TECHNICIANS *and* AIDES. *Downstage
is the suite full of TV screens; a console at which you can turn
the volume of the narrowcast up and down, and a microphone
to talk to studio.* PAT, BLAIR LOWE*'s assistant, is watching
the narrowcast – later, she will sit and work at her laptop.*
MICHAEL *stands there waiting.*

REBECCA (*continues, in Spanish*). Hola. Soy Rebecca
McKeene y me estoy representando sobre mi experiencia. He

sido honrada por los votantes de este estado, habiendo sido elegida como miembra de la Asamblea y dos veces Senadora del Estado. Como miembra del Comité de Educación del Senado he votado . . . [Hello, my name's Rebecca McKeene and I'm running on my record. I'm honored to have been chosen by the voters of this state to be an assembly member and twice a state senator. As a member of the Senate Education Committee, I've voted . . .]

Simultaneous with the above, BLAIR LOWE *walks forward, speaking on her cell phone. She raises a finger to indicate to* MICHAEL *that this will only take a moment.*

BLAIR (*phone*). Blair Lowe. Oh, hi. Yeah, sure, I got your spiel. Yeah, we will certainly want doorhangers and phonebanks, but we will need Mandarin as well as Cantonese.

MICHAEL. Blair.

BLAIR (*waves*). Hey, Michael.

Phone.

And, sure, yes, we are very interested in your doing us a lawnsign distribution program. But, no, we're not up for late voter reg. right now.

She hears something from REBECCA.

REBECCA (*continues, in Spanish*). . . . contra los vales y por la educación bilingüe. Estoy a favor de una política de inmigración justa y mi trayectoria demuestra que mi lucho contra el crimen es fuerte. [. . . against vouchers and for bilingual education. I'm for fairness in immigration policy and my record shows I'm tough on crime.]

BLAIR (*into phone*). Hey, I'm going to call you back.

As BLAIR *ends the call and talks with* PAT, REBECCA *continues.*

REBECCA (*continues, in Spanish*). Y por eso los departamentos de bomberos y policías me han endorsado, también los neg-ociantes y los líderes religiosos de la comunidad. Soy Rebecca McKeene, me estoy representando sobre mi experiencia.

[That's why I've been endorsed by firefighters and businesspeople, the police and religious and community leaders. I'm
Rebecca McKeene, I'm running on my record.]

Meanwhile:

BLAIR (*to* PAT). Pat, could you ask – Therese if I heard
'educación bilingüe' coming before 'contra el crimen fuerte'?

PAT (*heading there*). Sure. Did you say 'fuerte'?

BLAIR. Yes, it means 'tough'. As in 'tough / on crime – '

PAT. I think you'll find it's (*different Spanish pronunciation*)
'fuerte'.

PAT *goes into the studio.*

BLAIR. We're re-recording our grabber ad in Spanish.

MICHAEL. Was that the one with her striding along corridors?

BLAIR. And balancing the budget.

MICHAEL. But you've changed the issue, right? Now it's
crime and bilingual education?

BLAIR. Oh, shoot. You've caught us talking about things that
people care about.

MICHAEL. Blair, we need to talk about a meeting we attended
in the winter of 1972.

BLAIR. Yes. Yes, I know.

But PAT *has reentered.*

Well?

PAT. It's the candidate. She feels it's hotter education and then
crime and do you want to make an issue of it?

BLAIR (*shrugs*). On her own cabeza be it.

MICHAEL (*quizzically*). Uh, why would . . .

PAT. Blair's Law: the crucial thing in politics is not what you
say but the order in which you say it.

MICHAEL. That would presumably explain your current
silence on Prop. Ninety-Two?

Knowing where this is heading, PAT *moves away.*

PAT. Hah-ah.

BLAIR *sees* PAT *sit at her laptop.*

BLAIR. Now, I imagine that's a point of easy rhetoric, but in fact you're on the nose.

MICHAEL. Oh, yes?

BLAIR. What's our major problem fighting Sheldon Vine?

MICHAEL. Beats me. Blair, is there somewhere we can / talk?

BLAIR. Where would you place his views on economic questions?

MICHAEL. To the right of Vlad the Impaler.

BLAIR. While, on social matters . . . ?

MICHAEL. . . . he is unexpectedly benign.

BLAIR. And would we be advised to draw attention to his excellent positions on gay rights and choice?

MICHAEL. I would guess not.

BLAIR. But if we go for him on wanting to cut taxes then we make his positives our negatives which the manual specifically instructs us to avoid.

MICHAEL. So, why . . .

BLAIR. But he's in trouble too, on account of how his target voters like his policies on guns and offshore drilling even less than paying taxes. So thus far, he's happy to affirm his faith in the values we all share, while we . . .

MICHAEL. Keep marching along corridors.

BLAIR. Just so. And with regard to Proposition Ninety-Two, which I should point out we've not / endorsed –

MICHAEL. Blair, your folks were communists.

BLAIR. They always claimed that they misread the form.

MICHAEL. Mine didn't. So when they were asked if they were now or if they'd ever been, they refused to answer.

BLAIR. Yup. Mine too.

MICHAEL. In the Sixties we fought against a law which made it a criminal offense to counsel, aid or abet a person to refuse the draft.

BLAIR. We did.

MICHAEL. Proposition Ninety-Two requires all state employees, teachers, voters for Christ's sake / to pledge –

BLAIR. All new or re-registering voters.

MICHAEL. – to pledge their loyalty to the constitution and to affirm they're not a member nor supporter of a body which pursues its ends by force.

BLAIR. Just so.

MICHAEL. And if you refuse, then you can't vote.

BLAIR. That's right. So, obviously / it won't –

MICHAEL. So fuck 'not endorsing,' why on earth haven't you come out against it?

BLAIR *goes to select a videotape from a pile, and inserts it in a player.*

BLAIR. You won't have seen this. It's called 'Dirty Secrets'.

BLAIR *plays the tape. It's quite a rough tape, put together to show to focus groups. It begins with an unflattering picture of* REBECCA.

VOICE-OVER (*on tape*). *Rebecca McKeene says she's running on her record. But she's kind of coy about her past.*

A fuzzy Seventies picture of REBECCA *as a hippie, then a student newspaper headline 'Black Power Is Our Struggle by Rebecca McKeene.' As:*

BLAIR (*to* MICHAEL). As well she might be.

MICHAEL. Thanks.

VOICE-OVER (*continues*). *As a student she backed extremist groups who advocated violence.*

MICHAEL. Well, that's an exaggeration.

Footage of contemporary 'extremist' groups.

VOICE-OVER. *No wonder she's backed by extremist groups today.*

(Back to the McKeene Seventies shot, followed by shots of crazed druggies.)

She admits she abused so-called 'soft' drugs.

MICHAEL. This is a Vine spot?

VOICE-OVER. *But she won't answer questions about cocaine and LSD.*

(Pictures of anti-war demonstrations with 'Bring the Boys Home' and 'Hell No We Won't Go' placards.)

She campaigned for us to surrender to our enemies. Perhaps that's why she won't back loyalty to America today.

BLAIR *stops the tape. She is changing it for another tape, as:*

BLAIR. Financed by Americans In Broad Agreement With America.

MICHAEL. They aired that?

BLAIR. No. They didn't even make it. Though knowing my opponent, I would be staggered if / they hadn't made –

MICHAEL. So, who / did –

BLAIR. We did. To try out on the three Ls, and, more importantly, to test out our response.

MICHAEL. The three Ls?

BLAIR. Labor, Latinos and Ladies of a Certain Age. To a selected group of whom we showed first 'Dirty Secrets' then a little numero we call 'Ideals'.

She plays the tape, which shows REBECCA *talking over shots of the nice Sixties and its leaders, and over location shots of poverty, schools, clearcuts and polluted beaches.*

She herself appears talking to ordinary Americans and looking concerned.

REBECCA (*on tape*). *Yes, I'm one of the baby boomers who grew up in the Sixties, and like millions of others felt America wasn't living up to its ideals. I was inspired by leaders like . . .*

BLAIR *fast-forwards.*

BLAIR. Cesar Chavez, Martin Luther King . . .

Tape back to speed:

REBECCA.. . . . *if we still don't have a way to go. In this state, we rank nearly last . . .*

BLAIR *fast-forwards.*

BLAIR. Home-ownership, per pupil spending . . . destroy the forests and the seas…

Tape back to speed:

REBECCA. . . . *Yes I had an ideal then and I have it still today.*

MICHAEL. Don't tell me.

BLAIR. Betcha.

REBECCA. *That ideal is called America.*

BLAIR *stops the tape.*

MICHAEL. And does it work?

BLAIR. The fuck it works. We're smoked. And do you know why?

MICHAEL. No. Why?

BLAIR. Because after 'Dirty Secrets' we can show them 'Peace and Love and Bunny Rabbits' paid for by Flower Children for a Nicer Day but the people we need still see Vietcong flags and public enemies selling their kids crack. Which is why, no, we are presently not volunteering that we're down on loyalty.

MICHAEL. Blair, remind me, why did you buy into this?

A phone rings. PAT *answers.*

PAT. McKeene for Governor.

BLAIR. Oh, doubtless for the reasons you accepted the current governor's kind offer to lead a major state commission. Recommended as you know by the future governor. When I promised that if she did so I would never mention you again.

PAT (*phone*). Sure, I'll be right down.

BLAIR. Hey, what was it with you guys?

MICHAEL. You said she liked the report.

BLAIR. We liked the fact that, unusually, it didn't say it's all about bad teachers.

MICHAEL. Or bad kids.

BLAIR. Or the capitalist system.

PAT. Blair, they've brought over the new Vine ad.

BLAIR. Go get, girl.

As PAT *goes, to* MICHAEL.

We've got a mole in Fox. Now you've got till she gets back to explain what the fuck you're doing here.

MICHAEL *takes a sheet from a folder.*

MICHAEL. I'm here because the two of us were at a meeting thirty years ago. Along with someone who was snitching on us to the FBI.

BLAIR. This is your file.

MICHAEL. Yes.

BLAIR. What's it say?

He hands her the sheet.

MICHAEL. You know. It says, there was a mission to release . . .

BLAIR. Yeah yeah, OK.

She reads.

Well, they haven't got it quite right.

MICHAEL. No. But . . .

BLAIR. And you're sure the 'black militant' was . . .

MICHAEL. Tommy Lee Trayton. Who else could it be?

BLAIR. I don't know, Michael. There might have been a dozen plots. I wasn't like a leading cadre.

MICHAEL. This was the plot to kidnap a young woman who you shared a dorm-room with in order to exchange her for an imprisoned leader of the Black Panther Party.

BLAIR. Yeah, yeah, it's all flooding back to me.

MICHAEL. But which didn't actually happen. Because three days after we all met to plan it – that's the eight of us – Tommy Lee Trayton was shot dead in the prison yard while 'trying to escape'.

BLAIR. And you think that one of us . . .

MICHAEL. Why, do you have another explanation?

BLAIR *shakes her head.*

Did you get your file?

BLAIR. Yeah, I got my file. Like years ago.

MICHAEL. And is the meeting in your file?

BLAIR. Michael, Bad Moon Rising isn't in my file. Thank the Lord. Like I was, what d'you call us? 'Extra Vehicular Activity.' We used to call ourselves the little green cheese people.

MICHAEL. Do you have the file?

BLAIR. What, with me? Oddly, no. As you point out, it's not so great for a political consultant to have been involved in a criminal conspiracy. Particularly this consultant, running this campaign.

MICHAEL. You mean, because / of who –

BLAIR. Michael. One person knew me at that meeting. Please tell me there weren't any more.

MICHAEL. So who do you remember being there?

BLAIR. Well . . . there were two Panther guys. One was, the guy who's changed his name – Cedric Baptiste? He's still around.

MICHAEL. Kwesi Ntuli. Would he know you?

BLAIR. Possibly. Troy Practice knows me now, though he didn't then.

MICHAEL. You see him?

BLAIR. Frequently. He's hosting – fuck it – a big fundraiser in two weeks' time.

MICHAEL. Why 'fuck it'?

BLAIR. Because he *really* doesn't like to talk about that time.

MICHAEL. That's five.

BLAIR. Well, obviously, Ground Control.

MICHAEL. Remember who?

BLAIR. When did Jack Sand and Claudia Perowne go underground?

MICHAEL. Later that year. Just after the state assembly bombing.

BLAIR. Which reminds me why we have a hard time with amnesties for fugitives. Well, is that everyone?

MICHAEL. Don't think so.

BLAIR. Was Ira Kitchen there?

MICHAEL. Of course.

BLAIR. Well, there's your snitch.

MICHAEL Why?

BLAIR. Have you seen the dreck that he's been writing lately?

MICHAEL. And would he know you?

BLAIR. Michael, for Ira, I was plankton level.

MICHAEL. And, if the snitch had known you, then, the plot would be in your file.

BLAIR. And if I was the snitch, the meeting would be in yours.

MICHAEL. Not necessarily. You could have told the feds about the plot but not the people.

BLAIR. And it's so absolutely in my interests to shop you to the Senate Rules Committee. Having frankly put our ass online / for you –

MICHAEL. Blair, I obviously don't think it's you. But it was someone, and as you point out it's not in either of our interests for this to come out now, and so I'd kind of like to find out who it was. Plus the fact they indirectly wrecked my marriage, and more importantly than that my relationship with my son.

Pause.

BLAIR. Your marriage?

MICHAEL. I was up for tenure. Then I wasn't. And so fifteen years later, there we are, with a growing child, having to choose between his braces, our insurance and a car that starts up in the morning.

PAT *comes in with the tape, during:*

BLAIR. And what does – Abby think about your quest?

MICHAEL Well, actually, it was kind of her idea.

BLAIR. And she seemed so sensible.

MICHAEL. Her point entirely.

BLAIR (*to* PAT). What is it?

PAT. It says it's 'Vision'.

BLAIR. Doesn't mean it isn't really 'Dirty Secrets'. There must be someplace you can check it out.

PAT *could check it out here. But she realizes she's being got rid of.*

PAT. Ho. Right.

She picks up her laptop and goes.

MICHAEL. So you see why I'm / pursuing this?

BLAIR. You know she died.

MICHAEL. Who?

BLAIR. The 'woman who I shared a dorm-room with.' The daughter of the prominent Republican / candidate.

MICHAEL. Yes, I heard. Breast cancer?

BLAIR. Pancreas. I actually got quite close to her.

MICHAEL. What, afterwards?

BLAIR. Yes, and her brother. Her elder brother, but her brother. Pretty funny, eh?

Pause.

MICHAEL. I want to find out who it was. But of course I won't tell him or her or anyone who else was there.

BLAIR. Well, good. So, any thoughts?

MICHAEL. Well, you know what everybody says. Informers come from two groups: folks who were above suspicion by way of class or racial background, and folks who were adept at hiding things about themselves. Which might account for / Troy not being keen –

BLAIR. Well, that narrows it right down to all of us.

MICHAEL. What do you mean?

BLAIR. You know the thing I hated most about my commie childhood? The fact we had to be one thing at home and another thing outside.

MICHAEL. You mean, when they were asking / if your parents –

BLAIR. But then the Sixties happen, wild, it's let it all hang out, and do your own thing and I'm free to be me. Except, we weren't like actually free.

MICHAEL *looks questioningly. The* REVOLUTIONARY *from the first scene has appeared.*

I had a friend who was instructed to abort her baby on the grounds that 'motherhood's like counter-revolutionary, dig it?'

REVOLUTIONARY. Man.

BLAIR. I had another friend who told me that unless I undertook an act of personal betrayal against a 18-year-old coed then 'objectively, I was working for the enemy.'

REVOLUTIONARY. Uh – you?

MICHAEL. Yeah, well . . .

BLAIR. And so, I have to tell you, when thank God the plot fell through, I got on an airplane to New Hampshire and I signed up for McGovern.

BLAIR*'s phone rings.*

BLAIR. Hello? Yeah, sure. Hold on.

REVOLUTIONARY. *McGovern?*

BLAIR *down the intercom:*

BLAIR. Rebecca. It's a blue.

In the studio, REBECCA *nods, understanding, and leaves the studio, as the* REVOLUTIONARY *disappears.*

That's right, McGovern. Rallies. Fourteen hour days. Living on peanut butter sandwiches. We distributed ten thousand doorhangers on eve of poll. The best time of my life. 'Cause guess what, I discover you don't have to turn yourself into Sojourner Truth or Bonnie Parker or a Bolivian guerrilla in the hills, you can pursue the ideals of peace and justice and equality and still be you.

MICHAEL. And now you're paying people to distribute doorhangers and lawnsigns and do eve of poll.

BLAIR. Point?

MICHAEL. The things you did free for McGovern, you're paying people to do now.

As REBECCA *enters:*

BLAIR. Yes. You're right. The things I did free for McGovern,
I'm paying people to do now.

REBECCA. And Michael's thinking, oh, whatever happened to
the good old days?

MICHAEL. Hello, Rebecca.

REBECCA *takes* BLAIR*'s phone.*

REBECCA (*phone*). Hello? You're putting me *on hold*?

To MICHAEL*:*

When campaigning was all volunteers, and empowering the
party faithful. Now a party rally is three people watching 30
second spots on television and a campaign is the candidate
sitting in a room dialling for the cash to pay for them.

Checking the phone:

Hello? Why do they always play Vivaldi? But you know
what I say? I say this. Frankly, grassroots is expensive,
unreliable and pointless unless you're in a squeaker. And
actually the people who want to help me win this race are
money-rich and time-poor, and if I said, don't bother with
the hundred bucks, give me ten hours, they'd keep the cash
and wouldn't give the time. Why should they?

Checking the phone:

And why is it always Winter? Hey? Hello?

MICHAEL. Well, if you see / the process as –

REBECCA. I'm sorry. Walt? You caught me in mid-flourish.
I just called to ask . . .

You did.

You *did*. Maravilloso. No, end of story. Thanks a million.
Fine.

She ends the call.

That's twenty thousand from the Correctional Peace
Officers.

BLAIR. Hey.

MICHAEL. You mean the / prison guards –

REBECCA. Yes, pal o'mine, that's the prison guards. And
nobody likes doing this, but till we persuade the taxpayer to
pony up, that's the way it has to be.

She gives the phone to BLAIR, *turns to go, turns back.*

And, what's so wrong with thirty-second spots? Why
shouldn't people get my message in the same place as they
get their other messages? Why should that message be
mediated via a party, or a precinct boss? What we're doing
here is not manipulation. It's treating people like the adults
that they are. But of course, for Michael, that's a sellout.
Just as our platform is a sellout of the principles we fought
for all those years ago.

MICHAEL. Well, I didn't think you'd come out against
amnesty for fugitives. Or for workfare or the death penalty.

REBECCA. No. But then you don't know what a woman has
to do if she runs for an executive position in this country.
How before you say a word on choice or bilingual education
or gay marriage you have got to lay it on the line that if
you're faced with a tough call on budget cuts or crime or
terrorism then you'll stand and fight just like a man.

Enter PAT *with the videotape and a transcript.*

PAT. Hey, it isn't 'Dirty Secrets'.

BLAIR. Oh? What is it?

PAT. What it says.

REBECCA (*to* MICHAEL). Well, Mikey, you're looking
tediously well-preserved.

BLAIR. What, 'Vision'?

MICHAEL. As, of course, are you.

PAT (*hands over the transcript*). Oh, and it's a hundred and
eleven words.

REBECCA (*tapping his arm, as she makes to go*). Liked the
report.

MICHAEL. Well, thanks.

BLAIR (*looking at the transcript*). What, in a thirty second spot?

REBECCA. Great to have you in the real world.

She's headed off when MICHAEL *stops her.*

MICHAEL. So why not run 'Ideals' first?

REBECCA (*turns back*). 'Scuse me?

BLAIR. Mike . . .

MICHAEL. You made 'Ideals' as a response to 'Dirty Secrets' but it doesn't work because 'Secrets' had already clamped drugs and treason to the Sixties and to you. But surely, if you follow Blair's law and get your response in first, you define the Sixties on your terms, as the decade of civil rights and draft resistance and the principles we stood and fought for all those years ago.

REBECCA*'s thrown by this.*

REBECCA. Excuse me, Michael is now a campaign strategist?

MICHAEL (*to* BLAIR). Unless of course you want to be defined by what other folks want you to be.

Pause.

REBECCA. Well, thank you, Michael. Maybe we'll get back to you for the reelection. When Blair's my Chief of Staff and has better things to do.

REBECCA *glances at her watch.*

PAT. Eleven minutes.

REBECCA (*as she goes*). I am presuming, by the way, that there is nothing sinister or threatening about Mike's presence here. Or if there is, that my manager will tell me.

She goes out. PAT *follows.*

MICHAEL. You didn't tell her.

BLAIR. Only in the broadest general terms.

MICHAEL. Well, good.

Slight pause.

BLAIR. I wouldn't do it.

MICHAEL. Do what?

BLAIR. Run for public office. Imagine knowing you'll be judged on the worst thing you ever did.

MICHAEL. I'll try.

BLAIR *gets it, and looks at* MICHAEL.

BLAIR. In fact, you're wrong. They're still people who do grassroots for nothing. For instance, Kwesi Ntuli nee Cedric Baptiste.

MICHAEL. But as she says, it's 'unreliable and pointless unless you're in a squeaker.'

BLAIR. Well, we're sixteen points ahead.

Pause.

MICHAEL. And you say you can work within the system and still keep to your ideals. Just not right now.

BLAIR. And speaking of right now . . .

MICHAEL. I'm sorry.

BLAIR. Oh, what for?

MICHAEL. For what I asked of you back then. I'm sorry that I said you had to change yourself into another person to prove that you were serious about the revolution.

BLAIR. Well, just so.

MICHAEL. But I'm not sorry for believing there are things inside us we don't know are there till someone else discovers them.

BLAIR. Well, I guess that's why you became a teacher.

Reenter PAT.

MICHAEL. Yeah. Just so.

Pause.

PAT. Uh-huh.

BLAIR. Hey, you know what, Pat? I think I may want to get something into the rotation at around eight hundred points by Friday. Can you call and check it out?

Slight pause.

PAT. Uh – title?

BLAIR. 'Youthful Indiscretions'.

PAT (*getting it*). Ho.

PAT *turns on her heels and goes out.*

MICHAEL. Ideals.

BLAIR. The ones you fought for, and we call America.

Second linking sequence.

REBECCA (*McKeene 'Ideals' spot*). *Yes, I'm one of the baby boomers who grew up in the Sixties, and like millions of others felt America wasn't living up . . .*

KWESI. Michael, it's Kwesi. Surely for real. Hey, I'll call you back.

Ninety-Two spot: a picture of an ASIAN WOMAN *pans out to reveal that the* WOMAN *is hanging the picture on a wall.*

VOICE-OVER (*Proposition 92 spot*). *There's a proposition on the ballot which will allow all new and re-registering voters to declare their allegiance to democracy.*

ASIAN WOMAN. *I really felt, now, I'm an American.*

KWESI. Hey man, it would be good to know what this is all in aid of.

KWESI (*different call*). I see. Make that the morning.

Scene Three: Strategic Hamlet A

A neutral space: initially, we assume it's outside. In fact, it's a community hall in the poor district of a big city on a Saturday morning. A group is role-playing a grassroots voting drive. The group is EDDIE, an old Beatnik, JIMMY, a middle-aged man in a wheelchair, BETH, a life-long campaigner, now in her fifties, TRINA, a young, white working-class woman, and DARREN, a young, white working-class man. The session is being overseen by KWESI and YOLANDE. Currently DARREN is the activist (with clipboard). KWESI walks forward as a voter.

DARREN. Hey. Pardon me, sir. May I ask, are you registered to vote?

KWESI. Am I what?

DARREN. Are you registered to vote?

KWESI. Sure I voted. Why, what's up?

DARREN. 'Cause like . . .

KWESI. 'Cause like?

DARREN. 'Cause like some people like move and they don't know how they get to register again.

KWESI. So do I look like I don't know how to register?

DARREN. No. Sure. Great. Now, we got this proposition you might / care to sign . . .

KWESI. Me too. Get off my back.

He marches off. DARREN is seething.

DARREN. Yeah.

YOLANDE *comes by.*

Pardon me, ma'am, but are you / registered . . .

YOLANDE. ¿Qué dicés? [What are you saying?]

DARREN. Ah. Do you speak English?

YOLANDE. No te entiendo. ¿Qué quieres? [I don't understand. What is it you want?]

KWESI *is whispering to* BETH.

DARREN. Bitch.

YOLANDE. 'Bitch' tú también. [– to you too.]

KWESI *nods* BETH *forward as* J.C., *a young African-American, hurries in late.*

J.C. Hey, man, I'm . . .

KWESI *stops him with a finger on his lips.*

BETH. Young man.

DARREN. Yes, what?

J.C. Excuse me.

BETH. Are you selling something here?

DARREN. No.

KWESI. No?

DARREN. I mean . . . I'm wondering if you might be registered to vote, ma'am.

BETH. Well, you know, I'm not so sure. I was in my last place.

DARREN. Well, if you've moved, you need to re-register at your new address. Now, here's the form you need to fill in . . .

BETH. Thank you. What, I fill it in and mail it to that address?

DARREN. Sure.

Pause.

BETH. Uh . . . anything else?

DARREN. Oh, and also maybe you'd think about voting for a ballot measure here.

BETH. That's interesting. What about?

DARREN. Uh . . . low-rent housing for the poor.

BETH. Sounds good to me.

DARREN. Well, great.

BETH. Well, thank you.

DARREN. Thank you. Have a good day.

KWESI. Well done. Who's next?

> DARREN *tosses the clipboard to* J.C. YOLANDE *the voter.*

DARREN. The late fuck. She's all yours, brother.

J.C. Hey, 'scuse me . . . 'scuse me . . .

YOLANDE. Hey. You from the Moonies?

J.C. No.

YOLANDE. You from the Hare Krishnas?

J.C. No. I'm from the campaign for Measure Q.

YOLANDE. Oh, yeah? What's that about?

J.C. It's for . . . low-rent housing for the poor. Would you like a flyer?

YOLANDE. Hey, why not.

> *She takes the flyer and reads.*

J.C. Hey maybe like / you want to . . .

YOLANDE. Hey. This is Measure Q, right?

J.C. Right.

YOLANDE. Which hands my city tax to deadbeats, right?

J.C. Uh, no . . .

YOLANDE. Freebies for Freeloaders, right?

J.C. Well, no, that's kinda / not how –

YOLANDE. No? Ain't the Chamber of Commerce said this means a tax hike?

J.C. Well, maybe, but we / think . . .

YOLANDE. Ain't the police said it'll bring more winos, drug dealers and assorted crazies into town?

J.C. Sure, but that doesn't mean / it ain't –

YOLANDE. Hey, ain't this crazier than the Moonies and the Hare Krishnas put together? Ain't I the asshole of all assholes of all time?

J.C. Yeah.

Slight pause.

Um, I . . .

KWESI (*rescue*). Let's hear it for you wonderful folks.

He leads the applause.

Now what lessons can we learn from that?

DARREN. Get outta here.

KWESI. That is a lesson which we never learn.

EDDIE. Learn Spanish.

JIMMY. Don't start, 'like I've got this important proposition here.'

KWESI. Say what instead?

BETH. Say . . .

EDDIE. 'Don't you think rents are too high?'

KWESI. Great. That's the hook. And Darren's great ride?

J.C. Darren's easy ride.

KWESI. Anything he could do even better?

BETH. Get me to fill the form in then and there.

KWESI. Good. And when Beth said she was a 'yes' on Q, what else might Darren have done?

JIMMY. Given her a flyer.

KWESI. Sure.

BETH. Given me a button.

TRINA. Sold her a button.

KWESI. Good.

EDDIE. And a yard sign.

YOLANDE. Hey, I have a question.

KWESI. Yolande?

YOLANDE. Who's that gringo by the door?

They turn to see MICHAEL *who has been standing there for some time. Pause.*

MICHAEL. I'm here for Cedric. Kwesi.

YOLANDE. There is a lobby.

MICHAEL. There's nobody there.

KWESI. Let's take ten, huh?

EDDIE. Then it's prep for blitzing Prop Q?

KWESI. My brother, we're so down for Q.

As they go:

JIMMY. Miguel's?

BETH. I'm Dunkin' Donuts.

EDDIE *wheels* JIMMY *out,* BETH *following.* TRINA *hanging on for* J.C. *and* DARREN. *Meanwhile:*

J.C. I'm sorry.

KWESI. Why?

J.C. I fucked up.

KWESI. No you didn't. Hey, Darren, who's the man?

They do a little hand slapping.

Say, could you do me a latte and maybe something like a churro from Miguel's?

DARREN. No problem.

KWESI. Michael?

MICHAEL. I'm fine.

KWESI (*hands money to* DARREN). Thanks buddy. (*To* J.C.)
Hey, my brother. You got the asshole.

J.C. Story of my life.

> J.C. *and* DARREN *go out with* TRINA. YOLANDE *is*
> *preparing for the next session.* KWESI *to* MICHAEL:

KWESI. He's been into some shit.

MICHAEL. Which one?

YOLANDE. The white one.

MICHAEL. What kind of shit?

YOLANDE. Assault and battery.

MICHAEL. And the other one?

YOLANDE. Kwesi has an infinite faith in people's capacity
for self-improvement.

MICHAEL. And they're all volunteers?

KWESI. Of course.

YOLANDE. Like, we're still stuck in a Sixties time warp.

KWESI. Push comes to shove, it's the only way to fly.

> *Pause.* MICHAEL *and* KWESI *can't talk while* YOLANDE
> *is there.*

YOLANDE (*picking this up*). I'll see you guys.

KWESI (*glance at watch*). Eight minutes.

> YOLANDE *goes out.*

MICHAEL. Hey, man / it's good . . .

KWESI. So let me make a calculated guess here. It was the
meeting where we set up springing Tommy Lee.

> *Pause.*

MICHAEL. Yes. You remember it?

KWESI. Oh, just about. And you remember who was present.

MICHAEL. Think so. You?

KWESI. Well, you have – four, five? I was with a brother. And the woman who knew the kidnap victim, she was late 'cause she'd been waiting in the wrong part of the church and how the fuck was she to know.

MICHAEL. Yeah, I've seen her.

KWESI. And?

MICHAEL. I think it's most unlikely.

KWESI. And did you have a . . . a kind of thin-faced pale guy . . . name of, something mythical . . .

MICHAEL. Yes.

KWESI. Troy – something.

MICHAEL. Yes.

KWESI. And, uh . . . was Ira Kitchen there?

MICHAEL. Someone suggested he might be the snitch.

KWESI. Well, that would fit with what he's saying now.

MICHAEL. I'm going to see him.

KWESI. Lucky you.

MICHAEL. But of course, the common wisdom is informers come from two groups . . .

KWESI. People good at concealing things about themselves, and black guys.

Pause.

MICHAEL. Of course I don't think / it was –

KWESI. Well, it's true. The Panthers had their fair share of informers.

MICHAEL. Yeah, but / not the people –

KWESI. And there were two Panthers there.

MICHAEL. Who was the other guy?

KWESI. His name was Sonny Crane. Good cadre, came out west from Michigan.

MICHAEL. His name 'was'?

KWESI. One of many.

MICHAEL. I'm sorry.

Slight pause.

KWESI. And then . . . there was your leadership.

MICHAEL. Yeah.

KWESI. I guess – Jack Sand and Claudia Perowne?

Slight pause.

MICHAEL. I want to speak to them.

KWESI. So do the feds.

MICHAEL. But still.

KWESI. Not easy.

MICHAEL. Even so.

KWESI. And maybe . . . You should ask yourself, if you really want to.

Slight pause.

MICHAEL. Why? Do you know something?

Pause.

KWESI. I know what everybody knows. That America was engaged in a genocidal war, and the only thing to do was bring the war home, by any means necessary.

MICHAEL. Yes?

KWESI. And so a group of nice white idealistic kids decide to turn themselves into a revolutionary army and the best and brightest head off underground.

MICHAEL. What are you saying, Kwesi?

KWESI. I am saying that eventually wars end. And the revolutionary army's stuck there in the outer darkness and what does it do now.

Pause.

MICHAEL. Where are they?

KWESI. I told you, I don't know.

MICHAEL. But they're still alive.

KWESI. Who, Jack and Claudia?

MICHAEL. Yes, Jack and Claudia.

Slight pause.

KWESI. Oh, yes. They're still alive.

MICHAEL. But you're not suggesting either of them might have been . . .

KWESI. I'm suggesting this thing's going to be hard whoever it turns out to be.

MICHAEL *breathes deeply. During this,* YOLANDE *enters. She is cool, but angry.*

MICHAEL. There's something you should know. I was in jail, with a group of white idealistic kids who'd been busted for their very first campus occupation. And they were herded into vans and taken off to jail by the goon squad and they were terrified. Correction, we were terrified. And Jack was there. And he had us telling each other who we were and how we'd gotten into this. And he talked about the Selma March and Greensboro and stopping troop trains and how from now on this cell is Strategic Hamlet A. And, how things would be after the revolution if only we dared live it now. And how it *was* being lived now, in the movement. And how it had been, all the way back through the century, in strange cooperative utopias in secret valleys and abandoned towns. And then we started singing, 'We Shall Overcome' or Beatles songs or 'Bread and Roses' . . . And before my eyes that group of scared and isolated children turned into . . . the front line of the future. And I thought – hey – I've seen water turned to wine.

KWESI. And so . . .

MICHAEL. And I thought that doing that was the noblest thing one human being could do for another. And so I became a teacher. And ten years ago I realized I couldn't cut it any more. So I stop teaching and become a dean. I write a study of why poor kids don't go on from community college to the university. And, guess what, I find the problem wasn't with the system, it wasn't even with the teachers, or the kids. It was simply that their parents didn't teach them basic integrative skills.

J.C. *enters with* KWESI*'s order. Clearly something's wrong.*

J.C. Uh-huh.

KWESI *turns to* J.C.

KWESI. Hey, J.C., what's up?

YOLANDE. Just an incident.

KWESI. What 'incident'?

YOLANDE. In Miguel's.

J.C. Darren met some white boys.

KWESI. What kind of white boys?

YOLANDE. Well, they weren't selling buttons.

J.C. And he like needs some scratch, so he tries to 'borrow' it off Miguel.

KWESI. And what happened . . .

YOLANDE. What did you say? Push comes to shove.

J.C. And it's like no big deal, and no one's hurt.

YOLANDE. Well, no one's hurt *bad* . . .

J.C. Except he splits and goes off with the white boys.

KWESI. And the other folks?

J.C. Well, Jimmy like tries to calm him down, but he's all, hey, get off my back you cripple, and Jimmy's all, I don't need this and Eddie wheels him home. Hey, hc got your order. Thcy didn't have churros so he got you polvorones.

KWESI (*taking the order*). Thanks.

Hey, I . . . I understand . . .

Enter BETH *and* TRINA.

BETH. So is this where we prep for Saturday?

Pause.

YOLANDE. Maybe we leave it for today.

BETH. Yeah, maybe we do that.

BETH *gets her stuff.*

TRINA. I, uh . . . It was kinda fun. I mean, like I only show because . . . and he, well like . . . He splits. But it was fun.

TRINA *and* BETH *go out. Nobody wants to look at* KWESI, *who sits down, takes out a polvorone from the bag and eats it. After a pause:*

YOLANDE. But then, if we just told bad kids about the Selma March and / Vietnam . . .

MICHAEL (*suddenly*). Hey. J.C., did you do stuff on Ninety-Two?

Pause. J.C. *is thrown.*

YOLANDE. Yes, he did some role-play.

MICHAEL. And did you do good?

J.C. Did OK.

YOLANDE. Like it's hard, you have to argue . . .

MICHAEL. I'd sure like to hear the argument again.

J.C. What, now?

MICHAEL. Yes, now.

KWESI. Michael . . .

J.C. So who's the asshole?

MICHAEL. I'm the asshole. What's the worst question that you have to answer?

J.C. What, on Ninety-Two?

MICHAEL. On Ninety-Two.

Slight pause.

KWESI. Michael?

J.C. We're free democracy. Like you shouldn't have to be violent, like why don't you, like, I'll prove my aims through only peaceful means. Ain't that the tradition and the US way.

MICHAEL. OK. 'We're a democracy. Why shouldn't you commit yourself to act within the law? Isn't that the great American tradition?'

J.C. Yeah. Like I said. That's the hardest question.

MICHAEL. So then, answer it.

J.C. Uh huh?

MICHAEL. Presumably the purpose – when you talk to people – is to win them over.

J.C. Huh?

KWESI. Michael . . .

MICHAEL. Tradition? Really? Legal, always? Free?

Slight pause.

In 1960, four black guys in Greensboro, North Carolina, sat down at a lunch-counter, were told that they were trespassing, and refused to move.

J.C. Yeah, well, civil rights.

MICHAEL. What do you mean, civil rights? That's a law. It was passed by Lyndon Johnson.

J.C. But it . . . I mean, it wouldn't get to be a law . . . without . . . those brothers.

MICHAEL. That's one example.

J.C. And the lady on the bus.

MICHAEL. That's two.

J.C. And, yeah . . .

Waving at YOLANDE*:*

. . . Vietnam. Dudes who won't take the draft and block the trains and shit like that.

MICHAEL. Sure. But all of those examples are a long time ago.

J.C. So was the great and glorious American Revolution. But that don't mean it wasn't revolutionary.

MICHAEL. Go on?

J.C. I mean tax everything by who the dude was, like the English king, right? I mean, that was all legal right? And correct me if I'm wrong, but revolution is illegal, right?

MICHAEL. As a general rule.

J.C. This motherfucking country's founded on illegal action, right? Goddamn? The right to vote came because we took up arms, right? And we let that go? And like the right to sit down and protest and shit, and, sure, yeah, block the roads in defiance of unjust laws, then the next fine morning glory hallelujah we wake up and find there ain't no right to vote no more. I mean, like Florida. Huh? Right?

MICHAEL. Yeah. Right.

J.C. So I'm guessing that you won't be supporting Proposition Ninety-Two.

MICHAEL. No.

J.C. And Kwesi I'm gonna see you here next Saturday.

KWESI. Yeah. Sure.

J.C. (*to* MICHAEL). Asshole.

He goes out.

KWESI. Thanks.

Pause.

YOLANDE. Well, sure. Another blow struck for the eternal optimist.

KWESI. Guess so.

YOLANDE. Another sinner born again, hallelujah hallelujah.

KWESI. Inch by inch, then mile by mile.

YOLANDE. You know, he's at the Williamsville First Pentecostal every Sunday?

KWESI. Strictly for research.

MICHAEL. 'Inch by inch,' is that Fidel?

YOLANDE. Oh, yes. 'Fidel'. 'The Movement'. With its endless cycle of euphoria and despair.

MICHAEL. What do you mean?

YOLANDE. How you try to implement the law and you are thrown in jail for breaking it. How you work with the federal government and they don't protect you. How you have no leaders and nothing works. How you build your own leadership and you are accused of separatism. You defend yourselves, and you fail as victim. You don't defend yourselves, and you fail as hero. And sure, you get J.C. and you get young white college kids in jail, singing 'Hey Jude' or 'We Shall Overcome' or 'Puff the Magic Dragon'. Well, lordy, lordy. But in the end they cop out or they drop out. And we end up here.

Slight pause.

I'm sorry.

She goes out.

KWESI. She's pretty badly burned.

MICHAEL. So why does she come here?

KWESI. She's pretty badly burned.

Slight pause.

But, hey. You need to find somebody who told something to somebody else thirty years ago.

MICHAEL. I need to speak to Jack or Claudia.

Pause.

KWESI. There used to be a system. I think you went to a
motel and waited for a call. And they send you off to
somewhere else and you were blindfolded and taken to the
rendezvous.

MICHAEL. And you can get a message to them?

KWESI. I can try.

MICHAEL. Thanks.

KWESI. But I want you to do two things for me.

MICHAEL. What's that?

KWESI. Tell her – tell them exactly what I told you. Then ask
why Bad Moon chose to abdicate, from folks engaged in
real struggles, in the real world.

Pause.

Sometimes I'm jealous. Folks who cop out and go over.
Join the club just because they'll be accepted as a member.
But then I think, hey man, who'd want to be in that club
anyway?

Slight pause.

MICHAEL. And you know such people...

KWESI. Pretty close to home. So I know how tempting it can
be.

MICHAEL. She's wrong.

KWESI. So we must pray.

> KWESI *smiles and goes out.* MICHAEL *remembers the
> long chant from the end of 'Hey Jude'. He turns to see the
> young* REVOLUTIONARY.

REVOLUTIONARY. Hey, Mikey. You remembered.

MICHAEL. Yes, Jack. I remember.

And JACK SAND *disappears.*

Third linking sequence.

JACK (*the Meeting*). Daddy, the republican candidate for Senate.

SHELDON (*Vine spot*). *I want to talk to you about my vision for this state.*

REBECCA (*McKeene spot*). *I was inspired by leaders like Cesar Chavez, Martin Luther King and Robert Kennedy . . .*

LORIANNE. Yes, this is Ira Kitchen's residence. Though in fact it's Kirschenbaum.

Ninety-Two spot: An AMERICAN *standing outside his house, next to his flag.*

WHITE ANGLO MAN (*Proposition 92 spot*). *Hey, these new guys get to say the oath. So why can't I?*

VOICE-OVER (*Proposition 92 spot*). *America.*

NEWS ANCHOR. Our top story this hour. In a tragic end to what police describe as a protest against genetically-modified crops, a young woman was shot dead on a campus forestry test site earlier today.

VOICE-OVER (*Proposition 92 spot*). *Vote Yes on Ninety-Two.*

SHELDON (*Vine spot*). *It's the vision of the people . . .*

IRA. Well, why not tonight?

Scene Four: Wrong

The living room in IRA*'s house. A little dark and gloomy. Books and the appurtenances of an orthodox Jew. A dining table.* IRA KIRSCHENBAUM *appears with two candlesticks.* MICHAEL *joins* IRA. IRA *puts down the candlesticks.*

MICHAEL. Rosh Hashana.

IRA. Yes.

MICHAEL. I hadn't realized.

IRA. I had.

LORIANNE *enters with a tray of silverware and crockery to set a table for Rosh Hashana.*

MICHAEL. Look, Ira, I can / easily –

IRA. Nonsense. Have you met Lorianne Weiner?

MICHAEL. No, I haven't.

IRA. Contributing Editor, *The Outside Edge*. Daughter of Theodore, the noted neo-conservative. Herself a leading commentator on the vagaries and vanities of our benighted times. You will have doubtless heard her radio show.

MICHAEL. Um, I . . .

LORIANNE. *Don't Get Me Started.*

MICHAEL. What, on the 'vagaries and / vanities – '

LORIANNE. That's the title of my show.

IRA. Michael's been trying to find out who betrayed him to the feds in 1972.

LORIANNE. Well, gosh.

IRA. I'm the prime suspect.

LORIANNE. Even gosher.

MICHAEL. I didn't say that.

LORIANNE. Are you staying for the meal?

MICHAEL. Um . . . Look, I . . .

IRA. I don't think Michael's an observer.

MICHAEL. No.

IRA. You've not reverted.

MICHAEL. Nothing to revert to.

IRA. No?

MICHAEL. My parents were both communists.

IRA. Well, we've all got that in common.

LORIANNE. My dad was more a kind of radical progressive.

IRA. Until, like some of us, he saw the light.

> LORIANNE *senses the gauntlet has been flung. She takes the tray out for another load.*

Try saying it. 'We supported the wrong side in Vietnam.'

MICHAEL. I disagree.

IRA. Try saying it: 'The Americans were on the right side.'

MICHAEL. I don't think that.

IRA. Just say it: 'The North Vietnamese were totalitarian dictators. They behave like commies always do.'

MICHAEL. That doesn't mean that we were wrong / to fight against –

IRA. What, you mean, we *didn't* behave like commies always do?

MICHAEL. Well, not unless you think the New Left was a red plot.

IRA. Clearly you've not read what I've written recently.

MICHAEL. You're serious?

IRA. Michael, I was there from the beginning. Objectively, the New Left was the Old Left in tie-dyes and bell-bottoms. As it proved by its progression from the Student Non-Violent Coordinating Committee and Students for a Democratic Society into Bad Moon Rising into Workers' Vanguard, Workers' League and Proletarian Advance. Whereby the politics of 'Puff the Magic Dragon' degenerates into the Neo-Bolshevism out of which it grew.

MICHAEL. So here's your logic. You were a Marxist-Leninist. You were around when the New Left started. Therefore the New Left was Marxist-Leninist.

IRA. Stalin led to us. Lenin led to Stalin. Marx led to Lenin. Marx was a self-hating Jew.

MICHAEL. Well, he was a Jew.

IRA. So what am I describing? There is a movement, largely
Jewish.

MICHAEL. This is the New Left?

IRA. This is civil rights. It supports and works with another
movement, largely black, which then turns around and
expels it. Still the Jews support this movement, as it
gradually mutates into a party which supports the
elimination of the Jewish state. Finally, still with Jewish
backing, this movement turns en masse to the world religion
founded on hatred of the Jews and all their works.

MICHAEL. Come on.

IRA. Say it. They chucked us out because we were all Jews.

MICHAEL. They took the leadership of their own movement.
Painfully, but rightly.

IRA. Say it. Objectively, the Panthers were a criminal
conspiracy.

MICHAEL. They were a party forced by circumstances / into –

IRA. Say at least that Tommy Lee Trayton was a gangster and
a rapist.

MICHAEL. Of course. Then he wrote a book about his time in
jail called *Wait for Morning* which inspired a lot of kids
who would otherwise have ended up on drugs or dead, and
so they rearrested him on clearly trumped-up charges and he
was shot down, 'while trying to escape.' 'Objectively.'

LORIANNE *is coming in with the next tray.*

IRA. Aha. A hoodlum and a hero? A villain and a victim? Like
those particles of light in quantum physics that mysteriously
move through two slits simultaneously? The truth that may
be true and maybe not depending on who looks?

Slight pause. LORIANNE *sets the table.*

MICHAEL. So what exactly are you saying / isn't true?

IRA. I'm going to check on – what? March 1972?

MICHAEL. January. You kept a diary?

IRA. No. I kept my file.

He goes out.

MICHAEL. I haven't seen a man let a woman set a table on her own since 1964.

LORIANNE. Well, you're welcome to help.

MICHAEL *helps, not always accurately.*

Even, set yourself a place.

MICHAEL. Well, I don't really . . .

LORIANNE. So I guess you're thinking: hey, wow, what's happened to this guy?

MICHAEL. I read his piece on McKeene in *Common Sense.* I mean, you have to be pretty far to starboard to consider Rebecca J. McKeene a clear and present danger to national security.

LORIANNE. Well, we've established you don't listen to my show.

MICHAEL. Considering her positions now.

LORIANNE. Well, that begs the question, doesn't it?

MICHAEL. What question?

LORIANNE. Whether her positions now are in fact her actual positions.

MICHAEL. Oh, why shouldn't / they be?

LORIANNE. Or whether she's just turned herself around to face the same way as America.

Slight pause.

MICHAEL. What, you mean, like Ira?

LORIANNE. Oh sure, he writes for *Common Sense* so obviously he's sold out to the CIA.

MICHAEL. I didn't say that. All I said was that he's / changed his mind.

LORIANNE. Presumably you know the story of his daughter.

MICHAEL. Well, I know she died.

LORIANNE. Or more accurately, was murdered. Whereupon either bravely or bizarrely, depending on your point of view, Ira comes out against the chair for the young, poor, black, deprived, uneducated killer.

MICHAEL. Yes.

LORIANNE. Having been implored to do so by his old friend and comrade, Rebecca J. McKeene, then the candidate for the whatever district of the state assembly.

MICHAEL. Yes.

LORIANNE. Before she changed her mind.

LORIANNE *looks at* MICHAEL:

You see a woman in a quandary. I've been asked to do a job for Sheldon Vine. I'd written something – actually, about McKeene and her positions, in her voice, for satirical effect, which had drawn me to the Vine campaign's attention. But you know, I kind of didn't want to take the job. But then I walked into his room and Ira's gazing at a picture of the two of them when Harriet was twelve and he'd taken her to Universal Studios. And I thought, scruples schmuples, hell, why not?

MICHAEL. So, what's the quandary?

LORIANNE. Oh, of course, I'm a conservative. So naturally, I welcome any chance to sacrifice my independence and integrity.

MICHAEL. I didn't say that / you weren't –

LORIANNE. And in answer to the question that you haven't asked: because I think that having to admit you were that wrong for that long makes you a kind of hero.

IRA *comes back in again, with a few sheets of paper.*

IRA. What are you talking about?

Slight pause.

MICHAEL. McKeene.

IRA. Oh, yes. Weren't you two once . . .

MICHAEL. Yes. Yes, we were.

IRA. Well, she's in even deeper trouble now.

MICHAEL. In what respect?

IRA. Didn't you hear? She runs a spot extolling the ideals of
the Sixties, specifically citing the environmental movement,
and then an eco-terrorist breaks into an agricultural test
facility and attacks a university official with a chainsaw.

MICHAEL. Or put another way, a twenty-one-year-old,
female, unarmed activist is gunned down in cold blood by a
security guard.

IRA. That's a Latino guard.

LORIANNE. That's unarmed meaning, just the chainsaw.

MICHAEL. With which she was cutting down a symbolic
number of genetically-modified / poplars –

IRA. Hey, do you remember McKeene's finest hour? It was also
SAU. And we'd occupied – meaning violently invaded –
the ROTC building. And somebody had the bright idea of
raising the flag of our country's current enemy on what was
essentially an army building. And since she was decked out
in a very fetching skimpy top and leather miniskirt – this
was the early Seventies – Rebecca was selected for the
honor of running the Vietcong flag up the pole. Hey. If
someone had a photograph of *that*.

MICHAEL. Well . . . Well.

LORIANNE. Ira, it's nearly sunset.

LORIANNE *goes.*

MICHAEL (*nodding to* IRA*'s envelope*). Did you find
anything?

IRA. For 'found,' read 'located.' I already knew I was two
thousand miles away.

MICHAEL. You were what?

IRA. That week, I'd been assigned to consolidate the
Cleveland chapter.

MICHAEL. But surely, you were at the meeting?

IRA. Sadly not. My plane was grounded. January.

MICHAEL. But . . .

IRA (*looking at the file*). I mean, the plan is mentioned, in
broad, general terms. 'In pursuit of which objectives . . .
securing the release of specified Negro militants . . . '

He hands the sheet over.

MICHAEL (*taking the sheet*). Yes, that's the same as mine.

IRA. But of course I didn't know about it at the time.
Especially as by the time I'd got back, Sand and Claudia
Perowne had gone off underground. So it can't be Colonel
Turncoat in the conservatory with the lead pipe after all. I'm
sorry, what a disappointment.

MICHAEL (*wryly*). Well . . .

IRA. But of course, your real worry is, I know it *now*. And
here's you, on the brink of your escape from thirty years of
community college teaching, with just the Senate Rules
Committee in the way.

MICHAEL. In fact, it was twenty years. I got out of teaching
in the early Nineties.

IRA. Understandable enough. It must be damned dispiriting.

MICHAEL. What do you mean?

IRA. Month after month, year after year, so many disappointed
dreams, that many unfulfilled / hopes –

MICHAEL. Well, no, that wasn't / why I –

IRA. The great utopian experiment of postwar higher
education crumbling into dust before your very eyes.

MICHAEL. I don't think it's crumbling.

IRA. Well, of course not. Otherwise, you'd have to face up to the fraudulence of the creed you'd lived your life by.

MICHAEL. Oh, and what's that, Ira?

IRA. The myth that under every hoodlum lurks a hero. That, if you just remove the shackles of oppression, then everybody's Beethoven and Michelangelo.

Enter LORIANNE *with the final load.*

MICHAEL. No, Ira, I don't think / that everybody's –

IRA. While maybe the sad truth is that students fail not because of teachers nor of – what is it? Inadequate integrative skills? – but because they're just not up to it. Or they don't work hard enough. Or they spend too little time with their noses in the books, and too much time with their nose in something else. That there's this thing called water and this other thing called wine.

MICHAEL *is furious, but he can't speak.*

And what happens when you realize that awful truth that the oppressed aren't heroes after all? You turn upon each other. And the scapegoats are selected and the charges laid. And the renegades confess to 'opportunism,' 'sabotage' and 'treachery,' just as their fathers did before.

LORIANNE. Whose fathers, Ira?

IRA. Ah. Ms Weiner is a different generation. She thinks the Moscow trials are where they pick the Russian track-and-field Olympic team.

LORIANNE *has heard this joke before.*

Whereas *we* know, that what Stalin did to his old comrades in the Thirties was precisely what each generation of the left does to each other and itself when it realizes its whole life has been based upon a lie. Up to and including, naturally, Bad Moon Underground.

MICHAEL. Yes, so I understand.

Pause.

LORIANNE. Now, in fact, it's / nearly time –

MICHAEL. Lorianne was telling me about your daughter.

IRA. Oh, yes?

MICHAEL. Harriet, as in Tubman?

IRA. Yes. And now my name is Ira David Kirschenbaum.

MICHAEL (*a little blurted*). You know, there are no signs to this place. You have to know your destination before you set out. Just like a military installation.

Slight pause.

IRA. True.

MICHAEL. And when you find it, with its Florentine renaissance meets Antebellum clapboard meets Tudor England pastiche architecture, you have to show ID into a screen and tap a code into the buttons on the wall, and then the gates slide open and they let you in. That's through the razor wire, and underneath the watchtowers.

IRA. Yes.

LORIANNE. Ira, it's sunset.

IRA. Yes. Begin.

LORIANNE *pours the wine, lights the candles and sings the Rosh Hashana blessings.*

LORIANNE. Bo-Ruch A-ttah \ Ado-noi E-lo-hei-nu \ Me-lech Ha-olom \ A-sher Ki-dde-sha-nu \ Be-mitz-vo-tav \ Ve-tzi-vva-nu Le-had-lik \ Ner Shel Yom Tov.

After LORIANNE *has begun:*

IRA. Did Lorianne tell you *how* my daughter died?

MICHAEL. Well, I know that she was / murdered…

IRA. She was working with gang members in a ghetto area. Naturally, she assumed that once removed from their environment, they would blossom into, at the very least, a gang of Byrons if not Galileos. Naturally, she opened up her home. One young man observed the value of her jewelry. He brought three friends, unannounced and uninvited, one evening. She was alone. She tried to reason with them. Naturally. So now, I feel – we feel we have the right to live in our own home securely and at peace.

MICHAEL. No, I didn't know that. Naturally I'm sorry.

IRA. And now, I'm going to tell you the last thing you want to hear.

MICHAEL. What's that?

IRA. I wasn't an informer then and I'm not one now. Your secret's safe with me.

IRA *offers* MICHAEL *the wine.* MICHAEL *shakes his head.*

MICHAEL *looks up to see grainy, black-and-white footage of* JACK SAND *on the screens:*

JACK SAND. My dream. My revolution. Every black kid in the ghetto, every white kid in a project, every Chicano working in the field, gets to be a leader. Or a scientist, or an artist or a poet. Anything they want to be.

Taking us into the fourth linking sequence.

SONNY (*the Meeting*). So do these honkies have a plan?

AIDE. This is the office of State Senator Cal Rasky.

TROY (*the Meeting*). Like how were you to know.

AIDE. . . . it's with regard to Rules Committee hearings on October 3rd . . .

NEWS ANCHOR. Anger mounts at District Attorney Joe Vincenzi's shock ruling that the shooting of protestor Sarah Jane Polowski by security guard Fernando Martinez was an act of justifiable homicide.

VOICE-OVER (*Proposition 92 spot*). *One flag. One pledge.*

REBECCA (*McKeene spot*). *I was inspired by leaders like . . .*

SHELDON (*Vine spot*). . . . *the fishermen and trappers who first came here . . .*

TROY (*the Meeting*). Cesar Chavez is an enemy of the state.

Scene Five: Busted

Saturday, noon. TROY PRACTICE*'s substantial yard,*
overlooking the ocean, the site for a fundraising brunch.
TROY *himself is among the faithful, a group of largely thirty-*
to-fifty-something, well-preserved coastal Democrats. BLAIR
and ABBY *among those in attendance.* REBECCA *herself*
stands on a small platform in front of the brunchers, waiting
for applause to die down.

TROY. OK, folks, our next Democratic governor... Rebecca J.
   McKeene.

REBECCA. Or indeed your next governor of either party.

   Response. TROY *demurs.*

   But, hey, thanks for inviting me to visit with you this fine
   and lovely morning. An invitation I accepted entirely on the
   promise of Sam and Troy's eggs florentine.

TROY. Don't we know they're the best.

REBECCA. Now, this isn't a political occasion . . .

   Response.

   This isn't entirely a political occasion . . .

   Response. MICHAEL *enters, late. He sees and makes his*
   way to ABBY.

   But it's kind of hard not to look around and think how great
   places here and elsewhere in the state would be if we take a
   bath November 5th.

BRUNCHER. Shame!

   ABBY *sees* MICHAEL, *who puts his finger to his lips. She*
   is surprised but pleased to see him, and, during the
   following, they greet and whisper. At the same time, TROY
   notices MICHAEL *and asks* BLAIR *if she knows why*
   MICHAEL *is there.* BLAIR, *clearly embarrassed, whispers*
   back to an insistent TROY.

REBECCA. The breathtaking ocean view with its mighty
   platforms rising proudly from its depths. The simple beauty

of the eroded dunes with the faintest trace of long uprooted marram grass. The awesome vista across the clearcut to the silted rivers inching sluggishly down bare unwooded hillsides. Or bare unwooded landslides. Or what would be an awesome vista, without all those condos in the way. So does anyone want offshore drilling?

AUDIENCE. No!

REBECCA. Anyone want clearcuts in our ancient woodlands?

AUDIENCE. No!

REBECCA. Or dune buggies in state parks?

AUDIENCE. No! No!

REBECCA. So does anyone want Sheldon Vine to win?

AUDIENCE. No!

REBECCA. Well, I guess you don't need telling what to do about it. So Troy, do all these good people get to eat?

TROY's *back on the case. A sense of breakup.*

TROY. Well, thanks, Rebecca. And sure they all / know what to do . . .

A HECKLER *intervenes.*

HECKLER. So hey, is anybody going to *mention* Sarah Jane Polowski?

REBECCA. I'm sorry?

BLAIR *looks to* TROY. TROY *shrugs, he doesn't know who this is.*

HECKLER. This is the twenty-one-year-old shot dead while protesting the contamination of the planet.

REBECCA. Yes, I know who she is and what she was doing.

HECKLER. But I guess this didn't happen in the *Sixties.*

TROY. Hey, man, maybe this isn't the time –

REBECCA. And while I'm on the record against tolerance for terrorism, / I have also said . . .

A MALE BRUNCHER *moves to remove the* HECKLER.
BLAIR *picks this up and shakes her head.*

HECKLER. Oh, so protesting GM crops makes you a /
terrorist –

TROY*'s young partner* SAM *comes out of the house.*

REBECCA. . . . I don't think it's the time to exploit . . .

SAM. Hey, folks, the food's congealing.

REBECCA. . . . a family's grief.

HECKLER. OK. Forget about it. Let's go eat.

REBECCA. I'm not forgetting it. I'm just not commenting / on
it right now.

HECKLER. I mean, like one way of helping out that family
might be for the Democratic candidate to say her killer
should be charged with killing her. But, then, this is the
Democrat who won't come out against Prop. Ninety-Two, /
so I guess –

REBECCA (*stung*). OK. What do I say? I say this. Do I
respect her motivations? Yes. Do I have serious reservations
about GM crops? I do. Do I intend to make a snap judgment
on a tragic accident without knowing all the facts? No I do
not.

SAM. And the food is on / the porch.

REBECCA. But if you – or anybody else – feels it's
inappropriate to continue with this fundraiser then I'm quite
happy to go home.

*Some shouts of 'No.' Applause. Now the formality really
does breaks up. Some people head off towards the food.*
SAM *hurries out.* TROY *looks to* BLAIR *and shrugs.*

REBECCA (*aware of nearby listening people*). But, hey, if
Sam's not fixed those hash browns then I *am* heading home.

Laughter. As everyone except MICHAEL, ABBY *and*
TROY *goes:*

TROY. Hey, Rebecca, I'm . . .

REBECCA. It's all part of the dance.

She turns to BLAIR.

Close call.

BLAIR. Good call.

REBECCA. Really?

BLAIR (*not quite convincingly*). Really.

REBECCA. Right.

Spotting MICHAEL:

Hey, is that . . .

BLAIR. Yes, I'm afraid so.

REBECCA *goes over to* MICHAEL *and* ABBY. SAM
appears, waving for TROY *to come in. Seeing* SAM, TROY
goes into the house. BLAIR *comes over to join* REBECCA,
MICHAEL *and* ABBY.

REBECCA. Now, Michael. This is presumably a test of our
security procedures?

MICHAEL. Rebecca, this is Abby Palladine.

REBECCA (*with a nod to* BLAIR). What, her of the thirty-
five-plus Asian undecideds taster shot?

BLAIR. Just so.

MICHAEL. And actually . . .

REBECCA. Big Tip. Don't get him on to Woodstock versus
Monterey.

ABBY. Tell me about it.

REBECCA. Senate hearings next week, right?

MICHAEL. That's right.

REBECCA. You'll knock 'em dead.

To BLAIR, *affecting explanation for her benign attitude to*
MICHAEL, *with a nod towards where the* HECKLER *was.*

Hey, come on, Blair. At least, he didn't actually applaud.

She goes out.

MICHAEL. Though I might have.

ABBY. Blair. I didn't actually *know* / that Michael –

BLAIR. What on the grounds that the only good Democrat is a defeated Democrat?

MICHAEL. Blair, surely this issue plays right into your hands.

BLAIR. How so?

MICHAEL. Pro-environment, pro-law and order, anti-gun.

BLAIR. Yeah, well. The problem is that Ms Polowski wasn't like protecting trees, but destroying them. Which would be tough enough had the guard been named Joe Sixpack.

MICHAEL. But as in fact he's Fernando Martinez . . .

BLAIR. . . . we discover that, far from lashing the environment to the community to safety, what this incident has done is to clamp the flag to the Latino vote to eco-terrorism to make my day. Result? Without Rebecca opening her mouth, we're five points down and falling.

MICHAEL. So how do you lash environment to community to security to crime?

ABBY. Come on, Michael, McKeene just did it.

BLAIR. Did she? How?

ABBY. Condos: keep out suburban hoi polloi. Dune buggies: stop noisy nouveaus strewing beer cans from their ATVs.

BLAIR. Well . . .

ABBY. And 'no tolerance for terrorism' is I guess, 'what's so wrong with Proposition Ninety-Two?'

BLAIR (*angry*). No, Abby, 'no tolerance for terrorism' does not mean 'what's so wrong with Ninety-Two?'

BLAIR*'s anger has thrown* ABBY. *Ameliorated, but firm:*

People have the right to preserve the character of the place they've chosen as their home.

MICHAEL. That's pretty much exactly what Ira Kitchen said
about living in a mock-Italian renaissance prison camp.

Enter TROY.

BLAIR. Oh, you saw Ira?

MICHAEL. Yes. He said he wasn't there.

BLAIR. You're sure of that?

MICHAEL. The feds are.

TROY. Then it must be true.

MICHAEL. Troy. This is / my partner Abby Pall-

TROY. So. Anybody finger me?

MICHAEL. Blair told you what I wanted.

TROY. When I promised to remove the thumbscrew.

MICHAEL. No, no one fingered you. Or anyone involved with
this campaign. And of course I didn't volunteer anybody's
name.

BLAIR *squeezes* MICHAEL'*s arm and goes out.*

TROY. And this is?

MICHAEL. Troy, this is my partner / Abby.

TROY. Presumably not on the scene in the early Seventies.

MICHAEL. No, obviously.

TROY. So she won't know what happens when a rumor gets
around you're a snitch. On the other hand, you do.

Slight pause.

MICHAEL. What do you mean?

TROY. And will thus remember, come an outbreak of informer
paranoia in the chapter – the cry was 'find the fag.' 'Cause
everybody knows, if you're good at hiding what you are,
hey, obviously, you're bound to be in covert government
employ.

MICHAEL. No, I / don't think –

TROY. But, hey, come on, you must have worked out who it was by now.

Pause.

MICHAEL. No, Troy, I haven't.

TROY. At least you've asked yourself the obvious question.

MICHAEL. No, I'm not so sure I have.

TROY. Why didn't they arrest us?

MICHAEL. Well . . .

TROY. The feds know of a criminal conspiracy? Which they ignore? Hello?

MICHAEL. Well, they didn't / quite ignore –

TROY. They needed to protect their source. And with due respect to you – though you don't deserve it – I think that means they went right to the top.

MICHAEL. You mean you think . . .

Enter SAM.

SAM. Troy, someone's asking about credit cards.

TROY. I'll be two minutes.

SAM. They are very rich and very pissed off about dogs on the beach and very nearly gone.

He goes out.

TROY. And now, what's going through Mike's mind? Well, mercy, what's become of Troy? From revolutionary internationalism to Not In My Back Yard.

MICHAEL. I didn't say / that.

TROY. And why? Because, you know what?, you don't start where people aren't. You don't start out saying: first, destroy yourself, you say: first, be yourself. You start with trash disposal *then* you move on to GM crops. You start with the fouling of the shoreline *then* the polluting of the planet. You do HMOs *then* HIV.

ABBY. And casinos? Immigration? The death penalty?

TROY. You start where people are. You start by saying: here we are, living in a stunning natural habitat / let's –

ABBY. Let's keep it that way.

TROY. Yes.

MICHAEL. Inch by inch, then mile by mile.

TROY. Well put.

MICHAEL. So, you think that the informer was Jack Sand or Claudia Perowne?

TROY. I thought you weren't volunteering names.

MICHAEL. Well, they've both been underground for thirty years. I doubt if they'll be using those names now.

TROY. Yes, Michael, I think that in the absence of a better explanation for our not having been arrested for conspiracy, that the snitch was Jack Sand or Claudia Perowne.

MICHAEL (*to* TROY). I'm sorry.

TROY. Why?

MICHAEL. You're right. I hadn't thought of the effect that this might have on other people.

TROY *is a little thrown.* MICHAEL*'s phone starts to ring.*

TROY. Well, how were you to know.

TROY *goes out.* MICHAEL *answers his phone.*

MICHAEL (*phone*). Hi there. Yes, it is.

Pause.

Yes, certainly.

He ends the call.

ABBY. Well, thank God.

MICHAEL. For what?

ABBY. You're in the clear.

MICHAEL. How so?

ABBY. If the snitch is underground, they're hardly likely to be volunteering evidence to the Senate Rules Committee next Thursday.

MICHAEL. Blair will be pleased.

ABBY. I'm pleased. As presumably this means you can come home.

Slight pause.

And we can sell your house, and buy our house, and move into a future of achievement and success.

Slight pause.

Assuming obviously that's what you want.

MICHAEL. Abs, I can't.

ABBY. You can't? Why ever not?

MICHAEL. I've got to find them.

ABBY. Why?

MICHAEL. Because of what Troy said.

ABBY. Mikey, Troy said that the snitch / was someone who –

MICHAEL. Because I don't think you start with dog shit and end up protesting acid rain.

ABBY. What?

MICHAEL. Because my fear is, you start out where people are, you end up staying there. You treat the people as the adults that they are, and tomorrow you get tough on terrorism and the next day you repeal the First Amendment. And I look at this and of course I think it's rainbow nimbyism and I look at Camp Ira which is ditto but without the rainbow but I wonder if we're any different. Inch by inch, for sure. Hey, we've got a manual corkscrew *and* I ride a bicycle. Just as long as there's no question of that extra mile.

ABBY. Then change it. Change us, Michael.

MICHAEL. But I've been here before. When we were up against a huge injustice and a genocidal war. And we found that moving from the inches to the miles meant living other people's lives, because if we lived our own we'd run back home to daddy. And that ends up with a body called Students for a Democratic Society meeting in of all years 1969 and splitting down the middle over whether we should live like Ho Chi Minh or Mao Tse Tung. And I've got to find out why that happened. Because otherwise I'd have to think that Ira Kitchen's right, that it's vanity to think you can turn water into wine, and all that happens is, the wine turns into blood. And I really don't want to think like Ira Kitchen, now or ever. And I don't care who betrayed us, any more. I need to know why we betrayed ourselves.

ABBY. This is Jack Sand.

MICHAEL. Yes. How do you know?

ABBY. You told me. One night when we'd got back at some absurd hour from the eighteenth Who or Grateful Dead abso-fucking-lutely final concert, and we were both so up we couldn't go to bed so we sat down at the table on the deck and you opened up a bottle of red wine.

And you told me what had kept you going, through the long bleak years, which was a vision of a place. A new, free territory, independent of the national or state government, where drug offenders and draft evaders would be harbored and protected, people would work in voluntary cooperatives, the economy would be sustainable and free wild kids would learn in open schools. Where people would reinvent themselves through others, they arrive there naked and alone, and they dress each other up as anyone they want to be.

And I made some predictable remark about human nature and who picks up the garbage, and you said 'no, this kind of happened.' In of all years 1914, in of all places Southern California. Where a guy who'd nearly won the LA mayor's race – on a platform of graduated income tax and the public ownership of all utilities – how this guy had led a group of settlers off into a desert valley, where they build a colony. With schools, a library, a laundry, a rug-making shop?, a sawmill and a rabbit farm. And every May Day they would march behind the red flag and they'd chant 'If you have two loaves of bread, sell one and buy a rose to feed your soul.'

MICHAEL. It was a hyacinth.

ABBY. And the local ranchers cut their water and they up and moved to Louisiana, and they built the same thing up again. And they kept it up for a quarter of a century, and by then maybe there was something else and someplace else and you said: 'All I need to know is that somewhere, there's a frontier to the future.'

You told me what Jack Sand had told you in the jail, as we sat around the table . . .

MICHAEL. And we drank . . . our wine.

Pause.

ABBY. So what happens now?

MICHAEL. What, you mean, / with whether I –

ABBY. I mean, your call.

MICHAEL. Oh, well. If . . . It's a Denny's parking lot on Five. Where I go and as I understand it I get 'docked' by what is called 'the backup crew.' And they take me to the people who I want to see.

ABBY. These important people.

MICHAEL (*thinking* ABBY *is being sarcastic*). Well, to me.

ABBY. To me as well.

MICHAEL. Uh, why . . . ?

ABBY. Because that was the night I fell in love with you.

Pause.

MICHAEL. Uh – huh.

ABBY. Mike, I read the file. There was a list of three things you guys were planning. It was springing somebody from prison, 'targeting' a politician, and a kidnapping? And one of them freaked you out because it was something you did. And for reasons I've just stated, I'd like to know which one.

MICHAEL. It was raining. It was in the Chapel of the Holy Sepulcher, in the Cathedral Church of St. John the Evangelist.

The people there were Jack Sand, Claudia Perowne, Blair, Troy, Cedric Baptiste, Sonny Crane and me.

It was all three.

Thunder and rain. Now we're in MICHAEL's *memory.* BLAIR *runs on. Around her, through the darkness,* KWESI *and* TROY *appear, with the young* SONNY CRANE. *Unseen as yet, upstage, are the young* JACK SAND *and* CLAUDIA PEROWNE. *The voices echo.* ABBY *watches until she is swallowed by the darkness.*

BLAIR (*to* MICHAEL). I'm sorry. Fuck, like I . . . Hey. Michael, sorry.

MICHAEL. Hey, it's cool.

BLAIR. Sorry, your name.

SONNY. So this is . . .

BLAIR. Like I didn't realize . . . I been like in the place with all the stalls and stuff.

TROY. Like how were you to know.

CLAUDIA *and* JACK *come forward – clearly the great couple, clearly in charge.*

CLAUDIA. And you room with Deborah Vine.

BLAIR (*with a glance to* MICHAEL). Yeah.

JACK. Daddy, the Republican candidate for Senate.

BLAIR. Sure. Right on.

JACK. Calls for cops on campuses. Calls for 'rioters' to be expelled. Send pushers to the chair.

TROY. Cesar Chavez is an enemy of the state.

CLAUDIA. Hey, man, she doesn't need a gut-check.

SONNY. So what exactly do you have in mind?

CLAUDIA. The proposal is to kidnap Deborah Vine and exchange her for Brother T.L. Trayton, prisoner of war.

KWESI picks up BLAIR's nervous alarm, and pulls MICHAEL aside.

KWESI. And this chick sets it up?

MICHAEL. That's right.

KWESI. And she's prepared to do this?

MICHAEL. Sure. Sure, she's prepared.

He looks to BLAIR who smiles nervously. Louder, for the rest of the group, but particularly for JACK.

'Cause hey, man, anybody's not prepared for people's war . . .

BLAIR. Objectively . . .

MICHAEL. . . . they're on the other side.

SONNY (*to* KWESI). So these honkies have a plan?

CLAUDIA. Of course we have a plan.

JACK. The operation is codenamed 'Endeavor'. The prisoner of war is 'Falcon'. He is held in the Penumbra. Our objective is to blast the Falcon out of lunar orbit and to bring him safely back to earth.

Suddenly, the Cathedral disappears. Dark figures in motorcycle helmets rush MICHAEL. Thunder and rain.

MICHAEL. Now you're presumably . . .

MICHAEL is pinioned, blindfolded, and his arms tied. The dark figures disappear. Now MICHAEL is stumbling and blundering through the rainforest, surrounded by huge, ancient trees. Although the storm is subsiding he is dripping wet. He doesn't know if anyone is still with him. All he can do is call out:

Hello! Hello! Is anybody there? Hey, guys, what's going on?

Something falls from above, near enough to splatter MICHAEL.

What?

He manages to pull one hand free. Voices from above:

AQUARIUS. Hey! Motherfucker!

MICHAEL. What's that?

FIREFLY. Hey, man, you a ranger?

MICHAEL (*pulling his blindfold off*). Hello?

SNOWBIRD. Pig alert!

HULA HOOP. Repel invaders!

Another projectile splatters to the ground beside him. It's human excrement.

MICHAEL. Uh . . . is this stuff what I think it is?

MICHAEL *moves back to avoid another projectile, and falls over a stump.*

Fuck.

Above MICHAEL, TREE-SITTERS *are rappelling down the trunks of the trees, while others are emerging from the forest.* NO SHIT, SNOWBIRD, RAINBOW *and* AQUARIUS *are under twenty-five.* FIREFLY *is nearer thirty.* HULA HOOP *is older.* MICHAEL *gets to his feet, realizes he's twisted his ankle.*

NO SHIT. Hey man, name, rank and number.

MICHAEL. What?

FIREFLY. Are you a ranger?

MICHAEL. No, I'm looking for some people.

AQUARIUS. Oh, what people?

SNOWBIRD. Ranger? He's a spy.

MICHAEL. Look. Look, I may be in the wrong . . .

NO SHIT. What people?

MICHAEL. A woman, around fifty-five . . .

RAINBOW. And does this woman have a name?

RAINBOW, FIREFLY, NO SHIT and AQUARIUS *are moving in on* MICHAEL.

MICHAEL. I kind of . . . I don't know.

NO SHIT. No shit.

HULA HOOP. And you?

MICHAEL. My name is Benjamin Michael Bern.

AQUARIUS. Hey, man. Consider yourself busted.

End of Act One.

ACT TWO

Scene One: Endeavor

The Forest. Now, dappled with rich late-afternoon sun.
MICHAEL sits, in his T-shirt and shorts, with a tarpaulin
draped around him – his sodden clothes and his shoulder bag
hang on a branch to dry. Having just finished a bowl of food,
he and ASH are watching NO SHIT, RAINBOW, SNOWBIRD
and HULA HOOP cheer their guest up with a rewritten
Christmas carol, accompanied by guitar. As we join them, the
carollers have reached the twelfth verse:

THE SONG. On the twelfth day of Christmas
   Conn Pacific gave to me . . .
   Twelve saws clear-cutting
   Eleven raiders strutting
   Ten assets strippin'
   Nine hippies trippin'
   Eight sitters shittin'
   Seven poisons spreading
   Six slopes a-sliding . . .
   Five 'Acts of God'
   Four spawning fish
   Three Doug Firs
   Two spotted owls
   And the last remaining old-growth redwood tree.

HULA HOOP. So. Any questions?

MICHAEL. No.

SNOWBIRD. All clear?

MICHAEL. Well . . .

HULA HOOP (*hand out*). Hi, I'm Hula Hoop.

MICHAEL. Hula Hoop.

ZEE – *the oldest of the men – enters with elements – a blanket, emblems – that will be the centerpiece of a ceremony later in the scene.*

RAINBOW (*introducing*). Rainbow.

MICHAEL. As in 'coalition'?

NO SHIT. No Shit.

MICHAEL. And you're . . .

ASH. 'No Shit' is his name.

ZEE *smiles and goes back out.* NO SHIT*'s cell phone rings. He answers it.*

NO SHIT (*phone*). What's up?

MICHAEL *looks questioningly at* SNOWBIRD.

SNOWBIRD. Snowbird.

MICHAEL. Snowbird.

SNOWBIRD. It was that or Rosebud.

NO SHIT (*phone*). Yeah, far out.

MICHAEL. Wasn't that a wooden sled?

SNOWBIRD. Yeah, right.

NO SHIT. Sure, bye.

NO SHIT *ends the call.*

SNOWBIRD. In the last frame of my father's favorite film.

NO SHIT. Base camp. They've heard there's another storm a-comin'. And they're on their way.

SNOWBIRD. Far out.

They're going. NO SHIT *turns back, to* MICHAEL*:*

NO SHIT. Hey, man, like I'm sorry 'bout the . . . uh.

MICHAEL. It's cool.

RAINBOW. We kinda thought you were the Man.

MICHAEL. Blindfold. Hands tied. Obviously.

NO SHIT. It's a long way down.

MICHAEL. No shit.

NO SHIT, RAINBOW *and* SNOWBIRD *leave. As she goes,* HULA HOOP *turns back to explain a little more to* MICHAEL.

HULA HOOP. We've had some hassle. People turning up with money and engaging rhetoric and ten good things to do with monkey wrenches.

MICHAEL. I was invited. And as no one briefed me on how to recognize a Pacific tree-frog, and whose ancestral lands we're on, and the whereabouts of – Blaydon?, and the lyrics of 'God Rest Ye / Merry Lumbermen . . . '

ASH. Michael, you know why they had to check / you out . . .

MICHAEL. I mean, if you'd been any longer I'd have started singing 'Kumbay-fucking-yah'.

A moment then ASH *gets it, and smiles.* HULA HOOP *picks this up also, but decides to leave* ASH *and* MICHAEL *together.*

HULA HOOP. These lands belong to the Yawelmani Yokut people.

She goes.

ASH. Michael, I explained. You were landed in the wrong spot.

MICHAEL. And the right spot . . . ?

ASH. I live up a tree three hundred yards away.

MICHAEL *standing, testing his ankle which still hurts.*

MICHAEL. So what's the story? I thought tree-sitting was a solitary occupation.

ASH. This is a village. It's the second anniversary of the first tree to be sat here. That's why there's so many folks around.

MICHAEL. Veterans of sedentary wars.

ASH. You try perching on a door slung between two branches two hundred feet up in the air.

MICHAEL (*with a gesture at his foot*). Oh sure. And how many people . . . uh, like, permanently . . . ?

ASH. Three or four. Rotating.

MICHAEL *dresses, as:*

MICHAEL. What, so Soybean and Sapling hand over the watch to Termite and Tofu?

ASH. Michael.

MICHAEL. And you?

ASH. Round these parts they call me Ash.

MICHAEL. And when you're not around these parts?

ASH. Well, as you might imagine, my identity has had to change from time to time, but usually it's someone who was born in the late Forties and who died before they learned to drive.

MICHAEL. I'm sorry?

ASH. Didn't you know this? It's how the communists did it in the Fifties. You go round cemeteries and you look for gravestones and you write off for birth certificates and to their posthumous surprise, little Frankie Flu or Mary Meningitis or Rosie Carwreck finds herself selling chicken wings in Madison Square Garden or organizing janitors in Buffalo or disguising herself as herself and planting a Tampax pack of Semtex in the ladies room of the Chicago Stock Exchange. And I sometimes wonder how they'd feel about being reborn as a guerilla fighter but then I sometimes wonder that about me. So really, Michael, there's no need to be discreet.

MICHAEL. What do you mean?

ASH. I mean, the meeting you're concerned about was seven people: you, me, Jack, Troy Practice, Cedric Baptiste and another Panther who I never got the name of.

MICHAEL. Yes.

ASH. And the woman who was going to lead us to the target.

MICHAEL. That's correct.

ASH. Who looked a whole lot like a younger version of somebody working for the Democratic candidate for Governor, but more on that later.

MICHAEL. And Ira?

ASH. Wasn't he trapped in the Midwest?

MICHAEL. That's right. I've seen him.

ASH. Well, I'll bet that was a blast. And what did Ced – . . . uh, Kwesi say?

MICHAEL. He told me I should tell you what he said.

ASH. And what was that?

MICHAEL. That you had abdicated from the struggle.

ASH. Is that all?

MICHAEL. What, all you abdicated from?

ASH. No, all he said.

MICHAEL. Well, he implied there'd been bad stuff underground.

ASH. Oh, yes? And did he mention me?

MICHAEL. He mentioned both of you.

ASH. But no specifics.

MICHAEL. Only that you were both alive.

ASH. No shit.

MICHAEL. In fact, of course, I'd assumed that / I was meeting both –

ASH. So you want to know what I know.

MICHAEL. Mainly because Troy Practice thinks / the only –

ASH. But first we need to talk about what you can do for me.

Slight pause.

MICHAEL Oh, yes, of course.

ASH. Michael, this puts me at some risk.

MICHAEL. Considerably, I'd say. Isn't the safest place for fugitives the suburbs?

ASH. Here, I'm a visitor.

MICHAEL. Yes, I want to ask you about 'here'.

ASH. Well, Michael, as it happens, 'here' is largely People United to Liberate the Planet. Which is an offshoot of the Gaia Fellowship, which itself outgrew Citizens for a Sustainable America.

MICHAEL. Yes?

ASH. One of the differences of opinion between PULP and its progenitors is that, although itself committed to non-violence, it refuses to condemn groups who take a different position. Which if Proposition Ninety-Two goes through will make it kinda hard to fundraise for. And even riskier to join.

MICHAEL. I agree with that.

ASH. Thus far the Democratic candidate has refused to disavow it.

MICHAEL. So, is this right? The notorious revolutionary outlaw Claudia Perowne wants me to – what? – persuade the Democratic candidate's consultant to come out against a ballot *proposition*?

ASH. Yes, but that's not all you've got to make her do. You've heard tell of Sarah Jane Polowski.

MICHAEL. Yes of course.

ASH. An unarmed young women who was shot dead in cold blood at close range by a security guard.

MICHAEL. Most of that statement is contested, as you know.

ASH. No shit.

MICHAEL. What isn't contested is that it's made it a whole lot harder – 'as it happens' – to come out against Prop. Ninety-Two.

ASH. Well darn it why didn't we think of that before.

Pause.

MICHAEL. 'We.'

ASH. 'Fraid so.

MICHAEL. 'Here.'

ASH. Not many people here know that.

MICHAEL. And you . . . No, that I shouldn't ask.

ASH. No, you have to. Well, I have to tell you. There is an activist called Sarah Jane Polowski . . .

MICHAEL. Claudia, I don't . . .

ASH. . . . who is living at a base camp called Nirvana. And she has an action planned, but she needs a person who is good at cutting fences, and so someone who's aware of my experience calls me. Which is as it happens no bad thing, as I'm kinda getting worried 'bout a vulnerable ID, quite impeccably suburban, but I'm getting funny looks from the tenor section of the neighborhood light opera society, so I accept the invitation in exchange for refuge someplace where I won't stand out if I go by a false name. So there I was and here I am and darn it, you're complicit in a felony.

MICHAEL. Why tell me this?

ASH. You know the pigs' line. She had a chainsaw. It was self-defense.

MICHAEL. Yes.

ASH. In fact, she dropped the chainsaw. As it happens, at the first shot. Which misses her as do shots two and three, on account of how she's running pretty darn fast now, when it looks as if she turned her ankle. By the fourth shot, she'd dropped down to the dirt. And she turns towards him and he shoots her in the chest. From I'd say around eight feet. Then

he goes back to get the chainsaw, lays it down beside her
and goes and calls the cops. So instead of one shot fired in
panic at an intruder with a chainsaw it's five bullets fired at
a woman with no chainsaw trying to run away.

MICHAEL. Is that remotely provable?

ASH. Only if somebody picked up the casings of the first four
bullets.

*ASH reveals she is wearing a necklace hung with four
bullet casings. She rattles it at* MICHAEL.

MICHAEL. But you'd need to . . .

ASH. Yup. Give evidence in court.

NO SHIT, HULA HOOP, RAINBOW, ZEE, FIREFLY,
AQUARIUS *and* SNOWBIRD *enter to prepare for their
ceremony.* NO SHIT *passes by* MICHAEL *and the detritus
of his meal.* MICHAEL *drops his voice:*

MICHAEL. You know she's ruled out any amnesty for
fugitives.

ASH. 'No tolerance for terrorists.' I know.

MICHAEL. So you want me to get a promise from McKeene
that she'll offer you a pardon in exchange for giving
evidence against the guard.

ASH. Well, darn it, the boy's there. So are you going to do
this, Michael?

NO SHIT. Hey man. You kinda left a disaster area here.

NO SHIT *starts tidying up* MICHAEL*'s meal, meticulously.*

MICHAEL. Uh, I'm sorry, I . . .

ASH. It's a habit. Leaving places the way you found them.

NO SHIT. For future reference, that feller on the branch down
there's a Pacific tree-frog.

He's finished tidying.

So there we are. All neat and shipshape.

MICHAEL. Thank you.

NO SHIT *hands* MICHAEL *his detritus in a bag.*

NO SHIT. You're welcome. And you're standing on the huckleberry.

MICHAEL. So what and where is Blaydon?

HULA HOOP. It's a town, below the Cougar River.

RAINBOW. Now, literally.

MICHAEL. Why?

ZEE. It was the victim of a landslide.

FIREFLY. Caused by clearcutting the Cougar Old Creek Grove.

MICHAEL. So who lives there?

NO SHIT. A lot of seriously muddy people.

HULA HOOP. Mainly loggers and ex-loggers and their families.

MICHAEL. And did people talk to them about the clearcut and the river?

ZEE. Yes, sure, we talk to loggers.

NO SHIT. Some loggers.

FIREFLY. The ones who'd like jobs to hand on to their kids. As opposed to / cutting . . .

NO SHIT. As opposed to ones who put up signs, 'Another Logger Pissed With PULP.'

ZEE. Oh, and who maybe like to fish a little on the weekend so it would be nice if there was coho in the stream.

NO SHIT. Or 'Save a Logger, Eat a Spotted Owl.'

ZEE. And who understand that if the understory's fucked by burning off the snag with diesel, then there goes their livelihood.

NO SHIT. No shit. So why / the fuck –

The TREE-SITTERS *laugh at* NO SHIT *saying* 'No shit.'
NO SHIT *smiles.* MICHAEL *intervenes.*

MICHAEL. So you wouldn't stop all logging? I mean, you're
not the ones who don't believe in any cut at all?

MICHAEL *has picked up that there's a division in the group.
For instance,* NO SHIT *doesn't believe in any cut at all.*

NO SHIT. Hey, man. Your momma's going to fall and die. That
means it's right to chop her down?

Pause. Laughter. This has avoided the issue.

SNOWBIRD. Like, respect your elders.

RAINBOW. Hands off Momma Cass.

MICHAEL. Momma Cass?

HULA HOOP. The mother tree.

MICHAEL. The Mother Tree?

SNOWBIRD. Each grove's a family.

HULA HOOP. Of course it's got a mother tree.

MICHAEL. How do you tell?

AQUARIUS. You can hear them.

MICHAEL. Hear the trees?

HULA HOOP. Yes, and they can hear each other.

AQUARIUS. That's how they know that one has died.

MICHAEL. Uh . . . they can tell . . . ?

Pause. Everyone smiles cherubically at MICHAEL.

Even if . . . there's no one there.

RAINBOW. Oh, man. There's always someone there.

NO SHIT. 'Cause hey, like, trees are people too.

Pause.

FIREFLY. But of course this guy's a baby boomer brought up
in the Sixties. 'Wow, man, off the pig.' Hey, he spent his

adolescence taking on the running dogs of US Imperialism.
Or was it paper tigers? Whatever, of course this isn't serious.

MICHAEL. I didn't say that.

FIREFLY. No.

MICHAEL. But I'd sure like to hear the reasons why it is.

RAINBOW. What, now?

MICHAEL. Yes, now.

RAINBOW. You mean, like . . .

MICHAEL. I mean like, presumably, when you talk to loggers,
the idea is to win them over.

FIREFLY. So, 'win you over'?

MICHAEL. Yeah.

The TREE-SITTERS *look at each other. They haven't made
their case to outsiders for a while.*

RAINBOW. Well, like . . . there's the issue of who owns the
land.

MICHAEL. The – Yokut people.

RAINBOW. I was thinking of Connecticut Pacific.

SNOWBIRD. Huh.

MICHAEL (*to* SNOWBIRD). What's their story?

SNOWBIRD. Yeah, well . . .

ZEE. Old family firm. Started out back east.

HULA HOOP. No unions, but workers' rights, and putting
loggers' kids through college.

MICHAEL (*to* FIREFLY). Good firm?

FIREFLY. Good as a logging firm can be.

NO SHIT. Which isn't very.

ZEE. They never logged more than they grew.

SNOWBIRD. 'They' grew.

MICHAEL (*to* NO SHIT). So what went wrong?

NO SHIT. Oh, a corporate raider rides on in from Arizona with a pile of junk bonds.

MICHAEL. And?

NO SHIT. A pretty smile.

MICHAEL (*to* SNOWBIRD). And then?

SNOWBIRD. They say 'yes, please.'

MICHAEL. Who's they?

SNOWBIRD. The family.

MICHAEL (*to* FIREFLY). And then what happens?

FIREFLY. Well, the raider drains the pension fund, rips off the assets, sells off some of his old-growth to the government . . .

HULA HOOP. The pretty parts.

SNOWBIRD. Near to the freeway.

RAINBOW. National Tree Museum.

ZEE. And sets to clearcut the rest.

NO SHIT. And the family decides to use its ill-gotten gains to bankroll a run for governor.

SNOWBIRD (*sarcastic*). Right on.

FIREFLY. While Connpac expands into Chile, Canada and Thailand.

ASH. So it's hard to say that taking on Connecticut Pacific's 'liquidating the class nature of the struggle.'

HULA HOOP. When it's operating at its cutting edge.

MICHAEL. OK, but in the Sixties we thought we were creating an alternative / to the existing –

AQUARIUS. You know, sound moves at fifteen cycles per second through the air. In the forest it's three cycles.

MICHAEL. So?

AQUARIUS. So, yes, of course you can hear the trees.

Pause.

And we give the places names like Huckleberry Grove because otherwise they're Unit Five of THP Six-Seventy and a tree that started growing before Columbus is an estimate of a number of board feet. Forest names are for security. Some are chosen for you, some you choose yourself. But either way, your new name makes you a new person, so you trust each other, and you don't need leaders to tell you what to do.

MICHAEL. Yes, I remember.

AQUARIUS. And, as it happens, if I'd heard tell of a time of struggle and resistance, people operating at the outer edge of everything, knowing if they didn't build the future then it wouldn't happen, making a last stand, then I'd say, darn it, ain't that just like now.

MICHAEL. We didn't trust anybody over thirty.

AQUARIUS. Sure, and we respect our elders.

MICHAEL. We wanted to reject our parents.

ASH. Kill our parents.

AQUARIUS. And we listen to the Mother Tree.

MICHAEL. People starting out from where they are.

AQUARIUS. Not stopping there.

MICHAEL. No gut-checking.

AQUARIUS. Less gut-checking.

MICHAEL. Not giving up yourself.

AQUARIUS. But becoming a new person.

MICHAEL. What, like we . . .

AQUARIUS. And if you have two loaves of bread, sell one . . .

MICHAEL. . . . and buy a hyacinth to feed your soul.

AQUARIUS. 'Fraid so.

Pause.

MICHAEL. So what's your name?

AQUARIUS. So what's your name?

MICHAEL. It's Michael.

AQUARIUS. It *was* Michael.

RAINBOW. Hey he's 'Running Dog'.

FIREFLY. He's 'Paper Tiger'.

MICHAEL. Let's call it 'Paper Dog'. So what's your name?

AQUARIUS. When I first came to the forest, I was Poppyseed.

MICHAEL. And then?

AQUARIUS. Uh . . . Dreadlock.

MICHAEL. Then?

AQUARIUS. Aquarius.

MICHAEL. The age?

AQUARIUS. The spaceship.

MICHAEL. Yes. In which you fly off to the front line of the future.

AQUARIUS. Yes.

Slight pause.

SNOWBIRD. My father says the difference between trees and people is that trees have roots which bind them to the place they started. Whereas people are like birds with wings who can fly off anywhere they want.

MICHAEL. 'Snowbird.'

SNOWBIRD. Yeah, right.

MICHAEL *turns back to* AQUARIUS.

MICHAEL. So how does this go wrong?

BRANFLAKE *enters. She is in her thirties, carrying bags of provender, currently angry.*

BRANFLAKE. What's happening?

ZEE. What?

BRANFLAKE. Tie-Dye says there are new people. Where are these new people?

RAINBOW. These are they.

SNOWBIRD. They're cool.

BRANFLAKE. 'They're cool.' How do you know that?

NO SHIT. We checked them out.

BRANFLAKE. Amazing. Rather than asking them to leave.

Pause.

MICHAEL. Is there a problem?

NO SHIT. But then like he wouldn't recognize a Pacific tree-frog.

BRANFLAKE. Unbelievable. He looks like he's a federal agent, he knows like zilch about the forest, he drifts by and you welcome him with open arms. I mean, you know?

MICHAEL. I was invited here.

BRANFLAKE. By whom, may I inquire?

ASH. By me?

BRANFLAKE. And you are?

ASH. Ash.

BRANFLAKE. In-fucking-credible. And who invited 'Ash'?

ASH (*nodding to* HULA HOOP). She did.

HULA HOOP. So there's a problem here?

BRANFLAKE (*to* MICHAEL). I'm sorry. What was your name again?

MICHAEL. What's yours?

BRANFLAKE. It's Branflake. And for sure there is a fucking problem here.

Pause.

ZEE. What is it?

BRANFLAKE. Oh, only, first this woman shows up out of nowhere.

HULA HOOP. She's not out of nowhere.

BRANFLAKE. And just after a GM crop protest which turns into a chainsaw massacre, in the middle of a governor's election, hey, great timing, huh? Like how much would Connpac love it if they could tar us all with 'eco-terrorism,' now, you know? And so the thing we absolutely need is some guy named – what was it? Baklava or Bandana, with dreadlocks, Birkenstocks and free dope for all, going 'hey, man, what about the good old days when a spike's a long thin metal thing discovered by a sawmill worker in a tree?' Like an obvious provocation at two hundred paces on a cloudy day? Like people welcoming this guy with open arms, like you could describe as sabotage? Like you ask like which side are they on, objectively, you know?

HULA HOOP. This guy's not Bandana.

NO SHIT. Hey, they're cool.

BRANFLAKE. They're 'cool'.

HULA HOOP. They've got nowhere else to go.

BRANFLAKE. And neither of them was involved in any way in the circumstances . . . in what happened, like, with Sarah Jane . . . 'cause like if they were then they're outta here, you know, like now?

HULA HOOP. No, neither of them was involved with what happened to Witchhazel.

Pause.

BRANFLAKE. 'Consensus'?

She looks round the group. There is consensus.

FIREFLY. Yup.

BRANFLAKE. You know, the big mistake was letting guys back in.

BRANFLAKE goes and joins the group. ASH and MICHAEL are left alone. Drumming begins. Maybe there is singing. The TREE-SITTERS *form a circle round the shrine, beginning to hum and sway.*

MICHAEL (*Hula Hoop*). Good liar.

ASH. Yup.

MICHAEL. Why were the guys excluded?

ASH. I don't know.

MICHAEL. Was the view that they were more aggressive? More prone to laying heavy leader trips on people?

ASH. Well, we recognize the syndrome.

MICHAEL. But she's saying, this time, it'll all be different?

ASH. Who's she?

MICHAEL. Your daughter.

Slight pause.

She talks like you. She acts like you.

Slight pause.

And, am I right, Aquarius was the lunar module of Apollo Thirteen? The spaceship got them back to earth?

ASH. Michael, since I finished breastfeeding this is the ninth time that I've seen my daughter.

Pause.

MICHAEL. So who brought her up?

ASH. I have a terrible confession.

MICHAEL. Yes?

ASH. My daughter was raised by a woman known as Hula Hoop.

They both crack up.

MICHAEL. And is Jack her father?

Slight pause.

ASH. Yes.

MICHAEL. And does he... / see her –

ASH. No.

MICHAEL. But you know where he is?

ASH. Yes. I know where he is.

ASH looks at MICHAEL, firmly cutting off any further questions. MICHAEL acknowledges. Changing the subject:

Didn't you get married? Have a child?

MICHAEL. A son. Who I've hardly seen since his mother left me, took him back east, and persuaded him that I'd failed her and him and me.

ASH. And had you?

MICHAEL. Let's say, when I signed up to the real world, I got the pain but not the gain. Though that's about to change.

ASH. Oh, why?

MICHAEL. I've been asked to rescue the great utopian experiment of postwar education.

ASH. And it wouldn't help if anybody knew about your misspent youth.

MICHAEL. No, it wouldn't. But that's not the reason I'm here.

ASH. Oh?

MICHAEL. Or rather, it's not the reason any more.

Pause.

ASH. You want to know what happened underground. Deep down, you wish you'd lived like us and you've heard it all went wrong and you need to find out why. And now you've seen this, you want to know if this can go wrong too.

MICHAEL. Yes.

ASH *sees* AQUARIUS *and* SNOWBIRD *approach.*

ASH. The GM poplars action. She supported it. She agreed
with it. But she doesn't know I did it. So she's not complicit
in a felony and that's how I'd like it to remain.

SNOWBIRD *and* AQUARIUS *arrive.*

SNOWBIRD. Hey, like the consensus is, you're here, you join.

ASH. What, both of us?

AQUARIUS. 'Fraid so.

SNOWBIRD *and* AQUARIUS *lead* MICHAEL *and* ASH *to
join the circle that is forming round the shine.*

ZEE. What are we gathered here to do?

SNOWBIRD. To name this place.

ZEE (*to* BRANFLAKE). What is its name?

He turns to FIREFLY.

What is its name?

FIREFLY. Witchhazel Grove.

ZEE. So let us speak our names.

AQUARIUS. Aquarius.

HULA HOOP. Hula Hoop.

NO SHIT. No Shit.

RAINBOW. Rainbow.

BRANFLAKE. Branflake.

SNOWBIRD. Snowbird.

FIREFLY. Firefly.

ZEE. Zee.

ASH. Ash.

MICHAEL *doesn't want to say his name.*

(*An order.*) Michael.

MICHAEL. Paper Dog.

ZEE. Now let us speak the names of the living beings that surround us.

Each TREE-SITTER *goes to the tree they name and touches it.*

SNOWBIRD. Evergreen.

RAINBOW. Shiva.

HULA HOOP. Magic Dragon.

AQUARIUS. Protect you, Magic Dragon.

NO SHIT. Cleopatra.

SNOWBIRD. Love you, Cleopatra.

BRANFLAKE *goes to the mother tree. She looks questioningly.*

AQUARIUS. Momma Cass.

BRANFLAKE. Momma Cass.

FIREFLY. Momma Cass.

ASH *goes to a tree.*

ASH. What's this tree called?

FIREFLY. It doesn't have a name.

ZEE. You choose.

Slight pause.

ASH. Endeavor.

SNOWBIRD. That's like another spaceship?

ASH. Among other things.

ZEE. Now let us speak the names of our dead.

A moment. To start:

My daughter Sky Sarah, died of asthma, seven years of age.

RAINBOW. OK. My brother Nelson, died in a car wreck at the age of seventeen.

FIREFLY. David William Mackintosh a.k.a. Snafu. Fallen one-hundred-fifty feet, gave his life for the Scquoia Forest.

NO SHIT. Joy. Killed by person or persons unknown October 2000.

MICHAEL (*to* ASH). Is Joy a . . . ?

FIREFLY (*hearing*). Joy was a Douglas Fir.

RAINBOW. Ursa Major. Six-hundred-plus years old. Killed by employees of the Northwestern logging company.

HULA HOOP. All the many creatures who lived around her and inside her.

The circle waits for BRANFLAKE *to name Sarah Jane Polowski. A moment, then she does:*

BRANFLAKE. Witchhazel. Murdered by Fernando Martinez seven days ago.

NO SHIT. We love you, Witchhazel.

AQUARIUS. We love you, Branflake.

SNOWBIRD. My aunt Debbie. Pancreatic cancer. 1976.

Pause. ZEE *assumes that's it.*

ZEE. Let be. Let go.

ASH (*a decision*). I'm sorry, I've got someone.

ZEE. Yes?

ASH. He was killed in an autocrash five miles south of Devine, Texas on December 16, 1981. From the amount of liquor in his bloodstream, it was hard to consider it an accident. As it happens, it was not so considered.

ZEE. And his name?

ASH. Jack Sand.

MICHAEL. But . . . Jack Sand's still alive.

ASH. I'm sorry.

In fact, that was said to MICHAEL, *but* ZEE *chooses to read it as an apology to the group.*

ZEE. It's OK. We were done.

The circle breaks up.

RAINBOW. So shall we fix the food?

NO SHIT. There's supposed to be another storm.

BRANFLAKE. Who's on lookout?

NO SHIT. Tie-Dye. Then it's me.

ZEE, BRANFLAKE, NO SHIT, HULA HOOP, FIREFLY, SNOWBIRD *and* RAINBOW *go out, leaving* AQUARIUS *for a moment, with* MICHAEL *and* ASH.

AQUARIUS. Let be. Let go.

AQUARIUS *goes out.*

MICHAEL. What happened, Claudia?

ASH. What, to Jack?

MICHAEL. To you.

ASH. To me? Our greatest fear.

MICHAEL. Go on.

ASH. You know it.

Pause.

That the thing you see – the thing you want back – that revolutionary love we all felt, not as often as we'd like, but, oh, enough . . . it's that leads to the witch hunts and the purges and the burnings at the stake. That it did so in the Thirties, in Russia. In the Forties, for your parents. In the Sixties, us. And now, who knows.

MICHAEL. You don't think this. You know this.

Slight pause. ASH *takes an old envelope of papers wrapped in plastic from her bag.*

ASH. Every fugitive keeps something permanent. However dangerous. I mean, for Christ's sake, some people got tattoos. Some others, kept photographs or family jewelry.

She opens up the plastic covering and then the envelope,
taking out the papers.

This is the transcript of a meeting held by Bad Moon
Underground in 1980. I would prefer to confess to anything
but this. I would prefer to tell you what I think you want to
know.

MICHAEL. What's that?

ASH. That I was the informer.

MICHAEL. And you're saying that / you're not –

ASH (*interrupts*). Just read it, Michael.

> MICHAEL *starts to read the transcript out:*

MICHAEL. 'Q: Please state your name. A: You know my
name. Q: Please state your name. A: You mean my party
name? Q: You are suspended from the party. State your real
name. Blank, blank.'

ASH. Obviously.

MICHAEL. This is the transcript of – what, an interrogation?

ASH. Yes.

MICHAEL. And Q is Jack?

ASH. Read on.

MICHAEL. 'Q: Let us begin with the plan you hatched with
other members of the Right Opportunist Faction for the
Liquidation of the Underground.'

> *He shakes his head in disbelief at the language.*

And you say . . .

ASH (*memory*). 'There was no faction. There was no plot.'

MICHAEL. And he asks: 'Are you denying that you were the
author of the counter-revolutionary polemic *By Any Means
Feasible*?' And you say:

ASH. 'No, I am the author.' But I don't.

MICHAEL. You mean you aren't.

ASH. No, I mean you're reading it the wrong way round.

MICHAEL *reads the next question, the other way round. As he does so,* JACK SAND *appears, in the 'normal' clothes he wore as a fugitive in 1980.*

MICHAEL. You. 'Then let me ask you once again . . . '

ASH (*continues, from memory*). 'Then let me ask you once again about your plot to liquidate the revolutionary character of Bad Moon Underground?'

MICHAEL. 'That's not the way I'd put it.'

ASH. 'Then how would you put it?'

MICHAEL. 'I would say . . . '

JACK. . . . I was trying to initiate a conversation.

MICHAEL *turns the page.*

MICHAEL. You: 'In conversation with a comrade you were / heard to say …'

ASH. ' … 'we can't go on beating up on the working masses for not being lesbians.' What did you mean by this?'

JACK. It was a private joke.

MICHAEL *turns the page.*

MICHAEL. 'Do you admit …'

ASH. ' …. that these deviations form a pattern of opportunism and sensationalism in your work which stretches back to your advocacy of alliance with Black Revolutionary Leadership in a strategy of Custeristic Terrorism?'

JACK. Excuse me? 'Custeristic'?

ASH. 'How would you describe the plot to liberate Comrade T.L. Trayton from the clutches of the enemy?'

JACK. I'd describe it as a fuck-up.

ASH. 'Do you think that word is adequate?'

JACK. What word would you prefer?

ASH. 'Try saying it. My actions were objectively destructive of the party and its works.'

MICHAEL. 'Try saying it.'

ASH. 'Try saying it. The party is a revolutionary organization, thus to sabotage it is objectively to promote the counter-revolution.'

JACK *starts to sing the chant from 'Hey Jude'.*

MICHAEL. Just say it.

ASH. 'Just say it. I'm the enemy.'

MICHAEL. Objectively.

ASH. 'Say: Objectively, I was on the other side.'

Singing to blot out Claudia's words, JACK *disappears into the darkness.*

MICHAEL. And did he?

ASH. Did he what?

MICHAEL. Confess.

ASH. Yes, he confessed.

MICHAEL. You mean . . .

ASH. I mean, that I destroyed your hero.

MICHAEL. And you're sure he wasn't . . .

ASH. . . . what, the snitch? No more than me.

MICHAEL. Claudia …

ASH. So what went wrong? I'll tell you. What goes wrong is people telling people that 'objectively, they're on the other side.'

MICHAEL. Well, sure.

ASH. Did you hear her? 'I mean, the folks who welcomed – whatsisname, Bandana? Like you could describe as sabotage? Like which side are they really on? Like objectively, you know?'

MICHAEL. But 'Bandana' was on the other side.

ASH. Sure. Like the person who informed on you.

Slight pause.

So what am I describing. There is a wrong to right. You
march. You petition. Hey, you write your congressman.
Laws are passed. They are evaded or ignored. You go to
court. By the time you get there it's too late. You take a
little direct action. You get beat up. You create a culture to
encourage your supporters to continue getting beat up.
Increasingly you find yourself up against the law, not least
because the law makes what you do increasingly illegal.
While at the same time, anybody else who supports or helps
you gets to become a criminal themselves. You are isolated.
You are infiltrated. You're afraid. So what happens? You
turn into the thing the other side wants you to be. You don't
sell out to the FBI, you *become* the FBI. You turn against
yourselves. Now do you see why it's important that
Fernando Martinez gets charged? Now do you see why
Proposition Ninety-Two must fall? So my daughter isn't
turned into a criminal for supporting people who pursue
their ends by force? So this doesn't keep on happening?

Enter NO SHIT.

NO SHIT. Hey, guys. This is a bust.

*Suddenly, sound and light: searchlights, blaring music,
helicopters. It's a raid by* SECURITY MEN.

I'm up Geronimo.

He disappears.

ASH. What's up?

BRANFLAKE, HULA HOOP, FIREFLY *and* ZEE *rush in.*

BRANFLAKE. It's a bust.

ASH. Who?

ZEE. Private security.

MICHAEL. It's not . . .

ASH. Let's hope not.

HULA HOOP. I'm going back up Methuselah.

FIREFLY. There's no time.

ASH (*grabs the document from* MICHAEL). I gotta go.

> ASH *searching for her bag. Enter* SNOWBIRD *and*
> RAINBOW.

SNOWBIRD. They're coming up the other path!

MICHAEL. So you knew the snitch wasn't Jack.

ASH. Oh, yes.

ZEE. What about the drybed?

> RAINBOW *runs out with* SNOWBIRD.

MICHAEL. And there's only one way you could know that.

RAINBOW. Looks like they haven't found it.

MICHAEL. If you knew who the snitch was.

HULA HOOP. It's got cover.

ASH. So, Michael, are you going to do this thing for me?

ZEE. Let's *go*.

> SNOWBIRD *and* RAINBOW *run back on.*

SNOWBIRD. There's ten of them coming up there.

ASH. Michael, ask yourself these questions.

ZEE. Armed?

RAINBOW. Hey you know we didn't stop to ask.

> RAINBOW *runs out.*

ASH. What did Kwesi know? Why did he insist you told me
exactly what he said? And what he wanted you to think and
why.

BRANFLAKE. So who's up trees?

SNOWBIRD. Tic-Dye's up Crazy Horse.

ASH (*calls*). Hey, where's Aquarius?

FIREFLY. Don't know.

She runs out with SNOWBIRD.

BRANFLAKE (*to* MICHAEL). So what about you?

MICHAEL. I'm OK. (*To* ASH.). You know who did it.

HULA HOOP. He's a kidnap victim.

BRANFLAKE. What?

ZEE. Let's go.

ASH. If I knew, it's not my secret to reveal...

ZEE. Now!

ASH. Michael. You have the power to right a wrong. Do it.

She runs out with ZEE *and* BRANFLAKE.

HULA HOOP. Michael.

MICHAEL. You're right. I was kidnapped. Go.

SNOWBIRD *runs in.*

SNOWBIRD. Too late. They're all round Hemlock Grove. Hey, what about . . .

MICHAEL. Just go.

HULA HOOP. I'll . . .

MICHAEL. Go.

SNOWBIRD. Good luck, Paper Dog.

HULA HOOP *and* SNOWBIRD *run out.* MICHAEL *is alone.*

MICHAEL. I don't know how I got here. I don't know where I am.

NIGHTHAWK *enters. He's in his fifties, with one bad arm. He holds a Ruger Mini-14 rifle and he has a revolver in his belt.*

NIGHTHAWK. Freeze. Hands on your head. Turn around.

MICHAEL *obeys all these instructions.* NIGHTHAWK *speaks into his radio:*

Nighthawk to Arab.

We hear the squawk of ARAB*'s reply.*

ARAB. I hear you, Nighthawk.

MICHAEL. Look, I . . .

NIGHTHAWK. Hey, got me a hugger here.

ARAB. Any others? We got dozens runnin' round.

MICHAEL. Look, in fact . . .

NIGHTHAWK. No, just one. You want me to hold him for yer?

ARAB. What condition?

NIGHTHAWK. Wounded.

ARAB. Hold him.

NIGHTHAWK. Sure will. Nighthawk out.

NIGHTHAWK *clicks off the radio.*

Everybody's busy. I'm holding you.

MICHAEL. Are you the cops?

NIGHTHAWK. Forest Security. But if you're asking, 'is this guy arresting me?', this guy's arresting you. And the sheriff's headed up from town.

MICHAEL. Um . . . I'm not the only one.

NIGHTHAWK. Oh no?

Suddenly, something attracts NIGHTHAWK*'s attention. He turns towards it.*

MICHAEL. What's that?

NIGHTHAWK *raises the rifle into a firing position.*

Hey, man . . .

NIGHTHAWK. Stay still.

NIGHTHAWK *fires past* MICHAEL. *A screaming sound.*

MICHAEL. What the fuck –

MICHAEL *tries to hobble away.* NIGHTHAWK *fires again.*
The rifle jams.

NIGHTHAWK. Shit. I said, don't move.

MICHAEL. OK.

NIGHTHAWK *tosses the rifle on the ground, takes out his
revolver, goes over to the screaming animal in the
undergrowth and shoots it dead.*

Uh . . .

NIGHTHAWK. Raccoon. Rabid.

NIGHTHAWK *shakes his bad arm. He turns the revolver
on* MICHAEL.

Aha. Thoughts of the Ducksqueezer. This guy's jammed his
Mini, and hey he's got a busted arm. So maybe my odds
ain't so bad here. 'Specially if one of my fellow daisy-
munchers chooses to drop by.

MICHAEL. No, I wasn't thinking that.

NIGHTHAWK (*still aiming at* MICHAEL). Oh, no?

MICHAEL. And they're not . . . my 'fellow daisy-munchers.'

NIGHTHAWK (*still aiming at* MICHAEL). Sure.

MICHAEL. I mean, hell, do I look like . . . one of them?

NIGHTHAWK *lowers the revolver.*

NIGHTHAWK. So, what's the story?

MICHAEL. Could say, I'm a passerby.

NIGHTHAWK. So, you mean, you don't even have a funny
name?

MICHAEL. No, Nighthawk, I don't even have a funny name.

Pause. NIGHTHAWK *laughs. Then:*

NIGHTHAWK. Hey, 'passerby.' Know anything 'bout guns?

MICHAEL. No.

NIGHTHAWK. You're about to learn.

NIGHTHAWK *keeps* MICHAEL *covered with the revolver.*

MICHAEL. Uh, what . . . ?

NIGHTHAWK. Take the Ruger. Then sit down.

MICHAEL *takes the rifle and sits, follows* NIGHTHAWK'*s instructions.*

Watch that muzzle, keep it pointing up. There's a hot round in there.

MICHAEL. So you're still holding me?

NIGHTHAWK. We'll discuss it with the sheriff. Now take out the magazine.

MICHAEL. It's stuck.

NIGHTHAWK. Go easy. Push that lever by the trigger guard.

MICHAEL. Uh, how do I . . .

NIGHTHAWK. Your thumb.

MICHAEL. Done it.

NIGHTHAWK. Good boy. Pull the slide handle all the way back and hold it.

MICHAEL *pulls the slide handle.*

MICHAEL. What now?

NIGHTHAWK. Now press the bolt lock plunger, that little pin sticks up to the left.

MICHAEL. I got it.

NIGHTHAWK. Sure it's pressed?

MICHAEL. Sure as I can be.

NIGHTHAWK. Now ease off slow and let's see if she'll hold.

MICHAEL. What if she doesn't?

NIGHTHAWK. You don't want to know.

The plunger holds.

MICHAEL. OK.

NIGHTHAWK. Now look down the breach.

MICHAEL. There's a bullet in there.

NIGHTHAWK. Whatdja know. Now very gently, ease the round out, with your fingernail . . .

MICHAEL. You're serious?

NIGHTHAWK. I'm serious.

MICHAEL. OK . . .

He dislodges the bullet.

I've done it.

NIGHTHAWK. Now put the cartridge down in front of you.

He goes to pick up the cartridge.

'Know I can do that in the pitch dark with one hand.

MICHAEL. Oh, yeah?

NIGHTHAWK. You can say it. 'Well, you'll need to.'

MICHAEL. So what do I do now?

NIGHTHAWK. Look down the muzzle.

MICHAEL *moving to look from the slide end.*

Other end.

MICHAEL *nervously looks down the barrel from the other end.*

MICHAEL. Nothing.

NIGHTHAWK. Right.

NIGHTHAWK *takes a cleaning kit from his belt, takes out a set of rods and quickly and skillfully assembles them into a single long rod. As he does this:*

MICHAEL. I'd sure . . . I'd sure like to hear what happened to your arm?

NIGHTHAWK *considers this. Then:*

NIGHTHAWK. Ever heard of a company called Connecticut Pacific?

MICHAEL. Sure.

NIGHTHAWK. Got taken over.

MICHAEL. By some guys from Arizona.

NIGHTHAWK. Right. And they speed up the cut, and I'm setting choke-chain, log rolls on me, and smashes up my arm. Old management, they'd'a found me somewhere light and easy in the mill. New management, they fire me.

MICHAEL. Shit. What happens then?

NIGHTHAWK. I buy a tract of land.

MICHAEL. Oh yeah?

NIGHTHAWK. But the only way to make a living out of legal vegetation is to pay your debt off first by growing something else.

MICHAEL. What, dope?

NIGHTHAWK. Let's just say, when the Bureau of Land Management goes in for aerial surveillance, I'm forced to undertake some speedy and economically irrational crop rotation.

MICHAEL. Bad.

NIGHTHAWK. Then I lose my irrigation on account of the Fish and Wildlife wanting to protect some endangered sucker-fish upstream.

MICHAEL. Bummer.

NIGHTHAWK. And my tract of land is now owned by First Mutual of Houston.

He hands the rod to MICHAEL.

MICHAEL. What do I do with this?

NIGHTHAWK. You ease the rod down the muzzle till you feel something.

MICHAEL. Uh, is this safe?

NIGHTHAWK. Safer than what you were doing three minutes back.

MICHAEL (*as he pushes the rod down the muzzle*). And now you're protecting the property of the folks who fired you.

The jammed bullet dislodges and the rod slides through to the magazine well. MICHAEL *removes the bullet and hands it and the rod to* NIGHTHAWK.

Hey. Done it.

NIGHTHAWK. You know, I can field strip that mother down to the stock and put it back together in forty-seven seconds.

MICHAEL. Yeah. Sure.

Pause.

NIGHTHAWK. One day, I'm gonna get me back my tract of land.

MICHAEL. You are?

NIGHTHAWK. And I'm gonna build a fence around it and inside I'm gonna build me a new place to be.

MICHAEL. Oh, yeah?

Slight pause.

NIGHTHAWK. An independent state, seceded from the federal government. An association of independent men and women, who fear God and no one else, and who live towards their dream.

MICHAEL. What's that?

NIGHTHAWK. No drivers' licenses, IDs, birth certificates, social security. No taxes – voluntary tithes. Citizens' juries make the laws, based on the common law of England. Home schooling. Develop our own language. Produce our own money. Citizens' militias guard our borders from the gangs and ghetto-trash and the one-world conspirators who direct their actions. Inside, a free republic of free white citizens, liberated from the chains of federal tyranny. Whatja think of that?

MICHAEL. Uh – no.

MICHAEL *clicks the magazine back into the rifle.*

NIGHTHAWK. Gimme the rifle.

MICHAEL. Are you arresting me?

NIGHTHAWK. Looks like it.

MICHAEL. No.

NIGHTHAWK. No, what?

MICHAEL. You can't have that.

NIGHTHAWK (*with his revolver*). I'm faster than you, boy.

MICHAEL. No, I don't mean the rifle.

AQUARIUS. Hey! Paper Dog!

RAINBOW. Hey! Paper Dog!

Suddenly, NO SHIT *appears at the side.* RAINBOW *and* AQUARIUS *swing down on their ropes.* MICHAEL *drops the rifle, flings himself at* NIGHTHAWK, *knocking him down.* NIGHTHAWK's *radio falls a little way away from him.* MICHAEL *grabs the revolver, stands and moves back, hobbling.*

MICHAEL. Fuck.

NO SHIT. What's the matter?

MICHAEL. Ankle.

AQUARIUS. Hang in there, man.

NIGHTHAWK. Hey, uh . . .

RAINBOW (*reaching out for one of the guns*). Do you want me . . .

MICHAEL. No.

Keeping NIGHTHAWK *covered,* MICHAEL *goes and picks up* NIGHTHAWK's *radio, throwing it to* RAINBOW *who*

pockets it. AQUARIUS *takes the revolver and covers*
NIGHTHAWK. NO SHIT *strips* NIGHTHAWK *of his*
ammunition belt and equipment. As he speaks, MICHAEL
dismantles the rifle as quickly as he can.

I'm sorry. You can't have it.

NIGHTHAWK. Excuse me?

MICHAEL. You can't have that place. It's ours.

NIGHTHAWK. It's yours?

MICHAEL. And it wasn't just for patriots, and certainly not
just for whites. It wasn't about concocting fantasies about
sinister conspiracies between the secret masters of the
universe and the wretched of the earth.

In fact, it was for the wretched of the earth. And maybe
about making somewhere where they didn't have to be that
way. A haven of resistance to all tyrants and all states. It
doesn't yet exist, but we've been that close, and I want to
live as if it could. So you can't have it. Sorry.

He's finished disabling the rifle. He tosses the pieces aside.
He takes the revolver from AQUARIUS, *empties out the*
rounds, throwing the revolver down on a pile with the rest
of NIGHTHAWK'*s disabled weaponry. To* AQUARIUS:

We've got forty-seven seconds to get out of here.

AQUARIUS. OK.

MICHAEL. Will you see Ash?

AQUARIUS. Sure will.

MICHAEL. Please tell her that I'll do it.

AQUARIUS. Hey. No shit.

AQUARIUS *goes.* MICHAEL *gestures at the ropes:*

MICHAEL. Hey, thanks.

RAINBOW. Hey, people are trees too.

Scene Two: Heroes

Sunday morning. Outside a gospel church. MICHAEL *has pulled* KWESI *out of the church halfway through the service. We hear the singing from within.*

KWESI. You've got five minutes. I don't want to miss the preacher.

MICHAEL. So you really go for this?

KWESI. What do you want?

MICHAEL. I want to make sure I've got this right.

Pause.

KWESI. I'm listening.

MICHAEL. I saw her.

KWESI. How's she doing?

MICHAEL. Good. I think she told me the truth.

KWESI. Well, so did I.

MICHAEL. I didn't say you didn't. But I could have.

Pause.

KWESI. Why?

MICHAEL. You know Jack's dead, right?

KWESI. Yes.

MICHAEL. What you told me was a message.

KWESI. Yes.

MICHAEL. You wanted Claudia to confirm Jack was the informer.

KWESI. Michael, I said, it's going to be hard whoever / it turns out –

MICHAEL. Because it had to be one of the leadership. And you'd heard about the witch hunt, and like me you guessed

Jack was the Grand Inquisitor, with the rack and thumbscrews, and then he died.

KWESI *shrugs.*

But you got the thing the wrong way around.

Slight pause.

Jack wasn't the inquisitor. She was. She accused him of betrayal. He was the heretic, cast out into the darkness.

KWESI. You're sure?

MICHAEL. Oh yes, I'm sure.

KWESI. I didn't know that.

MICHAEL. And I think, shit, Jack is innocent, and if Claudia had said what you wanted her to say, then you'd have made him guilty.

KWESI. Well, I'm sorry.

MICHAEL. And I think – fuck – why would Kwesi of all people want me to get it wrong? Was it really Sonny Crane? Or you? Ira's in Ohio. Which of the seven people were you protecting? And then I realized – of course – that there were eight.

Pause.

I'm right? It must be Tommy Lee.

Pause.

KWESI. Why on earth would it be him?

MICHAEL. Because it's the only thing that makes sense of them not arresting us. I mean, the feds would hardly want it to be known they knew about a plot to spring a person they'd just shot for trying to spring himself.

I'm right?

And you told Claudia the truth.

Do you want to tell me why you lied to me?

KWESI. Have you read Tommy's book?

MICHAEL. Of course.

KWESI. So did the FBI.

MICHAEL. I'll bet.

KWESI. And there's a passage early on which I'm told is a very accurate description of the early signs of wire fever.

MICHAEL. Excuse me?

KWESI. Going stir-crazy. Tommy was inside for six years the first time round. He hated it. And when he came out, and he wrote the book, and became a movement hero, the feds worked out that this provides him with a pretty perfect cover. So they pull him in on a minor charge and outline the major charges that they're going to lay on him if he's not prepared to snitch. And he's cut off from his comrades, and he's lonely and he's in despair.

While simultaneously, those of us who also knew the early signs of wire fever realize it's pretty urgent that we get him out.

You guys want to help the Panthers. We meet. We plan. And to keep the lid on Tommy, we get news to him that, hey, we're working on this great plan with Bad Moon Rising, hey those crazy honky motherfuckers, they'll do anything, they got this kidnap plan, we'll get you out.

But of course, by now he's had his conversation with the feds, and he thinks, is this a test? And if it is, and I don't pass it on, do I fail the test and die in here?

So he tells the feds there is a plan, hatched by persons unknown, to kidnap an unspecified but prominent Republican in an election year. And sure, they can pick up anybody they can find. But unless they pick up everybody, that just increases the incentive. So they can let him go, or remove the problem. Which is what they do.

Pause.

MICHAEL. Why did you keep this secret?

KWESI. Michael, you ask me why I come here. Because like my friend Yolande, I too have observed an endlessly repeated cycle. How individuals undertake heroic acts in defiance of injustice. How they discover talents in themselves they never knew were there. How groups are built to find such strengths in other people. But how, one by one, those individuals are marginalized or undermined or demonized and those groups are harassed and threatened and eventually implode.

So, I tell the truth about Tommy's death. And the wickedness and evil power of the FBI is once again exposed. And we lose another hero.

MICHAEL. But . . . But, Jack.

KWESI. I didn't know he was the victim. I don't know what I would have done. Maybe I would have said, we need our heroes more than you.

He hears the PREACHER *asking questions and the* CONGREGATION *chanting back the responses.*

MICHAEL. So, why . . .

KWESI. So why do I come here? I want activism to be like church. As routine, as regular, as believed, as this. So I come here every week to try and find out how it works.

MICHAEL. And what have you concluded?

KWESI. You don't have to be a hero. You don't have to be a victim. Jesus died for you. But he lived for you also. You don't have to live like him, and if you want to, you don't have to do it every day. You do it here, in a special place, in your imagination. Where, once a week, the water turns to wine.

They say that communism is a lot of little truths which add up to a great lie. And that religion is a lot of little lies which add up to a great big truth. Well, maybe Jesus didn't rise again. Maybe when he said 'my God have you forsaken me?' he meant it. But I say, just because our heroes fail us, doesn't mean they're wrong.

KWESI *looks at* MICHAEL.

There are no angels. But we will be better people if we imagine that there are. And try to live that way.

Slight pause.

You coming in?

MICHAEL. No, I've a job to do for somebody. But thanks.

KWESI. 'By any means necessary.'

MICHAEL. 'Fraid so.

MICHAEL *goes out.* KWESI *goes back into the church. The church music gives way to a television trail.*

TV ANNOUNCER. Stay tuned to Statewide News, where in half an hour we present the leading candidates for governor in live face-to-face debate, followed by post-game analysis by strategists from both the Vine and the McKeene campaigns...

Scene Three: Right

Two days later. Late afternoon, in the holding room for the Democratic team at the location of the gubernatorial debate. On screens we see OFFICIALS and TECHNICIANS making final preparations for the debate. BLAIR and PAT enter. BLAIR has a checklist. During this, MITCHELL VINE enters. He is sixty years old.

BLAIR. Pencils, one sharpened and one blunt, two pens, one red one green.

PAT. Check.

BLAIR. One pad of lightly lined white paper with a spiral binding.

PAT. Check.

BLAIR. Handed to the debate commissioner at least fifteen minutes before curtain, to be placed . . .

PAT. Uh, Blair . . .

BLAIR *sees* MITCHELL.

BLAIR. Ah. Mitchell.

MITCHELL. Not an apparition.

BLAIR (*the room*). Now, this is kind of . . .

MITCHELL. Yes, I know.

BLAIR. Pat, this is Mitchell Vine.

PAT. Uh, that's the Chairman of . . .

BLAIR. Just so.

MITCHELL. Blair, I need to speak to you.

Slight pause.

PAT. I need to check levels.

PAT *goes out.*

MITCHELL. I called.

BLAIR. I know. Now I trust this isn't more about the color / of the candidate's –

MITCHELL. No, it's about a piece of information.

BLAIR. Well, we're always happy to / update our files.

MITCHELL. Which we both remember.

REBECCA *enters.*

Blair –

REBECCA. Um …

BLAIR. Ah. Rebecca, this is Mitchell Vine.

REBECCA (*hand out*). The reclusive Mr Vine.

MITCHELL (*shakes hands*). How do you do.

BLAIR. Mitchell's here to discuss last-minute proposals to overturn months of tortuous negotiations. So what's it now? We don't get a closing statement? You want props?

MITCHELL. Look, maybe we should find somewhere / a little more . . .

REBECCA. Isn't this something I should / to know about –

MITCHELL. I would like to speak with Blair alone.

Slight pause.

REBECCA. Yes, well. This is my . . . what do they call it?

BLAIR. Your retiring suite.

MITCHELL. We have one also.

BLAIR (*to* MITCHELL). Let's find a quiet corridor. I'll be back in five.

She goes out. MITCHELL *remains a moment.*

MITCHELL (*to* REBECCA). Good luck.

REBECCA. Thanks. And . . . same to Shel.

MITCHELL goes out. REBECCA, *alone, decides to run through an answer.* PAT *admits* MICHAEL *during this.*

So let's lock this down. I'm for national registration of all guns. My opponent thinks this is a terrible idea. I want to close the gun-show loophole. My opponent wants it kept wide open. I don't think anyone outside the military needs an M-16. And this makes me a harbinger of tyranny? Oh, really?

PAT. I don't think so.

REBECCA. Why not?

MICHAEL. I think she means that's better than 'Oh, really?'

REBECCA. Michael. How the hell did you get in?

They both look at PAT.

PAT. Ho. Right.

PAT goes out.

REBECCA. Well, this is becoming something of / a leitmotif –

MICHAEL. Becc, I need to speak with you.

REBECCA. You realize of course this is the worst / possible moment –

MICHAEL. That's why I need to speak with you.

REBECCA. Mikey, this has to be so fast and it has to be so good.

MICHAEL. I've just seen Claudia Perowne.

REBECCA. Michael, please don't tell me this.

MICHAEL. And I want you to promise me that if you're elected you'll do a deal with her.

Pause.

REBECCA. What deal?

MICHAEL. A pardon.

REBECCA. You do know what I've said / about this?

MICHAEL. 'No amnesty for fugitives, no tolerance for terrorists.'

REBECCA. And how vital it is that a woman candidate …

MICHAEL. …. be tough on crime. Good.

REBECCA. Why good?

MICHAEL. Because she's got evidence about the GM poplar case.

REBECCA. Please, I shouldn't know/ this.

MICHAEL. She knows that Martinez shot Polowski in cold blood.

REBECCA. There's only one way she / could know –

MICHAEL. So obviously she needs a deal.

REBECCA. Michael, have you come across the concept of the second term?

Pause.

No, I'm sorry, but / I have to ask –

MICHAEL. Well, I'm sorry too.

MICHAEL *takes out an envelope, and slides a photograph out of it. He shows it to* REBECCA.

I was listening to A.M. Radio. They say that Sheldon Vine
may call for a re-investigation of the shooting. And come
out against Ninety-Two.

REBECCA. Where did you get this?

MICHAEL. I didn't need to get it.

REBECCA. Ah.

MICHAEL. What is it?

REBECCA. You tell me.

MICHAEL. It's you, running a Vietcong flag up a flagpole on
the top of an illegally occupied ROTC building. Which is
why most people have handkerchiefs across their faces.

REBECCA. Not me.

MICHAEL. No. It would be bad for you.

REBECCA. It would be very bad.

MICHAEL. Though for me, of course, it's one of the best
things you ever did.

Pause.

REBECCA. Yes, I need some clarity here, Michael. You're
saying – threatening – that if I don't amnesty Perowne,
you'll – what? – give this to the newspapers?

MICHAEL. Persuade me not to.

REBECCA. How can I do that?

MICHAEL. By calling for a prosecution in the Polowski case.
By coming out against Prop. Ninety-Two.

REBECCA. In other words, by losing.

MICHAEL. In other words, by leading.

REBECCA. Leadership? What, a member of the Sixties left is
demanding leadership?

MICHAEL. Why not?

REBECCA. What, after glorifying it and following it slavishly,
then spurning it and overthrowing it and defining it as

inherently imperialist or white or male, and finding finally
you need it after all . . . you make impossible demands on it
and challenge it and never actually accept it and so
Woodstock Nation morphs into the Khmer Rouge.

MICHAEL. I don't think that's why it happened.

REBECCA. And it would be nice to think that this is all because
you were real anarchists or even genuine collectivists in
your communes and your tribes, but the truth is more
prosaic. You are terrified of winning. You'd hate to be a
member of a club that might accept you. You base your
politics on dressing up as other people because you rate
what isn't higher than what is. You don't know what you're
for but you sure as hell know what you're against, because
it's everything. What would you say, romantic? No. Heroic?
No, not really. I would actually call it dilettante.

MICHAEL. As opposed to being so obsessed with winning
that you end up to the right of the Republican.

REBECCA. Michael, you listen to the radio. You know that
Sheldon Vine wants to sell the welfare system off to
Pepsico.

MICHAEL. And thus far he's not come out for Ninety-Two.

REBECCA. Ninety-Two is rhetoric. In practice, it doesn't add
up to a hill of beans.

MICHAEL. Nor has he called Sarah Jane Polowski a terrorist.

REBECCA. Michael, let me lock this down. Are you endorsing
Sheldon Vine?

MICHAEL. Yeah, that's the thing. The endlessly repeated
mantra. I'm preferable to my opponent, but so I can beat
him, I need to trim what I believe so I don't scare off the
undecideds. And you get elected, great, but the story isn't
over because there's reelection, so you're careful not to do
anything that might offend the voters that you'll need to
gain to make up for the base support you'll lose. And you
do get reelected, wonderful, and *now* at last you really could
do something. But this means you'd have to 'fess up to the
party and the voters and yourself that you hadn't said or

done what you believe in on the way-up or the stay-up. So you have a chance to make a real difference in people's lives and you decide you can't, because if you do you won't get reelected not to do it one more time.

REBECCA. Yes, you see, behind everything you say there's an assumption that what I think now is some form of cynical and cowardly retreat. That deep down there's a pure set of beliefs – the ones you've stuck to – which I've run away from, for reasons of expediency. But, in fact, I hated being in a club where the admission fee was demanding the impossible and defending the intolerable. My new club's better. I like being there. I don't want to live in a society where people won't take responsibility for their actions. I think we told America: we're the ones who stand up for the feckless and freeloaders and we should have said: we're down on being ripped off by the corporations *and* by deadbeat dads and welfare queens.

MICHAEL. Oh, what, you mean, you actually believe / in all this stuff about –

REBECCA. Because someone has to say that social justice isn't about defiance of the rule of law, it's about upholding it. This country has this unique capacity to reinvent itself because of individual freedom not despite it.

MICHAEL. No. I think it's actually because, from time to time, there's groups of people in this country who're prepared to come together, to break the chains of history and try to live the future in the here-and-now. A place where every black kid in the ghetto, every white kid in a project, every Latino working in the field, gets to be a leader. Or a writer or a doctor or a teacher. And I've been saying that for thirty years and I had doubts about it then and God knows it's hard to think that now. But I need to act as if it could be true, because otherwise it never will be.

BLAIR *has entered.*

BLAIR. Rebecca.

REBECCA. Blair. Mike and I / have been debating –

BLAIR. Yes. Look, we need to have a conversation.

MICHAEL *puts away the photograph.*

REBECCA. What about?

BLAIR. I've been speaking to Mitch Vine.

MICHAEL. *Mitchell*?

BLAIR. Yes, Sheldon's elder brother.

REBECCA. Michael, what say we talk about this later.

BLAIR. No, I'd like him to stay. In fact he has to stay.

Pause.

REBECCA. Tell me.

BLAIR. Mitchell has a piece of information.

REBECCA. Oh?

BLAIR. Which he's threatening to use.

REBECCA. What is it?

BLAIR. Unless we do what he wants us to do.

REBECCA. Which is?

BLAIR. Come out against Prop. Ninety-Two at the top of the debate.

MICHAEL. Great.

BLAIR. No, Michael, it's not great. If we come out against it, he comes out for it and, as the polls make clear, we're toast.

REBECCA. So, what . . .

BLAIR. Do you know what Michael's been trying to find out?

REBECCA. Only that it's something from your past.

BLAIR. Good. Mitch Vine knows about it.

Slight pause.

MICHAEL. How?

BLAIR. I told him. Many years ago. When we were – close. For reasons that seemed valid at the time.

MICHAEL. What?

REBECCA. And is this / serious –

BLAIR. I was involved in a conspiracy to commit a felony.

REBECCA. What felony?

BLAIR. Come on.

REBECCA. And if we endorse . . .

BLAIR. Sheldon: 'I'm surprised my opponent has endorsed this proposition, opposing the use of force for political ends, since her campaign manager was involved in the planning of precisely such an act.'

Pause.

REBECCA. Yuh. So, how . . .

BLAIR. You, first question. 'Well, Bob, I'm really glad you asked me that, but first there's something else I have to say. Half an hour ago, I was informed that my campaign manager was involved, peripherally and many years ago, in discussions which might have led to the commission of a felony.'

REBECCA. Blair, surely, you don't have / to do this . . .

BLAIR. 'I have not inquired about the details of this felony and she has not volunteered them. She has offered me her resignation and of course I have accepted it. Now, I'm sorry, Bob, what was the question?'

REBECCA. But, Blair, that lays you wide / open –

BLAIR. Or even better. That, and then: 'This incident has reminded me of the importance of distinguishing between expression of political opinion and supporting or condoning acts of violence. So I call on my opponent, here this evening, to join with me in endorsing this exemplary proposition.'

REBECCA. And what's Vine say?

BLAIR. 'Oh, right. Hey, you know what? Great idea. Fine. Why don't I endorse it too.'

Pause.

MICHAEL. So you're saying, she dumps you and comes out for Prop. Ninety-Two.

BLAIR. Yes, Michael.

MICHAEL. And Vine's skunked.

BLAIR. Just so.

MICHAEL. And because actually your resignation doesn't kill Rebecca . . .

BLAIR. Which it doesn't.

MICHAEL. Then you've won. In the sense of, her.

BLAIR. Well, bingo.

REBECCA. And they didn't work that out?

BLAIR. They didn't work that out.

REBECCA. Why not?

MICHAEL. Because they didn't think she'd tell you.

Slight pause.

Right? They were counting on her saying: 'Look, I can't tell you what this is, but it's bad, and we're going to have to do what they want.' They were counting on her saying that, to save her skin.

Pause.

BLAIR. He said . . . He suggested that I say there was a compromising photograph.

MICHAEL shows *the photograph to* BLAIR.

How did you get hold of this?

REBECCA. He took it.

BLAIR. And he's saying . . . What, he'd use this?

REBECCA. Well, I think that Michael feels that I should come out against the proposition. And promise to reinvestigate Polowski. And . . . call their bluff on you.

MICHAEL. And you'll prevent a manifest injustice. And you'll right two wrongs. Hey, you know what? I'd just do it.

Enter PAT.

PAT. Rebecca, make-up's threatening to go out and catch a movie.

REBECCA. Right.

PAT. And the chairman's sent a huge bouquet.

REBECCA. Then he must never know about my allergy.

Slight pause.

And Michael must do what he thinks is right. Having thought about the consequences of his actions. For me. For Blair. And most of all, for him.

She goes to BLAIR.

BLAIR. 'Half an hour ago, I received a piece of information. Half an hour ago / I was informed – '

REBECCA *interrupts, hugging* BLAIR.

REBECCA. I think the person who comes out best from this is you.

REBECCA *leaves.*

PAT. Uh, what's . . .

BLAIR. It doesn't matter.

PAT *goes out.*

MICHAEL. So you told Mitchell Vine?

BLAIR. You know, you can't do this.

MICHAEL. Blair, you were safe.

BLAIR. Oh, yeah?

MICHAEL. Oh, yeah. I can't tell you who the snitch was. But I know, and you were safe. And all you have to do is persuade your candidate to do the right thing and you'd be safe now.

BLAIR. I'm sorry, Michael.

She makes to go, then turns back.

Hey. There's something you should know about your hero.

MICHAEL. Uh, 'my hero'?

BLAIR. As you're aware, we talk to prison guards. There's a guy who was around when Tommy died.

MICHAEL. Was murdered.

BLAIR. Well, that's the thing. He says that what the prison said was true – Tommy had been trying to escape. But it was like cockamamie, in the middle of the afternoon, no plan, he just starts running for the wire and they shot him down. Like it was a – kind of, cop-assisted suicide.

MICHAEL. What?

BLAIR. But being what he was, nobody was going to believe that. But still, some kind of fucking hero.

MICHAEL. You mean, he wanted it to happen? You mean, he sacrificed himself?

BLAIR. Yes, Mike. Just like you're planning sacrificing us. And yourself, of course.

MICHAEL. But, Blair . . .

BLAIR. You realise – what you're doing to us now – is exactly what the informer did to you.

She goes out, quickly. MICHAEL *stands there, holding the photograph.*

MICHAEL. Yeah, right. Some kind of fucking hero.

He starts to tear up the photograph. As he does so, the stage is flooded with the debate teams on either side: SHELDON VINE, *his wife* CONNIE *and campaign manager* DON

D'AVANZO; PAT, REBECCA; REPORTERS; MAKE-UP
PEOPLE; TECHNICIANS. *We see the debate podiums and
the moderator's table.* MICHAEL *finishes tearing up the
photograph and tosses the pieces into the air. Amid the
swirling chaos, we pick up some of this:*

M.C. Ladies and gentlemen, on behalf of the League of
Women Voters, it's certainly our pleasure here to welcome
you to tonight's live gubernatorial debate. All campaign
teams are reminded that from now on there is no member of
the teams on stage.

PAT (*to* 1st REPORTER). Hey, everybody thinks she's great at
this. But we take Vine very seriously.

DON (*to a* 2nd REPORTER). No, as far as we're concerned,
we're way behind. It's hers to lose.

As DON *passes the* 1st REPORTER.

1st REPORTER. So how did Vine prep, Don?

DON. He shaved.

MITCHELL *is talking to* DON *and then they go over to
meet* SHELDON *and* CONNIE. PAT *goes to* BLAIR.

PAT. Blair, someone overheard Bob Lejeune saying he's going
to go big on coastal access.

BLAIR. Pat, we are so up to speed on coastal access.

As SHELDON *heads towards the stage:*

DON. Hey, Mr Vine. What do we not repeat?

REBECCA. Blair, look . . .

BLAIR (*to* REBECCA). No. You go girl.

SHELDON (*turns back*). What, the question?

BLAIR (*as* REBECCA *heads up on to the stage*). Deep
breaths.

DON. No. The charges.

CONNIE *kisses* SHELDON *who follows* REBECCA *on to
the stage.* BOB LEJEUNE *walks out, shakes hands with*

both candidates, is applauded, acknowledges lightly, and sits. A TECHNICIAN *is counting down to airtime. As* BOB LEJEUNE *clears his throat and shoots his cuffs,* SHELDON *nods to* REBECCA *who nods back. They are both at their podiums.*

TV ANNOUNCER. Co-hosting with the League of Women Voters, Dateline Pacific presents, live, the Gubernatorial Debate between Sheldon Vine for the Republicans and the Democratic candidate Rebecca J. McKeene. Here's your moderator, Bob Lejeune.

BOB LEJEUNE. Good evening. On November 5th, the voters of this state are going to the polls to elect a governor. The two leading candidates for this office are with us for a live debate.

As the debate begins, we see BLAIR *looking fixedly across at* MITCHELL. MITCHELL *doesn't want to catch her eye, but eventually he has no choice but to look back.*

Ms McKeene. You started out with a double-digit lead. Now everybody has this race as too close to call. How d'you plan to turn this thing around?

REBECCA. Well, Bob, I'm obviously glad you asked that question good and early. First of all, however, there's something else I have to say. Half an hour ago, I received a piece of information from the manager of my campaign.

Blackout. In the change, we hear:

TV ANCHOR. Here's how it looks this election night November 5th. With forty percent of precincts reporting, this year's nail-biter of a governor's contest seems set for a photo-finish. Meanwhile, exit polls are encouraging to supporters of a controversial proposition to require all new and re-registering voters . . .

MICHAEL (*talking to an answering machine*). Hi, this is Michael Bern, calling for State Senator Cal Rasky. It's with regard to tomorrow's Rules Committee hearing. Look . . .

Scene Four: Arrivals

ABBY *and* MICHAEL*'s house, the morning after the election. Most of the luggage is assembled.* MICHAEL *stands looking at a pile of last-minute stuff from which he will select what goes in the last, open suitcase and his hand-baggage – including, currently concealed, his FBI file.* ABBY *calls from offstage.*

ABBY. OK. It's ten of ten now. *Five* of ten. The shuttle. And we leave EPX – whenever. And we're there at approximately lunchtime.

MICHAEL (*calls*). Tickets!

ABBY (*calls*). Virtual.

MICHAEL (*calls*). The email!

ABBY (*calls*). Did you check the drugs?

MICHAEL (*calls*). The *drugs*?

Enter ABBY *with her hand-baggage.*

ABBY. But in fact, it's fifteen hours ahead. So we actually arrive at 3 a.m. the day after tomorrow.

MICHAEL. Ab, you do know where we're going?

ABBY. Tylenol. My antihistamine.

MICHAEL. And we're being met?

ABBY. We're being met.

MICHAEL. At 3 a.m.?

ABBY. Yes, Mike. Your son will meet you.

MICHAEL *goes off.* ABBY *kneels and goes through the pile, rejecting.*

MICHAEL (*calls from off*). And he's working for a bank?

ABBY (*calls*). He lends money to small businesses.

MICHAEL (*calls*). My son's a money lender?

During this, ABBY *finds the FBI file and puts it in the 'no' pile.*

ABBY (*calls*). Particularly cooperatives. Especially when run by women. Exclusively in poorer areas, and focused on ecologically sound projects. Like, in Jack's case, sustainable teak harvesting in the forests of North Thailand. So that small foresters don't have to sell their land off to the running tigers of US Imperialism.

MICHAEL *has returned, with two big books.*

MICHAEL. OK.

The doorbell rings.

ABBY. The shuttle.

MICHAEL. Yes. Abs, d'you think I / did the right –

ABBY. And yes, it was hard to sit there, watching the debate, and the Democrat comes out for something you think sucks, and the Republican comes down against it. And the Democrat evades the Polowski thing, while the Republican appeared to back reopening the case. But still, you did the right thing, Michael.

ABBY *takes the suitcase out, passing the entering* JACK SAND *but not seeing him.* MICHAEL *finds his FBI file in order to pack it, but stops when* JACK *speaks.*

JACK. Did you?

MICHAEL. Well, all in all I didn't think I could deal with contributing to the election of a conservative republican.

JACK. Even if it means the murder of a woman called Witchhazel will go unavenged.

MICHAEL. Or opening the newspaper to see that photograph.

JACK. And a woman called a tree may spend her life pretending to be someone else.

MICHAEL. But mostly because the man we called the Falcon changed himself from a rapist and a gangster into a writer and a leader, and the FBI tried to turn him into an informer.

And he was lonely and despairing and foresaken and he cut a deal. But he realized that to betray the cause was to betray himself. And I guess the reason why I couldn't live with betraying Rebecca J. McKeene was because I'd be betraying my last thirty years. Does that make sense?

JACK. Oh yes. Oh, that makes sense to me.

ABBY *comes back in and sees* MICHAEL *with the file.*

ABBY. Michael, you aren't taking that.

MICHAEL. I thought that Jack might like to see it.

ABBY (*the books*). And you're definitely not taking those.

MICHAEL. I need them to prepare. I start class the morning we get back.

ABBY. It's entry-level sociology.

MICHAEL. Exactly.

Slight pause.

ABBY. And because it is the great utopian experiment of postwar education.

JACK. And the noblest thing one human being can do for another.

MICHAEL. Yes. And you don't mind / about the job –

ABBY. And because there's ways to keep our promise to each other which won't require you giving up the best part of yourself.

JACK *goes.* MICHAEL *takes* ABBY*'s hand.*

MICHAEL. What's that?

ABBY. The piece he handed on to you.

MICHAEL. And who might 'he' be?

ABBY. Well, I'd say, the person who you named your son for.

MICHAEL. Yup.

ABBY *stands. Briskly:*

ABBY. So, Paper Dog. Let's *go*.

ABBY *goes out.* MICHAEL *stands, looking down and around at his past. Then he picks up his bag and follows.*

End of Play.

A Selective Chronology from JFK to GWB

1960 Sit-in protests against segregated restaurants in Greensboro, North Carolina.

Students for a Democratic Society is founded to promote 'a responsible left in the universities'.

The Young Americans for Freedom founded to campaign against communism and for the market economy.

John F. Kennedy elected president.

1961 Freedom Riders campaign for desegregation of transportation in the south.

1962 American/Soviet face-off during the Cuban Missile Crisis.

1963 Martin Luther King delivers his 'I have a dream' speech.

John F. Kennedy assassinated and Lyndon Johnson takes over as president.

1964 'Mississippi summer' campaign against racial oppression and for the registration of black voters.

The Gulf of Tonkin resolution commits Congress to all-out war in Vietnam.

Free Speech Movement at the University of California at Berkeley wins the right to raise money for civil rights campaigns on campus.

Conservative Barry Goldwater loses heavily to Johnson in the presidential election.

1965 Under the leadership of Cesar Chavez, the United Farmworkers strike in California begins.

Race riot erupts in the Watts district of Los Angeles.

1966   Black Panther Party founded.

Pledged to counter campus radicalism, Ronald Reagan is elected governor of California.

1967   Race riots in Detroit, Newark and other American cities. Mounting protests against the war in Vietnam.

First national conference of the National Organization for Women.

The FBI starts a 'Rabble Rouser' (later 'Agitator') Index to 'expose, disrupt and otherwise neutralize' the New Left.

Anti-Vietnam War March on Washington is held.

1968   Faced with growing opposition to the war, Lyndon Johnson declares he will not run for reelection.

Martin Luther King and Robert Kennedy are assassinated.

Police attack demonstrators at the Democratic Convention in Chicago.

Richard Nixon is elected president.

1969   Young Americans for Freedom splits into libertarian and traditionalist factions over the issue of the military draft.

Students for a Democratic Society splits between the Maoist Progressive Labor faction and a Revolutionary Youth Movement which later forms the basis of the urban guerrilla faction the Weathermen.

Woodstock rock festival is held.

1970   The Weathermen go underground and mount a campaign of bombings in protest against the Vietnam war.

Following the invasion of Cambodia, six students are shot dead by National Guardsmen on two campuses.

1972   The Democrats select an anti-war candidate for president, George McGovern, who is defeated by President Nixon in a landslide.

1973   American troops leave Vietnam.

'Roe vs. Wade' Supreme Court decision legalises abortion throughout America.

1974   Newspaper heiress Patty Hearst is kidnapped by the Symbionese Liberation Army and subsequently takes part in a bank robbery.

Facing impeachment, Richard Nixon resigns over the Watergate scandal.

White protests in Boston against the busing of black pupils to achieve racial desegregation of schools.

1975   The Senate's Church Committee condemns excesses by the security services, directed against the Black Panthers and the anti-war movement.

1976   Jimmy Carter defeats Nixon's successor Gerald Ford for the presidency.

1978   Campaigning for family values, the Moral Majority gains strength. California passes Proposition 13, restricting property taxes.

1980   Ronald Reagan defeats Jimmy Carter in the presidential election.

1984   Ronald Reagan is reelected in a landslide.

1987   Iran-Contra hearings probe the Reagan administration's involvement in a secret arms-for-hostages deal which financed anti-government forces in Nicaragua.

1988   Following a negative campaign against 'the liberal Governor from Massachusetts', Vice President George Bush defeats Michael Dukakis for the presidency.

1990   Environmental movement Earth First! mounts 'Redwood Summer' protests against clear-cutting of ancient redwoods in northern California.

1991   American-led forces expel Iraq from Kuwait, but leave the Saddam Hussein regime in power.

1992   George Bush runs against Bill Clinton on a socially conservative platform and fails to secure re-election.

1994   The Republicans win a majority in the House of Representatives on the basis of a conservative program titled 'Contract with America'.

1995   Right-wing terrorist Timothy McVeigh kills 169 people in a bombing attack on the federal building at Oklahoma City.

1996   Bill Clinton wins reelection.

1999   Bill Clinton faces a senate impeachment trial over his affair with Monica Lewinsky.

2000   Despite losing the popular vote, George W. Bush wins the presidency on a vote of the Supreme Court.

2001   The September 11th attacks take place against New York and Washington. The USA PATRIOT Act gives increased powers to security services.

2002   Former Symbionese Liberation Army members are tried and convicted for crimes committed in the mid-70s.

2003   American forces invade Iraq, take Baghdad and overthrow the Saddam Hussein regime.